# Word of Mouth

# WORD OF MOUTH

## AN ANTHOLOGY OF GAY AMERICAN POETRY

## EDITED BY TIMOTHY LIU

Talisman House, Publishers
Jersey City, New Jersey

Published in the United States of America by
Talisman House, Publishers
P.O. Box 3157
Jersey City, New Jersey 07303-3157

Manufactured in the United Sates of America
Printed on acid-free paper


Library of Congress Cataloging-in-Publication Data

Word of mouth : an anthology of gay American poetry / edited by Timothy Liu.
    p.  cm.
Includes bibliographical references (p. ).
ISBN 1-58498-007-9 (acid-free paper) — ISBN 1-58498-006-0 (pbk. : acid-free paper)
    1. Gay men—Poetry. 2. Gay men's writings, American. 3. American poetry. I. Liu,
Timothy.

PS595.H65 W67 2000
811'.50809206642—dc21

                                      00-055960

## Acknowledgments

"The Hurricane Lamp," "In the Next Room," "A Reading of This Poem," "True Loves," "A Lecture on Avant-Garde" from *Selected Poems* by Jack Anderson (Release Press). Copyright © 1983 by Jack Anderson. "A Way of Happening," and "A Partial Index" from *Field Trips on the Rapid Transit* by Jack Anderson (Hanging Loose Press). Copyright © 1989 by Jack Anderson. Reprinted by permission of the poet. ● "They Dream Only of America" from *The Tennis Court Oath* by John Ashbery (Wesleyan University Press). Copyright © 1962 by John Ashbery. Reprinted by permission of the University Press of New England. "Sortes Vergilianae" from *The Double Dream of Spring* by John Ashbery (Dutton). Copyright © 1967, 1968, 1969, 1970 by John Ashbery; "The Ice Cream Wars" from *Houseboat Days* by John Ashbery (Viking). Copyright © 1975, 1976, 1977 by John Ashbery. "Forgotten Sex" from April Galleons by John Ashbery (Viking) Copyright © 1984, 1985, 1986, 1987 by John Ashbery. Reprinted by permission of George Borchardt, Inc. for the author. "The Laughter of Dead Men" from *Wakefulness* by John Ashbery. Copyright © 1998 by John Ashbery. Reprinted by permission of Farrar, Straus and Giroux, LLC. ● "Three Posthumous Poems" from *W. H. Auden: Collected Poems* by W. H. Auden, edited by

*Continued on pp. 455-458, which constitute
an extension of the copyright page*

# CONTENTS

# Timothy Liu

# PREFACE

When I was an undergraduate, I remember browsing through the poetry section at the Brigham Young University Bookstore—bookcases that ran a good forty feet or so. Beginning with the letter "A," I opened a book to a page that read: "Once I let a guy blow me. / I kind of backed away from the experience. / Now years later, I think of it / Without emotion." You could say I got hooked. I quickly, furtively, made my way through the rest of that "Poem in Three Parts" and felt those words planting something inside of me that would take years to reach fruition. I would not officially come out of the closet until I found a way to disentangle myself from the circumstances that brought me to Provo, Utah, in the first place, having just served two years as a Mormon missionary in Hong Kong—a period of my life in which I was asked to refrain from reading anything except the holy scriptures and church-related publications. Of course, John Ashbery's *Self-Portrait in a Convex Mirror* would not have made the officially sanctioned list. Nor would his work turn up in any of my literature classes at Brigham Young. But there it was before me at the BYU Bookstore, the sexy bulge in his pants on the full-length black and white photo enticing me to buy the paperback edition. I couldn't help but wonder, "Is he gay?" having been seduced by both body and text and feeling a need to know just where I stood. Ashbery would remain a mystery to me in the years that followed, never appearing in gay anthologies, though later I would learn that indeed he was gay through word of mouth.

Recently, I was invited to edit an anthology for Talisman House, an independent poetry press making its home in Jersey City, a press well-known for publishing innovative anthologies that have included: *An Anthology of New (American) Poets* (edited by Jarnot, Schwartz, Stroffolino); *Moving Borders: Three Decades of Innovative Writing by Women* (Sloan); *Primary Trouble: An Anthology of Contemporary American Poetry* (Schwartz, Donahue, Foster); *Postmodern Poetry: Interviews with Contemporary Poets* (Foster); *Crossing Centuries: The New Generation in Russian Poetry* (High); *Decadents, Symbolists, and Aesthetes in America: Fin-de-Siècle American Poetry* (Foster); and *Poetry and Poetics in a New Millennium* (Foster). After some thought, I decided that an anthology of gay American poetry would best suit my energies. Certainly in the last decade, many anthologies of gay poetry have appeared, including: *Gay and Lesbian Poetry in Our Time* (Morse, Larkin); *Gents, Bad Boys and Barbari-*

*ans: New Gay Male Poetry* (Kikel); *The Name of Love* and *Eros in Boystown*, both edited by Michael Lassell; *The Bad Boy Book of Erotic Poetry* (Laurents); and even one titled *Queer Dog: homo/pup/poetry* (Pearlberg), an anthology of dog poems written by gay and lesbian poets. So why do another anthology of gay (male) poetry? What audience(s) would such an anthology serve? Would it only serve the poetry-reading sector of the GLB community? Most of the gay anthologies aforementioned have nobly and ably focused on work that (re)presented gay experience in lines of verse, making lives and acts visible that some might continue to deem "unspeakable." Also, as if by word of mouth, the sexual identities of poets who chose to participate in such anthologies became known to the world. And yet, I felt that those anthologies limited themselves in regard to the kinds of poetry found therein, poems that seemed more daring by way of content than by choice of form or even by way of poetic lineage.

Any serious poet in America, gay or straight, is likely to have read the work of straight poets like Sylvia Plath and John Berryman as well as gay poets like Elizabeth Bishop and James Merrill. Why then all this fuss to isolate and segregate something like sexual orientation? Why not just leave them all together in anthologies like *The Harvard Book of Contemporary American Poetry* (Vendler) or *The Vintage Anthology of Contemporary American Poetry* (McClatchy) and let individual readers sleuth out private histories of the represented poets if they feel so inclined? After all, are we primarily dealing with poets who happen to be gay or straight, or are we dealing with gay and straight poets (not to mention anyone else up and down the Kinsey continuum)? None of these questions are merely rhetorical. Rather, they are essential, especially in a time when battles are being waged in academia over turf eroded by identity politics. Issues concerning race, gender and sexual orientation are raised with no less vigilance than melees over poetic theories and practices that range from traditional to radical forms. Out of these various intersections, my anthology came into being. Well-known for showcasing innovative writing without eschewing work steeped in tradition, Talisman House seemed like the ideal press to stage such a gathering of gay poets whose poems represent a plurality of forms, poems that may or may not directly traffic in "gay experience" per se.

I return to the case of John Ashbery, a poet whose œuvre is as likely to be lauded by Harold Bloom or Helen Vendler as by Marjorie Perloff, and yet a poet who has refused to be represented in a gay anthology in much the same was that Elizabeth Bishop refused to be included in any women's anthology of poetry, let alone a lesbian one. And indeed, not a few revisionists have come under fire for trying to wedge Uncle Walt and Aunt Emily into Gay and

Lesbian Studies course syllabi. Aren't poets free to choose what labels get attached to their names, or must Bishop and Ashbery too be subjected to being "outed," and to what purpose? To be an anthologist comes the burden of a responsibility, for what is an anthology if not an editor's "word of mouth" in print, hot gossip that says, "Read this! Now this!" My original working title was *Homotextual: A Talisman Anthology of Gay American Poetry*, a title that was met with both cheers and jeers by those who were asked to contribute. For some, the term "homotextual" was both too trendy *and* passé. Others were simply baffled by its denotation, a term that had previously appeared in Shoptaw's book of criticism on Ashbery's work that Ashbery himself reportedly found to be a nuisance. So after some deliberation, I've opted for the more down-home title of "Word of Mouth," especially since it has been through the "word of mouth" of many contributors herein that has led me to others I might have otherwise overlooked. Like an underground railroad, so much of the gay writing community has flourished both in public and in private. For years, one of Auden's most outlandishly gay poems, "The Platonic Blow," existed only in manuscript copy, carefully passed on from one poet to the next, until Ted Berrigan finally got a hold of it and had it published himself. Being in penurious circumstances, Berrigan feared nothing by way of potential litigation since there was nothing to be had! After having left Brigham Young to start a graduate program at the University of Houston, I had the good fortune to work with Richard Howard, a mentor cum role model who helped me with my poems even as I struggled with coming out to myself as a gay poet. It was also through his generosity that Auden's poem first came into my hands, a poem reprinted as a pamphlet by Orchises Press. It was but one station along a path that so many others had already come.

I began this project with a list of over a hundred living gay poets. Having been given a four-hundred manuscript page limit, I had to decide what was possible and desirable in terms of breadth and depth. I decided to work with fewer poets but to give each one more room—up to ten manuscript pages. Only poems written or published after 1950 were to be considered and only by poets who had published at least one full-length book. Of course, I wanted to include poets who not only identified themselves as gay but were willing to participate in a gay anthology. In addition to the fifty or so poets included herein, I also include a "recommended reading list" to document noteworthy titles by other gay poets that readers might wish to pursue.

Many lineages are gathered here, the poets themselves often belonging to more than one distinct camp. From the Formalists, we get Auden, Campo, Gunn, McClatchy, and Merrill; from the San Francisco Renaissance, we get

Duncan, Spicer and Ginsberg, San Francisco being the gay mecca that not only served as a stomping ground for the Beats but also for many poets then and now like Bowers, Broughton, Chin, Gunn, Johnson, Killian, Powell, and Shurin; others influenced by Olson and Duncan stayed back east (Jonas, Lansing, Wieners) or attended to The Jargon Society, a press not far from Black Mountain (Meyers and Williams); and of course, there's the New York School with Ashbery, O'Hara and Schuyler at the helm, a cultural hub that magnetized artists (Brainard), composers (Cage), librettists (Elmslie, Koestenbaum, McClatchy) and dance critics (Anderson, Denby) alike, a world that inspired the high camp of Field, the pop of Trinidad, the itinerant journals of Mead and the political activism of Giorno whose love of Zen is also shared by Schuyler's muse Carey, now a Franciscan brother in the Society of St. Francis in Brooklyn; and of course there remains a generation brought up through graduate writing programs, some who are also now teaching in academia: Cassells, Davis, Doty, Phillips and Shepherd.

The poets who participate here are more or less donating their work as they will only receive five contributors copies in payment. My budget for reprint rights was virtually non-existent, so I ended up spending as much time editing the book as securing permissions, tenaciously going to the begging bowl again and again in order to adequately represent many of the poets listed above. Many of the poems I had initially chosen (i.e. "This Lunar Beauty," "As He Is," "Heavy Date," "The Hidden Law" and "The More Loving One" by Auden or "The House Fly," "The Kimono," "Volcanic Holiday"and "164 E. 72nd St." by Merrill) were ultimately dropped due to prohibitive reprint fees that went as high as $15/line. When intellectual property becomes corporate capital, the endangerment of our first amendment rights is not far off. For most independent houses, the books of poetry they publish are hardly able to recoup their own printing costs, let alone the hundreds of hours that amount to little more than a great big labor of love. By working closely with both the poets and literary executors, I have hoped to remain sensitive to how each poet would like to be represented, that is, with works that may or may not be "about" being gay. A few of the poets invited to participate in this project opted out for reasons that ranged from "having recently gotten married to a woman and together (happily)raising a family" (therefore not knowing if he could still be considered a "gay" poet) to another writer who preferred to have his work "be read and judged in a broader historical and cultural context" rather than by "the narrow context of his sexuality." One writer declared he would only take part if the anthology precluded the word "gay" in its title, himself preferring the more clinical term "homosexual." And there was one executor who shamelessly insisted on the inclusion of his own work as a condition for including works by the writer that he represented.

After all is said and done, I still question the notion of a "gay sensibility." One gets tired of the cultural stereotypes surrounding sexuality itself, although most gay men do pride themselves on using their own "gaydar" to sniff out their own kind while cruising down the streets. But are there signs as concrete as a colored handkerchief, or even a gaze that lingers a little too long, to mark a poem written by a gay man? Of course there are poems that overtly flaunt their sexuality as if really working it atop an arena-sized speaker, but there are so many quieter poems (and poets) who might elude the most finely-tuned gaydar. Indeed, an Orphic poet like Robert Duncan could easily be read as either flamboyant or utterly closeted depending on what poems one chose to represent him with. One could also argue that the mythic resonance in so many of his poems might confound the very categories of sexuality itself. But for now, I am simply interested in documenting a particular and peculiar time in contemporary American Poetry, turf notwithstanding. And I hope that *Word by Mouth* will find a welcome audience in literary and cultural studies classes alike as well as the general poetry-reading public, even as it complicates the issue of just how useful the term "gay American poetry" is for our own time and for generations to come.

# Word of Mouth

## ❧ The Subway

The subway flatters like the dope habit,
For a nickel extending peculiar space:
You dive from the street, holing like a rabbit,
Roar up a sewer with a millionaire's face.

Squatting in the full glare of the locked express
Imprisoned, rocked, like a man by a friend's death,
O how the immense investment soothes distress,
Credit laps you like a huge religious myth.

It's a sound effect. The trouble is seeing
(So anaesthetized) a square of bare throat
Or the fold at the crotch of a clothed human being:
You'll want to nuzzle it, crop at it like a goat.

That's not in the buy. The company between stops
Offers you security, and free rides to cops.

## ❧ Summer

I stroll on Madison in expensive clothes, sour.
Ostrich-legg'd or sweet-chested, the loping clerks
Slide me a glance nude as oh in a tiled shower
And lope on dead-pan, large male and female jerks.

Later from the open meadow in the Park
I watch a bulging pea-soup storm lie midtown;
Here the high air is clear, there buildings are murked,
Manhattan absorbs the cloud like a sage-brush plain.

In the grass sleepers sprawl without attraction:
Some large men who turned sideways, old ones on papers,

A soldier, face handkerchiefed, an erection
In his pants—only men, the women don't nap here.

Can these wide spaces suit a particular man?
They can suit whomever man's intestines can.


## ∾ Venice

She opens with the gondola's floated gloze
Lapping along the marble, the stir of swill
Open to night sky like in tenement hallways
The footfalls, and middream a bargeman's lone call;
Sideways leading to her green, like black, like copper
Like eyes, on tide-lifted sewers and façades
Festooning people, barges a-sway for supper
Under hunched bridges, above enclosed pink walls;
And crumbling sinks like a blond savory arm
Fleshed, a curled swimmer's pale belly that presses
And loosens, and moist calves, then while the charm
Subsides, Venice secrets pleases, caresses;
The water-like walking of women, of men
The hoarse low voices echo from water again


## ∾ Villa d'Este

Beneath me this dark garden plunges, buoyant
Drops through the trees to basins furtive below
Under me wobbles the tip of a mast-thick fountain
I laugh and run down; the fat trunks heavily grow;
Then cypress, ilex rise reflected immense
Melancholy, and the great fount thrusts forceful
Tiny, their seclusion perches over the plains
For plains billow far below toward Rome remorseful;
But rilling streams draw me back in, up above
To the spurt, dribble, gush, sheath of secret water
Plash, and droves of Italians childish as love

Laughing, taking pictures of laughter, of water
Discovering new fountlets; so dense, so dark
Single on a desert mountain drips the locked park

ॐ

Neighbor sneaks refuse to my roof
Cat snores—that's a winter landscape
Newcomers shining in the loft
Friends' paintings—inattention to cope
With the rest—the tap's voice, the street
Trucks, nextdoor coffee, gas from drain's
Hole, the phone's armorplated speech
Snow's hush, siren, rain, hurricane
Nature crowds, big time, into, out
The building and of the man I'm
I do with nature, do without
Penetrated, also sublime
I'd like the room mine, myself me
But as facts go, neither's likely

ॐ

At first sight, not Pollock, Kline scared
Me, in the Cedar, ten years past
Drunk, dark-eyed, watchful, light-hearted
Everybody drunk, his wide chest
Adorable hero, mourn him
No one Franz didn't like, Elaine said
The flowered casket was loathesome
Who are we sorry for, he's dead
Between death and us his painting
Stood, we relied daily on it
To keep our hearts on the main thing
Grandeur in a happy world of shit
Walk up his stoop, 14$^{th}$ near 8$^{th}$
The view stretches as far as death

EDWIN DENBY                                                      3

∿ Three Posthumous Poems

I. GLAD

Hugerl, for a decade now
My bed-visitor,
An unexpected blessing
In a lucky life,
For how much and how often
You have made me glad.

Glad that I know we enjoy
Mutual pleasure:
Women may cog their lovers
With a feigned passion,
But males are so constructed
We cannot deceive.

Glad our worlds of enchantment
Are so several
Neither is tempted to broach:
I cannot tell a
Jaguar from a Bentley,
And you never read.

Glad for that while when you stole
(You burgled me too),
And were caught and put inside:
Both learned a lesson,
But for which we well might still
Be *Strich* and *Freier*.

Glad, though, we began that way,
That our life-paths crossed,

Like characters in Hardy,
At a moment when
You were in need of money
And I wanted sex.

How is it now between us?
Love? Love is far too
Tattered a word. A romance
In full fig it ain't,
Nor a naked letch either:
Let me say we fadge,

And how much I like Christa
Who loves you but knows,
Good girl, when not to be there.
I can't imagine
A kinder set-up: if mims
Mump, *es ist mir Wurscht.*

*March 1965*


## II. AUBADE

At break of dawn
he takes a street-car, happy
after a night of love.

Happy,
but sleepily wondering
how many away is the night

when an ecto-endomorph
cock-sucker must put on
The Widow's Cap.

*July 1964*


W. H. AUDEN                                                    5

## III. MINNELIED

When one is lonely (and You,
My Dearest, know why,
as I know why it must be),
steps can be taken, even
a call-boy can help.

To-night, for instance, now that
Bert has been here, I
listen to the piercing screams
of palliardising cats
without self-pity.

*? 1967*

## ∾ Afternoons in Ceylon

I

Luncheon had made us hungry
    for one another
After the curry and fried bananas
we added our own heat to
    the hot afternoon
simmering in sweat and coconut oil
as our two humidities rose
    high   higher        Bang!
    outside the window     Bang Bang!
and the houseboy's laughing shout

He had been tossing firecrackers
    at the roof
to dislodge itinerant pigeons
But at his feet had fallen
    a passing oriole
shocked into gape    beak ajar

Hurrying from the bedroom
    half-saronged
we saw him kneel to the yellow bird
fondle   cajole   kiss it   offer it
    back to the sky
Still it sat rigid in his hand

Chuckling then   you said
    Is this a golden trophy of
    our shooting match?
At which the oriole blinked
stretched and puffed
    spurted into the air
vanished beyond the papaw tree

II

Remember
in the breeze from the lagoon
    by the surf at Trincomalee
our pyramided tent of white
    mosquito netting
invited us in to romp
as naked pirates
celebrating freedom
from our woes of inland
    I triumphant over
buttock sore and anal ache
    you redeemed of
itches  chills  and sneeze
    both of us restored to
    plundering desire
    by the surf at Trincomalee
while monkeys thumped on the tin roof
and the German couple next door
    dismembered their marriage
in the breeze from the lagoon


## ∾ Wondrous the Merge

Had my soul tottered off to sleep
taking my potency with it?
Had they both retired before I could
leaving me a classroom somnambulist?
Why else should I at sixty-one
feel myself shriveling into fadeout?

Then on a cold seminar Monday
in walked an unannounced redeemer
disguised as a taciturn student
Brisk and resolute in scruffy mufti
he set down his backpack  shook his hair
and offered me unequivocal devotion

He dismissed my rebuffs and ultimatums
He scoffed at suggestions of disaster
He insisted he had been given authority
to provide my future happiness
Was it possible he had been sent
from some utopian headquarters?

I went to his flat to find out

.     .     .

He had two red dogs   a yellow cat
a girl roommate   an ex boyfriend
and a bedroom ceiling covered
with blue fluorescent stars
But he was ready to renounce anything
that would not accommodate me

He said I held the key to his existence
He said he knew when he first saw me
that I was the reason for his birth
He claimed that important deities
had opened his head three times
to place my star in his brow

This is preposterous   I said
I have a wife in the suburbs
I have mortgages   children   in-laws
and a position in the community

I thoroughly sympathize   said He
Why else have I come to your rescue?

These exchanges gave me diarrhea
I tried leaving town on business
but I kept remembering the warmth
that flowed through his healing fingers
We met for lunch at Hamburger Mary's
and borrowed a bedroom for the afternoon

JAMES BROUGHTON                                    9

He brought a bouquet of blood roses
and a ruby-fat jug of red wine
He hung affection around my neck
and massaged the soles of my feet
He offered to arrange instant honeymoons
and guarantee the connecting flights

Are you mad?  I said   You are half my age
Are you frightened of your fate?   said He

•    •    •

At Beck's Motel on the 7th April
we went to bed for three days
disheveled the king size sheets
never changed the Do Not Disturb
ate only the fruits of discovery
drank semen and laughter and sweat

He seasoned my mouth
  sweetened my neck
  coddled my nipple
  nuzzled my belly
  groomed my groin
  buffed my buttock
  garnished my pubis
  renovated my phallus
  remodeled my torso
until I cried out
until I cried
  I am   Yes
  I am   your Yes
    I am   I am   your
    Yes   Yes   Yes

•    •    •

He took a studio of his own
on the windward slope of Potrero
where I spent afterschool hours
uprooting my ingrown niceties
and planting fresh beds of bliss
His sheets were grassy green

   •     •     •

    In his long bathtub
    he sat me opposite him
    and scrubbed away my guilt
    With a breakfast of sunbursts
    he woke the sleeping princess
    in my castle of armor

    Waving blueprints of daring
    for twin heroes
    he roused my rusty knighthood

    To the choked minstrel
    aching my throat
    he proffered concerts of praise

    Off the tip of his tongue
    I took each tasty love word
    and swallowed it whole
    for my own

Are you my Book of Miracles?   I said
Are you my Bodhisattva?   said He

   •     •     •

Ablaze in the thrust of desire
we scathed each other with verve
burned up our fears of forever
steamed ourselves deep in surrender
till I lay drenched under scorch
and joy cried out through my crown

JAMES BROUGHTON

Wondrous   Wondrous the merge
Wondrous the merge of soulmates
the surprises of recognition
Wondrous the flowerings of renewal
Wondrous the wings of the air
clapping their happy approval

.    .    .

I severed my respectabilities
and bought a yellow mobile home
in an unlikely neighborhood
He moved in his toaster   his camera
and his eagerness to become
my courier   seed-carrier   and consort

Above all he brought the flying carpet
that upholsters his boundless embrace
Year after year he takes me soaring
out to the ecstasies of the cosmos
that await all beings in love

One day we shall not bother to return

## ❧ "In Our Image, After Our Likeness"

In what image? Michelangelo
of course, his Adam, one thinks of that, of all
that flesh, serene, symmetrical, fresh
from the hand of God without intervention; one hears
the body's innocent, pleasant harmonies.
There is this to be said for it, that everywhere
his image is always in our presence: one sees
such figures, part by part, at least, and in need
of composition, but still they are always there.

Is this what was meant, this image? This, man?
The greedy mind that eats all kinds
of phantasies refuses this one. No,
go hungry, rather. We go hungry. Man,
your image eludes the flesh as though the flesh
were a bad camera, or a slick craftsman with a quick,
dashing facility and a sure eye
for the grotesque, but little depth and out
of fashion soon, regrettably, because
the perfection and morality of the flesh can move us so.

The moral and perfect, however, are not the point.
The intrinsic image of man is what we hope
to find, and while we hope are afraid to find.
One would as soon confront God as man.

## ❧ Colloquy on a Bed

Listen, the celestial motions, though they make
an order of sorts, and this is an order in part
accessible to the mind, it is not to be thought
that this is a rational order. Not to our mind.
How should the scale, alone, make any sense?

There is evidence to be seen in addition to this
that, like it or not, this place, this universe,
in any rational sense is hopelessly
insane. Hopelessly: the saving word.
How should it otherwise be meaningful?

No, I do not love you, though the small hairs
around your eyes can make me tremble, stop
me talking, thinking even. You can go.
But you remind me passion does exist
as hopeless and meaningful as the universe is.


## ∾ The Wall

Watching the curve of the long line of your back,
desiring, I said in my mind that each of us
is alone forever, forever. We live with this.


## ∾ My Shoulder for Robert. Help Us Both

What, this world? Of course. It is
that terrible. The curious thing,
—we come back and back to think or pretend to think
there was some mistake, some fault, and it isn't so.

We think our attitude was wrong: no trust
or too much trust, lazy or not relaxed
enough. Did we have the chances? Did pampering
spoil us? We refuse to believe it really is.

It is, though. So what do we do? There must
be something to do, some way to make it right.
We refuse to believe there isn't a remedy.

Well, we may be right. You know though

I don't believe we are. You know my mind
is somewhere else. Another world. No world.


## ∾ In April

Spring again and the intensification of love.
So we term it. Of desire? Well yes, desire.
Even in terms of each other. In those terms.
How else in other terms? What else do we know?

But we feel. Oh, love, if we could tell
what we feel to someone, if someone were there
to tell to, that would be love indeed
and what we feel. Listen, I am talking to you.


## ∾ Bare

Why should it always be the beautiful
we have to talk to, especially since
the beautiful hasn't really much interest in us?
To say what we have to say to anyone else

would hardly seem worth doing even if
we said it all there. The beautiful
is unreceptive, hasn't much virtue or power.
What does it have? We take it our naked pleas.


## ∾ What You Can Do

I used to think it was impossible with boys.
It is impossible with girls too.
Oh, you can do it but if you think that that's what it is
you have to deceive yourself. It isn't that.

## ∾ Scanning

Fucking is nothing. There are times and ways
better than others. Even so. Then what?
I think sometimes I break apart to say,
looking wherever for it, trying to see.

## ∾ The Near Beyond

I want the impossible, (you, e.g.)
and if, as I imagine, by the farthest chance,
you proved possible, I'd have to say
it wasn't ever you I wanted at all.

## ∾ 17 March

I met a young friend on the road with his girl whom he hugged.
He turned and hugged me. Love hasn't much
to do with whom. I glorify the God
for this. And there are ages, times of the year.

## ∾ Friendly Greeting

All love is self-love; the other is not.
It is ourselves we particle.
Love has to have something. There is nothing more.
Hello, we say, I have been waiting for you.

## ∾ Questions for Eros

I know my loves—hah, my loves—are my loves
and have come to nothing and will come to nothing more;
and my mind makes up stories to say
who they are and why, maybe, and all about
their nature, mine, the nature of love,
because we don't know anything
—anymore than we know about anything else—about
these things and make up stories to know
as if we knew what the stories are about,
knew that even, as if we knew about love.

Eros, have I ever called your name?
Always, in all the calling, I had thought
to call you. Is there a name? Or have
I always called it wrong? Wrong? Is
there a right? What name is not diminishment?

Eros, if there be truly various gods,
there is one who is other than you
and he is nameless. Loving you, I love
the nameless one. All gods are one.
I call the names, none of them the name.

## ∾ Duplicity

Order, our order, is to deny
our nature; yet order is not to be denied:
we want an order. We want to respect our wants:
what else do we want?
                        Well, the something else we want
is that our nature is orderless; that want,
itself, is our want for an order: one we can feel.

WILLIAM BRONK

We mistrust an unfelt order, strange to us,
though it is ours.
                          Complex, we wish for things
more simple and, infinite, we want the things
which are finite, contrary things. Acknowledging both,
we wish our nature were not the doubleness
we are coupled with, with which we have to live.

There are no accidents, unnatural acts;
the horror of human doings is the nature of us:
our impossibility; our need to destroy
ourselves, all finite things; our helpless loves
for our half, our helpless half, the half we destroy,
helplessly, with that intent; and the grief
of that intent, of that finite order's loss
our infinite intention's nature it is to lose.


## ∾ Your Way Too

The way Swann, his whole life, loved
Odette and she not even his type, is the way
contrarily, we, each of us, love,
in spite of natural inclinations, our lives.
We trust the tact of others because we know
they know and won't speak of it. Things are far
more complicated than we say they are.


## ∾ Lucifer

Shun me. Adam's fall was trivial
to mine. I am too proud to contend His power,
will not be less and, as less, be least as known
beloved. Secret love is my desire.

## ❧ Anyway

I want to cry my wild happiness
—wild because it hasn't anything
to do with the cultivated ways: not sex
or Zen or Jesus or even as though
I thought that happiness was a place to look.
It wasn't and I didn't and here it is.

## ❧ For My Friend, Jerry, He Drunk

Yes, but there's something more than
the rational life and it asks us kill
me, kill yourself, kill the life where you are;
There's life and a better one on the other side.
You want this shit? You can have it: be good.
And even if there's not another life . . . this?

God give me love; it's what I have.

WILLIAM BRONK

## ∾ Circulations of the Song
### after Jalāl Al-Dīn Rūmī

\*

If I do not know where He is
    He is in the very place of my not knowing.
If I do not know who He is
    He is the very person of my not knowing.

His is the Shining Forth I know not.
My heart leaps forward   past knowing.

\*\*

Would I prune back the overgrowth of yearning?
Free today from the shadows of what has been?
    Cut away the dead Love-wood?

It is as if Christ-rood never perisht.
It is as if the God at Delphi still returnd.

Even now, new shoots are returning   toward Shrovetide,
fresh, tender.   In the fullness of summer
    they too will be rampant.
A thousand roots of feeling tamper the ground
    for this abundance,  this
        spring water.

Ten thousand leaves of this green
work in the free flow of the sun's light.

\*

Do you think I do not know what the curse of
    darkness means? the power in confusion?
Do you think I do not remember
    the tyranny of establisht religions,
the would-be annihilating cloud of lies
    and the despairing solar malevolence
that is rumord to lie back of these?
    the madness of kings?


But now, in thought of Him,   the Lord of Night
    stirs with verges of a radiance
that is in truth dark,   darkening glances of an obscurity
    Love seeks in love,   Eros-Oberon
whose Palace is Night.    Did I tell you,
    as I meant to,   He is all about me?


It is as if Night itself
            meant to cherish me.


                ✶✶


The body of this thought must be a star.

This Mind is that fathomless darkness
    racing out beyond itself,    Time
            pouring beyond time,

in the cast of whose scatterd sparklings,
            seed drift of suns,
I am all water.      I reflect
    passages of what is moving as I catch it,
the shadow of the expanding depth,
the glance fugitive and sparkling
    of but one among a million promises.


                ✶


ROBERT DUNCAN                                        21

In this world without kings
secretly in every thing    kings are preparing.
See!  a single leaf the chance light enhances
        is annointed and    *commands* my regard.
I am in the realm of this attention *subject.*

See!  over there  as if hidden  an other leaf
        in obscurity     as from the depth of its darkness
comes to light    and therein     sets up
                rule over my seeing;
all the mass of foliage I see are members now
        of this courting.    I shall derive
where I am      a court     and pay court to this
                courtesy.


                *


How happy I am in your care, my old companion of the way!
The long awaiting,  the sometimes bitter hope,
        have sweetend in these years of the faith you keep.
How completely I said "yes" when it came to me
and continue.   Each morning awakening you set free
        another day for me.   How has your face
aged over these years to keep company with mine?
ever anew as I waken endearing.    Each night
        in the exchange of touch and speech blessing,

prepared thruout for rest.    Is it not
as if He were almost here?    as if we were


                already at rest?


                **


The rest is an Artesian well,  an underground fountain.
The level of the water is so close,
up-welling in every season,   rising thru me

the circuit Jalāl al-Dīn Rūmī
in which    at last!    I come to read you,  you
      come to be read by me.    Releasing
freshets of feeling anew I come from.

                    *


But if you are the lover,   how entirely you are *He.*
How entirely He is here;   He commands me.

A blazing star in the southern hemisphere
      shines in my thought in the north
and I go forth to find rumors of him.

I am like a line cast out
      into a melodic unfolding beyond itself
            a mind hovering ecstatic
above a mouth in which the heart rises
      pouring itself into liquid and fiery speech
for the sake of a rime not yet arrived
      containing again and again resonant arrivals.

Fomalhaut,   guardian splendor of the other "sky"!
in reflection my mind is crowded with splendors.

                  **


Are you my soul?    my love?    my redeemer?
O no!    My soul rushes forward to you!
And, in the rushing,     is entirely given me anew.

                    *


The veil of speech I meant to be so frail    I
      meant to be transparent that the light
      were you to read there would reveal me,
thruout waiting,   thruout about to be naked,

ROBERT DUNCAN

thruout trembling,    has become a net
wrapping you round about in my words
    until I cannot see you.

        Now I would tear speech away.
I want you to find me out
with none of my leads in the way.
I want you to seek my being ready
    in your own way.

      \*\*

Because He was there where deep drunk I
    yet rememberd him,
because He was ever in the lure of the moment
    awaiting me,
because *His* are the eyes of my seeing you,
yours was the mouth of the wish the tongue of my speech sought
that may never actually    have been  yours
was the sweet jet from sleep's loins
    night stirrd to arousal
in the seed of the hour I came upon;
for the glorious tree of that long ago
    acknowledged need
bursts into a like-sweet abundance of leaves,
    as if from utter Being
risings of odors and savorings
    feeding full the inner song in me.

      \*\*

Have we lived together so long,  the
    confluent streams of each his own life
into one lifetime "ours" flowing,
    that I do not yet ever know the first
pang?    the confused joyous rush
    of coming to myself in you?

the leap at the brink of being
left alone?     the solitary on-going
      before you?     I am ever before you,
even in the habit of our sweet marriage
      of minds.     Yet I am not
            so sure of finding you
that I have no need for this
      reassurance,
for the embrace of our two bodies,
      for the entwining of bodies,
for the kiss,  even as the first kiss,

for the memorial seal into silence the
      lips bound,
the joyous imprint and signature of our
      being together     one
            in the immortal ellipse.


            *


For how entirely mortal is the love I bear for you.
I bring it forward into the full fragrant
      flare,  the rosy effulgence     of a perishing tree.

As in Oz or in fairyland,   the fruits of that
      arbor     are ever changing.
All the flowering specters of my     childhood and manhood
      come into and fade into     that presence,
perilous thruout,   essential thruout
      —apple, cherry, plum—deep purple
      as night and as sweet—quince and pear—
we know they are all there     all ready,
      in each ring,  each year
they belong to the tree's inner preparing.

For how entirely a door has been flung open in me
            long prepared!


ROBERT DUNCAN                                                          25

How each season of the year,    a thief,
    goes in and goes out,
bearing transgressions of tastes and odors,
    traces of me lost,
imprints of thee,   stolen hours,
    stored among my secrets.

          **

Stand by me!    you wingd and
          dark ascendant!
Attend me!    Here!    Falling!

        *

For I am falling out into that Nature of Me
    that includes the Cosmos it believes in

as if it were the smallest thing,    an all but invisible
    seed in the cloud of these seeds scatterd,
ever emerging from belief    beyond belief.

I shall never return into my Self;
that "Self" passes out of Eternity,   incidental!

*He* too seeks you out.   He too
    dreams of coming to this fugitive morning,
of finding His "Self" in a Time so personal
    it is lost in our coming into it.

        *

Again you have instructed me to let go,
to hold to this falling,   this
    letting myself go.
I will succumb entirely to your intention.

Word of Mouth

*Contend with me!*
you demand.   And I am surrounded by wingd
   confusions.   He
is everywhere,    nowhere
   now where I am.


In every irreality there is Promise.
   But there
where I am not   *He*   really is.


   In Whose Presence
it is as if I had a new name.


     **


I am falling into an emptiness of Me,
every horizon    a brink of this emptying,
walls of who-I-am  falling into me.


How enormous to come into this need!


Let us not speak then of full filling.
In the wide Universe
   emptying Itself into me, thru me,
in the myriad of lights falling,


let us speak of the little area of light
   this lamp casts.
Let us speak of what love there is.
Let us speak of how these perishing
   things
uphold me    so that


   I fall


     into *Place.*


ROBERT DUNCAN

The child I was has been left behind.
Those who first loved me have gone on without me.
Where they were    a door has been left open    upon a solitude.
In the midst of our revelry I find myself waiting.

Every day the sun returns to this place.
Time here advances toward another summer.
These fruits again darken;   these new grapes
will be black and heavy hang from their bough.   The heat at noon deepens.

Sweet and pungent each moment ripens.
Every day the sun passes over this valley.
Lengthening shadows surround me.
All day I waited.   I let the sun and shadow   pass over me.

Here    a last clearing of sunlight is left amidst shadows.
The darkest shadow falls from my pen as it writes.
In this farewell the sun pours over me
hot as noon at five o'clock.

But in Rūmī's text it is dawn.    At last
    he will come for me!
*"He has climbed over the horizon like the sun,"*  I read.
    Where have you gone?
*"He is extinguishing the candles of the stars."*

Come quickly here where the sun is leaving me, Beloved,
for it is time to light the lovely candles again!

        **

For a moment did Beauty pass over my face?
I did not have to reach for *your* beauty.
Radiant, it entirely flowd out and thru me.

WORD OF MOUTH

Were you talking?    Were we discoursing
    upon the mercurial Hermes?

The mysteries of quick-silver and the
    alchemical gold,
the transports of Beauty,    dissolve themselves
    and are nothing,
—are resolved again,  everything—
    a wave of my own seeing you
in the rapture of this reading.

    What were you saying?
An arrow from the shining covert of your gaze
    pierced me.    Molten informations of gold
flood into my heart, arteries and veins,
    my blood,    racing thruout with this news,
pulses in a thousand chemical
    new centers of this learning.

              *


How long ago I would have been your target!
every line of my young body alert to be drawn into your sight!
All of my youth was meant to be your target.

Now so late that my body
darkens   and the gossip of years
goes on loosening the tides of
my body,    now so late that
the time of waiting itself loosens
new pains in me,   I hear
the sound of the bow-string.

    Swift, swift,  how again
and again that arrow    reaches me

    and fails to reach me!

ROBERT DUNCAN                                             29

How I long for the presence of your eyes,
for in your eyes gnostic revelations
    come to me,    Hermes
darkens and quickens my speech.

I will take up geometry again.
The mysteries of here and there,   above and below,
    now and then,   demand new
figures of me.     A serpent intuition
    flickers its tongue upon the air.

Mine now the quickening of that
    shifting definition I am swaying in whose

    fascination suspended     before striking

which now opens out radiant and singing petals from itself
    so that I am lost in its apparition,
distracted in this looking into the time-sway.

I am like a snake rising in the
    mirage of the sun where
everything is swaying,     to and fro,
    noon visual dancing and,
beyond my hearing,   in seeing   I over-hear
    the messengers of the sun buzzing,   wingd.

I see and am held here in my seeing   before striking
    the honeyd glow of the woodwind dance

        singing.

    *

In each House    He has a different name.
In each    He is expected again.

And I too change,  but you in all
    these years remain
true to me so that it most seems,
         sweet constancy
    in you I have come true
and all the rest is range.

Then *He* is range.    And from this  household ours
    Heaven is range.    In the Grand Assemblage of Lives,
        the Great Assembly-House,
this Identity, this Ever-Presence,    arranged
    rank for rank,   person for person,   each from its own
sent out from what we were  to another place
    now in the constant exchange

        renderd true.

        &ast;&ast;

## ∾ A Head

A dead boy living among men as a man
called an angel
by me, for want of a word,
spaniel-eyed: wet, with bits
of gold deep in the eyeballs
hidden, like a mysterious ingredient
(c'est là, le mystère)
fringed with black and with black,
thick-grown, delicately thumb-smudged eyebrows
and brown cast on the face
so the lips are an earth red
and the rings or pouches under the eyes
are dark, and all the blue
there is hovers in the hollows
under the ridges of the cheekbones
as, in fall haze, earth,
broken into clods, casts shadows on itself:

except what, in the small hours, shows
the razor's path, its wide swaths
along the cheeks and down below
the strong and bluntly heart-shaped chin
where the taut flesh loosens and softens,
heaviest at the comers of the mouth
turning petulantly down from the fold
that lifts the upper lip and points
to the divider of the nostrils.

This so-called angel
who steps back into the shadows of an empty door
and staggers on short flights of stairs
is filled with a kind of death

that feeds on little things:
fulfilled plans that no longer suit the hour,
appetites that sicken and are not slaked
(such as for milk-shakes),
lost or stolen handkerchieves,
invisible contagion
(such as the common cold).

Within this head where thought repeats
itself like a loud clock, lived
the gray and green of parks before spring
and water on a sidewalk between banks of snow,
a skylit room whose windows were paintings
of windows with views of trees
converging in the park all parks imply;
in that head a million butterflies
took flight like paper streamers and bits of paper
a draught lifts at a parade.

Then they went away.
They went away in a dance-step
to the tune of *Poor Butterfly*
played on a wind-up phonograph
of red mahogany stuck with bits
of gold: right stele for him.

When night comes and lights come on
after the colors fade in the sky,
may he minister as he can to whom he may,
himself or other, give what grace
all the little deaths he stands for,
to me, have left him. He is an angel
for his beauty. So what
if it fades and dies?

JAMES SCHUYLER                                                    33

## ҂ Letter to a Friend:
### Who Is Nancy Daum?

All things are real
no one a symbol:
curtains (shantung
       silk)
potted palm, a
bust: flat, with pipe—
   M. Pierre Martory
a cut-out by Alex
             Katz:
Dreaming eyes
         and pipe
Contiguous to
*en terre cuite*
         Marie
Antoinette
her brown and seeming
living curls
and gaze seen as
Reverie: *My Lady*
*of My Edgeworth*
("Prince Albert in
the can?" "Better
let him out, I . . .")
pipe dream. Some
Vitamins; more
Flying Buzzard
      ware:
a silver chain—my
silver chain
from Denmark from
you by way
of London—
(I put it on: cold
and I love

its weight:
  *argento*
    *pesante*)
a *sang de boeuf*
      spitoon
or Beauty bowl,
a compact
with a Red Sea
    scene
holding little
pills (Valium
for travel strain),
this French
   lamp
whose stem of
  glass
Lights softly
        up
entwined with
autumn trees
(around the base
     are reeds)
its glass shade
  slightly oiled
as is the dawn
above a swamp
lagoon or fen where
    hunters lurk and
    down *marc* or *cognac*
or home-made rotgut
  of their choice,
I—have lost
     my place:
No, here it is:
   Traherne,
*Poems, Centuries*
  *and Three*

     *Thanksgivings,*
a book beneath
      the notebook
in which I write
     Put off the light—
the French lamp
  (signed, somewhere)
and put it on:
the current
        flows.
My heart
beats. Nerves,
    muscles,
the bright invisible
red blood—sang
*d'homme*
    helps (is
that the word?)
      propel
this ball-point
      pen:
black ink is
   not black
     blood.
Two other books:
*The Gay*
      *Insider*
—good—*Run*
*Little Leather*
*Boy* awaits
assessment
on my Peter Meter.
A trove of glass
  within a
   cabinet
near my
    knees

I wish I were on
my knees
embracing
   yours
      my cheek
against the suiting of
        whatever
suit—about now—
or soon, or late—
("I'm not prompt"
   you said, rueful
       factual
"I" I said, "climb
walls")
O Day!
  literal
and unsymbolic
       day:
silken: gray: sunny:
   in salt and pepper
tweed soot storm:
guide, guard,
    be freely
      pierced
by the steel and
gold-eyed
needle passes—stitches
—of my love, my
      lover,
        our love,
his lover—I
      am he—
  (is not
at any tick
each and every life
at hazard: *faites*
*vos jeux,*

JAMES SCHUYLER

*messieurs*)
. . . Where am I?
   en route to
      a literal
Vermont. It's
          time
            to
—oh, do this
      do that—.
I'll call.
Perhaps we'll
  lunch? We
already
said goodbye a
long farewell
for a few weeks'
     parting!
My ocean liner,
  I am your
tug. "Life
is a bed
    of roses:
rugosas,
nor is it always
    summer."
Goodbye. Hello.
      Kiss
Hug. I
  gotta
run. Pierre
Martory,
his semblance,
smokes a St.
      Simonian
pipe and thinks
Mme. de Sévigné
-type thoughts.

He was, when
             posing,
perhaps, projecting
A Letter to a Friend.
             (signed)—

all my
—you know—
         ton
                  Dopey.
PS The lamp is
    signed, Daum,
          Nancy.
Hence I surmise
     she made
or, at least,
designed it.
Who *is* Nancy Daum?


## ❧ Poem

Your enchantment
enchains me, stretched
out there, planked
like a steak or
a shad in season.
And there, where
you flower there.
You're cool to my
touch, soon growing
warm, smooth but not
sleek. I love you—
too much? Not quite
possible. The thought
of harm from you is
far from me as those

Vermont hills, en-
flamed, in October,
as I by you, in their
seasonal rush. To
go up in leaves! I
wish I could, as I
sink down beside you.


∾ Tom

*They told me, Heraclitus,*
*they told me you were dead.*

A key. The door. Open
shut. "Hi, Jim." "Hi.
Tom." "How didja sleep?"
"I didn't. And you?" "A
log." Blond glory, streaked,
finger-combed, curling
in kiss curls at the nape.
A kiss, like bumping fore-
heads. A god, archaic Greek
Apollo in a blue down
jacket. Fifteen degrees
no snow. Tom hates that;
me too. "French toast?"
"Of course." With apple-
sauce. The *Times*, the
obits, a great blues singer
has been taken from us
and a businessman. OJ,
coffee with milk, lecithin
to control mouth movements,
a side effect of Thorazine.
At the stove Tom sings the
release of his rock song,

"Manhattan Movie." His voice
is rich, true, his diction
perfect. I'm so in love
I want to die and take
my happiness to heaven!
No. To be with Tom, my
assistant, three hours
a day four days a week.
(Tom likes "assistant"
I
prefer "secretary."
No sweat: "Ain't no
flies on the lamb
of God." Ahem. Phlegm.)
Tom's eyes are "twin
compendious blue oceans in
which white sails and
gulls wildly fly." We'll
never make it. Tom's
twenty-eight, I'm fifty-
six: he isn't Proust's
"young man born to love
elderly men." He loves E.
an eighteen-year-old
poet whose mother feels
concern at Tom's two-
year pursuit (they only
lately made it). I'm
going to tell her how
lucky her son is, if he
is to have a homosexual
episode (or be one, as
I think he is, pretty
boy), to have a lover so
kind, so loving, so
witty—that thrash-about
laugh—I've said it

JAMES SCHUYLER

and I will. At Number
One Fifth Avenue I tell
E., "You should un-
reservedly make love
to Tom and be cosy and
tender." "I'm sorry, I
don't feel that way
about him." Later
he tells Tom,
"We had a man-
to-man talk." Sad.
I only care about Tom's
happiness. "He's not
very sexually oriented.
Here." The French toast
and applesauce are
delicious. We settle down
to read: he, a Ross
Macdonald, me *Phineas
Redux.* How superb is
Mme. Goesler when she
repudiates the Duke of
Omnium's bequest of priceless
pearls and diamonds and
a fortune (she already
has one) so they will
go to Lady Glencora, the
rightful heir, and no one
can ever say her three years'
tenderness to the dying
man was motivated. In
Tom's book a corpse is
found in corrupt upper-
middle-class L. A., where
he comes from. Beauty.
We might some
day shower

together, wash
each other's back.
Travelling share a bed.
Flesh on flesh,
a head pillowed
on an arm. Touch.
Running from a cab to
the deli, the energy
(graceful) of youth.
Thomas Paul Carey of
Sherman Oaks, California,
who writes and sings
his own rock songs, the
son and grandson of two
great movie actors, the
two Harry Careys. Love
is only and always beautiful.


## ∾ A View

*Little Portion*
*Tuesday, May 10, 1988*

How come a thickish tree
casts so thin a shadow
and that sign-supporting pipe
none at all? (here comes Tom)

The road dries off, lighter
and lighter (there goes
Tom, in the red car, after
flour). In the further

distance, a baby-blue camper,
after reeds and dead tree trunks,
peeled and weathered,
and the creosoted phone poles

JAMES SCHUYLER

Closer, on grass, the sunlight
breathes: fades and brightens,
brightens and fades, sparkles
yellow-green on green

Out of nowhere, a breeze
tosses the junk (soon
to be leaves) on twig ends.
Here comes Charlie, the cat.

Closer, window screen and
a six-light window sash
pushed part way up another
makes a fifteen-light window

framed by thick white net.
Closer, a bag says, The Cellar.
Closer, a pair of slippers, and
(khaki canvas) a Maine hiking shoe

invites my foot to go
out there, into the view
of May 10<sup>th</sup>, 1988
                    Here

comes Tom (he
got the flour) and there
sits Charlie, a white
cat on a green hummock.


WORD OF MOUTH

## ∾ Dietrich

She never had to make up
for not being popular at school—
she started out well beyond all that.

She was never a bobbysoxer, for example,
nor one of those girls fighting
against going all the way—
you don't go from that to where she is.

When she sings "My ideal is a big blond man"
or "Every night another bliss"
you know just what she means by this.

Ancient in Paris,
perfect setting for monuments
where the boulevards culminate
in a granite bust,

where the populace adores
the will that invents an inviolable mask—
still she writes "This rotten world,"

as if tied to a mast and forced
to witness, as she always has—
her eyes windows
with the shades permanently up.

## ∾ Garbo

Her eyes never blink—
higher beings do not blink,

nor people in remote lands
who stare at you from the fields—
but that's innocence, like animals.

If blinking is a kind of flinching,
she never flinches.
She doesn't adopt any facial expression—
it's her feelings she shows
or none at all. Nor does she put on
mannerisms like we do, meaning
we're desperate for attention.
If she says she wants to be alone
she's the only one we believe it of.

It's no devices then that make her beautiful
but the lack of them. Still, the awkwardness
of her grace shows that being graceful
is not an easy victory—
there's the permanent mournfulness in the mouth
and the testimony of those eyes—
no blinking it back,
it's all there.

Can't we make the same commitment,
risk shedding evasions, devices, defences
—in short, our faces—
and look unblinking at each other, vulnerable
to what in our hearts we long for,
whatever the cost, wherever it leads?

Or does she affirm that for mere mortals
the price is too great,

though for herself
she could not, would not, choose another fate.

# ∾ Callas

The voice that came out of her
chose her as its earthly vehicle,
for reasons only the gods can know.

She spoke of it as separate from her,
a wild creature she had to struggle to master.

It floats like an unwieldy bird with a small head,
whose wings can't quite control the over-large body
soaring dangerously low above jagged peaks,
wobbling in the updrafts.

An Egyptian sculpture of a priestess,
she held up her large, arresting hands,
invoking the authority of the ancients—
hawks, serpents, bulls and suns surrounded her as she sang,
cut into stone.

She had that specialized genius for song
birds have, an intelligence of too high a vibration
for the practical matters of life.
But she was unfaithful to her gift—
even if for the perfectly understandable reasons
of being fashionable and getting a man—
otherwise she would never have dieted down,
but stayed fat for those spectacular tones,
living only for art.

It was an operatic fate
that the man she suffered over
was one of the great rats
who dismissed the most magnificent voice in the world
as just a whistle in her throat.

EDWARD FIELD

But after her sexless marriage, this was probably
the first man with a hard on she got together with,
and duck-like, fixated on, as is so common with us ordinary slobs.
With some men, whatever they are besides, the cock
is the best part of them, even if they are monsters
and, like him, supremely ruthless.
And perhaps his selfishness is what ravished her,
for it was sex in the raw, the one thing
singing wasn't.

Like Norma, the Druid nun, who broke her vows
for the love of a mere mortal,
she, too, was cast aside,
not for any high priestess, but a more
earthly rival, famous widow, jet set icon,
who didn't need his powerful cock, just his power,
and to get her hands on his bank account.

She threw away her magic voice for a man who threw her away,
*thunderclap in the heavens, an accusing dagger of lightning,*
and her crystal brain—
whose single-minded command like a bird's
was to soar, to sing—
shattered, and she fell.


## ∾ Whatever Became of: Freud

Has the age of psychology really passed?
Aren't people interested anymore
in how toilet training shaped them?
Nowadays, nobody talks of their "analysis," or even
the less respectable therapies that came into fashion
about the time we gave up on the couch—
encounter groups, group gropes, group games, and finally
just lying on the floor, screaming out the pain.
Or even, on the lowest level

(which we all descended to in desperation),
self-help books: How to Overcome Depression,
Get More Confidence, Be Popular.

But usually, we were safely in the hands of Freud,
whose theories, a whole generation beyond Marx swore,
would rescue mankind from its lot,
and even, in the views of Reich, end war
when we liberated our sexuality
by working through the body's armouring
to release our soft and loving primal selves—
war and love supposedly being incompatible—
also by sitting for hours in the orgone box to absorb
the sexual energy of the universe.

Those were the years when we were all convinced
we were "neurotic," discussed our neuroses passionately,
analyzed our dreams with friends over coffee
and endless cigarettes—we were fiendish smokers—
talked of breakthroughs, insights, and sometimes with awe
of "graduation," when the "neurosis"
would finally be "cured," which meant
you had worked through your blocks, your inhibitions,
and were no longer Acting Out Negative,
but had found your niche in society—
marriage, a career, and forgiving your parents—
and worried whether this meant the end of creativity.

The air is clearer since "phallic symbol"
has gone the way of "penis envy" and "Freudian slip."
Nobody nowadays blames their failures on their neuroses,
and if you say "transferences," everyone assumes
you're talking about your bank accounts.
It's no longer news the discovery
(and Freud deserved the Nobel Prize for it)
that people's minds are always on sex.

EDWARD FIELD

But with the same obsession we had with Freud,
and the same narcissism (how we beat each other
with that faded cry), people nowadays are able to simply
turn away from "problems" and wallow in their pleasures,
making a cult of health, often devoting themselves
just to working on their bodies. Did I say "just"?
Even Freud was always looking for the roots
of neurosis in the body. And as Claudette Colbert said
on observing Marilyn Monroe's buns,
"I would have had to start at thirteen."

Sadly, true. For us old devotees of the therapies,
the cornerstone of our faith, You can change your history,
proved to be bad Freud, and even worse, a fraud—
far more expensive than the gym. Years of talk,
and nothing got solved. Except the language of it
seemed to define the losses of a generation,
and for all its radiant promises, that was all.


ॐ Post Masturbatum

Afterwards, the penis
is like a girl who has been "had"
and is ashamed.

Sudden neglect, you goose,
after all those romantic promises
carried off by soft caresses,
before the hard ramming
when you bit your lip until it was over—
foolish one who gave in, went all the way . . .

until the next time,
when the nudge of a lover's ardor,
or the sight of it,
and the memory of something

genuine if painful,
are again convincing.


## ∾ Getting To Know You

Like the hard-on,
the asshole is another level of being.
It's me, but a me
even I must negotiate with,
especially when washing after shitting,
as civilized life demands.
For it does not allow the soapy finger in,
presenting an impenetrable surface.


Do not be misled.
It is offering the coy resistance
it would to a lover. Therefore,
with a lover's singlemindedness,
remain stalwart in seeking entrance,
probe for a crevice
until the fingertip,
with a delicate wiggle,
pries open the curl of muscle
and slips in,

and miraculously, you will find
that the whole organ relents,
goes soft for the soaping,
with a sappy grin.

EDWARD FIELD

# \infty from *The Poetry File*

## Secrets of the Closet

Rupert Brooke was one of my earliest poetic loves, as much for his legend as his poetry. As with so many poets, the legend lent his poetry an extra dimension. He was such a famous beauty he expected every man to make love to him, but I heard that when he met Henry James, poor James, though smitten, had to stammer through his famous excuse about an accident, reported variously as stepping over a stile or stumbling off a streetcar, which left him incapable.

On picnics, Rupert Brooke displayed an unusual talent—after jumping into an ice-cold pond, he emerged, not shrivelled up like us normal men, but with a hard-on, which he displayed proudly to the girls and boys of the party. Not the usual Victorian scene.

Modern poetry was supposed to be a rebellion against the "poetical" language of Victorian sensibilities, but gentility keeps creeping back in. It's the curse of poetry. That's why I like to publish in little magazines like *Exquisite Corpse* and *Chiron Review* and *5AM* where they are open to the new low-down, vernacular poetry, and everything is allowed. I did have a poem about my cock in an academic quarterly, the *Michigan Quarterly Review* (I praise the editor; Laurence Goldstein for this)—the subject of the issue was The Male Body. But there are still plenty of restrictions in this country.

John Crowe Ransom, editor of *Kenyon Review,* to Robert Duncan, 12/6/44, rejecting a poem. "I read the poem as an advertisement or a notice of overt homosexuality and we are not in the market for literature of this type."

In the early sixties, one of Alfred Chester's stories was also rejected by *Partisan Review* on the grounds that it "celebrated homosexuality instead of being analytical about it." Even today plenty of censorship exists. What's so terrible about the word "hard-on," for instance? But try to get a poem published with that word in it.

It often depends on the political views of the editor. The Boston gay paper, *Bay Windows,* not long ago refused to print a poem of mine because I used the word "queer," which was unacceptable to the editor.

Back in the 40s and 50s, homosexuality was okay in poetry if it was veiled by metaphor, ambiguous pronouns, and verbal brilliance. I was a passionate admirer of the poetry of Dunstan Thompson, with its unmistakable homo-erotic content. But after Senator Joseph McCarthy and HUAC got done with the universities and intellectuals and made them knuckle under, poetry was not considered a medium for anything more than spiritual subject mat-ter—nuns, swans, carousels, etc. Or philosophizing. Academic and establish-ment poetry was reinforced in its gentility. Then the Beats came along, a breath of fresh air. But essentially they didn't change the poetry world, which is a very conservative establishment.

With its dedication to ambiguity, Modern Poetry fit right in with the need of gay poets to be closeted. Poets in the past have often changed the sex of the lover addressed—Byron's love poems to Lord Clare, for example, to the feminine pseudonym of "Thyrza." Of course, one can always address the lover with the anonymous "you" and it can be taken by the reader according to his own sexual preference. Hart Crane, openly gay in his life, in his work was cautious. But one can learn to read through the veils of metaphor.

Even straight poets found the devices of Modern Poetry useful. Henri Coulette was obsessed in his poetry with the secret world of spies, agents, traitors. "War of the Secret Agents," a marvelous sequence of poems about spies in occupied Paris, seemed to be his metaphor for human relations, where nobody knows the truth of anybody else and what secrets are hidden, with betrayal a constant. Was life under an oppressive occupying army also a metaphor for his own secret life, the betrayal he himself might have been forced to commit? His mysterious poem "Chicken Rampant, Bar Sinister," suggests an adolescent hustler phase, a court case where he had to testify against one of his johns, a spell with a psychiatrist.

CHICKEN RAMPANT, BAR SINISTER

I tell him my thirteen secret names,
and I say
"All my decisions are committee decisions,
and some of my selves,
Doctor, are always out of town."

Rich as Onassis, I count my fears.
In my dreams
I see the hard-hearted and familiar strangers
circling around me,
and I don't know if I'm their king

or their victim. Chicken rampant, bar
sinister—
my family coat of arms hangs invisible,
in an empty room.
Memory's a form of simile:

I am like all my unknown and frightened fathers.

Surely, I am not making up the plot I discern through the fragmentary technique, a teenage boy caught hustling in a gay bar, and sent to a psychiatrist by the family, thereby being frightened into conformity.

When I stopped over in L.A. on a reading tour, Coulette came to interview me for a book of interviews of poets. He was dressed academic conservative-style, with horn-rimmed glasses, appropriate to a professor at the U. of Southern California, not in the least California-casual, even slightly stuffy in manner. He gave nothing away, if there was anything to give away.

I've written to his friend, Donald Justice, to ask if he knew anything about Coulette's early life, but he didn't. Coulette was a very private man. But perhaps I am reading into this poem what I want to find there? In the other poems I can find no other references to a gay past or a double life, and even in "Chicken Rampant, Bar Sinister" it takes close reading to dig out the story, and what one gets is merely tantalizing.

*

Helen Vendler writes approvingly of: "The visible estrangement of poetry from prose." Odd that critics should try to make rules for poets.

Actually poetry and prose draw closer together on the West Coast, draw further apart on the East Coast, where poetry becomes more literary, moves toward artifice.

WORD OF MOUTH

When poetry is talked about by critics like Vendler, I rarely recognize myself.

> I'm the Eileen Farrell of the poetry world.
> A glorious voice, but low class,
> living with her policeman husband
> on Staten Island,
>
> Staten Island, for God's sake,
> prole heaven—
>
> and far too low class for the Met.

The problem I've had from the beginning was that I wrote for people like myself, assuming they were out there, but the poetry world says, You must write for Us.

I see poetry as a *vehicle*, but there are many different possibilities: Ashbery for instance, writes in the *manner* of someone writing a poem. It is an act that sometimes breaks down into giggles. With the Beats, the *impulse* to write poetry was demonstrated, emphasizing verbal improvisations. Now Helen Vendler, as premier critic, celebrates the *means* of poetry: language, form, diction, metaphor. I think she misses what poetry is really about.

> Mannerisms
> do not make it poetry,
> but sometimes they succeed.

Charles Reznikoff on the difference between formal and free verse:

> "Not like flowers in the city
> in neat rows or in circles
> but like dandelions
> scattered on a lawn."

Maybe what it comes down to is Do you like the sensibility?

*

## HOLY MEN, ALL

Rilke in religious mode
minimized our mortal ills.
Wordsworth in his greatest ode
chortled over daffodils.
In Dylan Thomas' poetry
Christmas was holy in his town.
Poets always claim to be
enlightened, God-struck, never down.
I try, I try but this morning I
only see God in a stream of shit—
alas, again denied me. Why?
And why scorn my laments for it?
If poets fill their poems with praise
of angels, mystic visions, flowers,
Field sings of constipated days
wasted on toilet seat for hours.
Such honest songs will never win
a MacArthur prize, and even worse,
the critics will never let him in-
to *The Oxford Book of Modern Verse.*

~ Chaco Canyon

Plato, my lord, might wonder, if he saw,
As we saw, from the cliff, the holy city
Built like a cave, its front shaped to the arc
The East's bright arrow follows in its flight.
And there, within, since daylight heat and glare
Are freshened by no breeze like the one that shoreward
Accompanies your mother on her shell,
Its people waited, fearful, for a brightness
Down from the mountain, in a violence
Of dark drums and of torches, suddenly
Out of an earth unburdened of its gift.
But then he might recall its wise men, watching,
Silently, each new solstice, for the sun's
Quick step upon the mark high on the butte
Or under unborn night, observing midnight
Against a cloud of stars and shooting stars
By Mercury's approach to Mars, as we
Observed the night before, a satellite
Conjured by his enraptured new disciples
Wavering across the axis out of sight.
Eleusis, Athens, and Delos! Consciences
Alive, in the particulars of place!

The moon shone full and whiter than the dawn,
My lord. Along the cliff the stony lichen
Seemed kin to the snake that Christopher awakened
From sleeping in the torpor spirits share;
While, fastened to the rock, the lunar flowers
That open in the dark gave off a scent,
When we stooped low to smell them, as of fields
Transcendent, where the blessed spirits gaze
Long on the smooth bright tables of desire

Expressive of the fortunes you prepare.
Along the path, under a meager growth
Of creosote and scattered in the powdery

Grey laval dust, were sherds, angled design
From some old common syntax of the mind;
And, on a wrinkled tree trunk near the fort
That overlooks the washes to the north,
Two lizards, male and female. Steven and Christian,
Red hair and black, almost thirteen and twelve,
Embarrassed, fascinated, boyishly obscene,
Kneeled to behold the prehistoric trance
Of roseate pale bodies pressed together,
Bellies moon-white and green and visions fixed
On rituals mysterious as air,
Hesitant, ardent, indifferent, all at once.
I thought of you, on Bacchus' arm, asleep.
Back in the valley, hot, in high noon's heat,
We played, too boisterous, under artesian streams
As fresh and cold as happiness, and soon
Were reprimanded by a uniform.

Later that night, around the fire, we two,
Happy again in our new dialogue
With you and Plato, heard Christian and Steven call
Their names from where they scrambled on the hill,
Until they met a girl in the next campground.
They moped back severe, furious with each other
And hating her, tormented, Christian threatening
To kill her the next day and, from his bed,
Cursing his friend, his enemy, his rival.
After breakfast, they climbed the hill again,
Challenging all the campground with their cries,
Tarzans, without a need or care for Jane.

If I have ever pleased you, give me, this once,
Unspirited by what has happened since,

To see distinct and honestly the truth
Of our adventure, not as Georgia O'Keeffe
Collected from the moon-dry sand a skull
As final as a piece of broken light
For her mimesis, but with such circumstance
As Plato keeps vivacious for his memoir
And such light as in oaks above Jalama
Is part shade and reflections of the shade.

We stopped, on our way back, to try the springs
At Ojo Caliente. Naked, we entered
Slowly, with short sharp cries of pain and pleasure,
An iron water hotter than human blood
And drank the slow pulse hot from the mineral vein.
Dizzy with heat, maybe hallucinated
By smelling the jimson flower back on the cliff,
Time shrunk into a white cloud far away,
I thought I had received the gift of tongues
And called out in the murk, "I have a vision
Requiring me to tell why all things are.
In the undark untime, long before *Don Giovanni*
And the *B Minor Mass* were natures, the moon
Fell for the sun. Round and round the abyss
She chased him, till desire was so intense
That, from its center, through the gathering blue,
A youth appeared. When, past the seas of crisis
Aud the deep lake of dreams, he reached the small
Sea of tranquility, then, on its bed
They knew such joy that the one became the many
Divided and distributed in time
And every habitation of the seas
Of air and earth and water, as a fire.
You are the fire, my lord: your quickening step,
Your ankle curved up sweetly to the calf,
Your ass cheeks poised together for your stride
Proud beneath the body's pathos, your arms
Triumphant and throat smoother than the dove's,

Your face divine, from whose smile comes the tender
Intimate voice, the body's echo, and
Your hair, still brushed by traces of the sun."

Steven and Christian jeered, though, as boys are,
Made reckless by exuberance. Christopher,
Though pleased to know I took him for a model,
Upon the cruel mirror offered him
Saw, opening his pale wing, your younger twin
Haunt love and beauty with old age and death;
And, feeling that embrace within the car
To Santa Fe, heard his new sorrow sung,
As if without redemption, in one man's
"*Ach, kennst du nicht dein Kind?*" played on a tape.
The highway seemed the future. Steven and Christian
Stirred in their sleep, exhausted. Night wore by.
Though Plato's eyes were open, in a dream
Remembering the canyon, he foresaw
That, in the time to come, a man, encamped
For years beside a ruin once a city
Exposed to the indifference of the sun
And moon, inquiring of the breathless dust
That covers all things made of it, one day,
Among the ashes, bones, and sherds, will find
Preserved by an egyptian air a memoir,
And, bringing it to the light, will read of us,
Dazzled by time and by what time provides.

## ∾ Even on Sunday

I don't know anything about God but what the human record tells
me—in whatever languages I can muster—or by turning to
translators—or the centuries—of that blasphemy which defines god's
nature by our own hatred and prayers for vengeance and dominance—
that *he* (lower case and questionable pronoun) would destroy by a
hideous disease one lover of another   or by war, a nation for what
uprightness and economic hide-and-seek—and *he* (lower case and
questionable pronoun) is on the side of the always-ignorance of politics
in which we trust—the *polis* is at the 'bottom of the sea,' as Hannah
Arendt noticed—and *he* (lower case and interrogated pronoun) walks
among the manipulated incompetences of public thought

where I had hoped to find myself ordinary among others in the streets—
a 'murmuring voice of societies'

and so one thinks them over—blasphemies all, against multiplicity,
which is all anyone knows about god—and one can only hate them
so much without becoming *halt and lame in their kingdom of single
mindedness*—their having taken a book to have been once and forever,
the language behind language that no one has ever spoken god's
what-knot and *mystical rags* we call flags

as a friend said, 'I'm going to become fundamentalist and call
everybody asshole'

and what would the gods be if l asked them—our nakedness didn't
quite fit—out, as it is, of nature—yet, there is a sentiment at *the
intersection between life and thought*—streaks of beyondness in that
careless relation

October came in August and petunias straggled,
sprawling white faces one at a time, lobelia browned and continued

blue   the neighbours cut down the sexual cottonwood which kept the
whole block from repainting door-steps for over a month—by the
fluffs of its happiness—

so we are in the midst of a metaphysical washout —take for example,
Verlaine and Rimbaud—as Hans Mayer says: *Being shut out of the*
*social order, they sought to heighten their condition by, say publicly embracing*
*in Brussels and thus providing the formula for a new 'condition humaine'*
*that called out to be created*—both failed—both remained in *outsiderdom*
—one continued to rhyme, the other gave up the whole damned
creation   behind this, an Enlightenment, which I'll return to
          and Sylvie asked,
*'But what became of the Man?'*
*'Well, the Lion springed at him. But it came so slow, it were*
*three weeks in the air—'*
*'Did the Man wait for it all that time?'* I asked.
*'Course he didn't'* Bruno replied, *gliding headfirst down the*
*stem of a fox-glove for the story was evidently close to its end.*
*'He sold his house, and he packed up his things, while the Lion were coming.*
*And he went and lived in another town. So the Lion ate the wrong man.*
          *This was evidently the Moral . . .* said Lewis Carroll

the moral is that something does devour the existential given—
Rimbaud, Mayer writes, *does not intertwine with visions of Sodom in order*
*to provoke heavens' fire; it is simply the sole possibility of his own self-acceptance*

*being shut out of the social order*   Rimbaud writes *de posséder la verité*
*dans une âme et un corps,* which Mayer interprets to say *being alive*
*in the full sense of body and soul*   the truth is being alive, until you break
on it

ah, Laius, when you ran off with the youth Chryssipus, the Sphinx
flew to a whistling stop in Thebes—and fire fell on Sodomites, on
each one of them, and, I'll be damned, almost everybody—tell me a
tale to explain sublime biology—then, tell me another to explain
sublime human nature—and murder, unmythologized, fell on 20th-
century outsiders   pollution of what in the momentary hangup of

the vast biology of things, desiring?    a covenant with whom?

    androsphinx, recumbent lion with the head of a man, answer me—
that is to say, each one of us

the sublime, dear everybody and everyday, is not so simply human—
overwhelms—*uncanny* is Hannah Arendt's word for the face of it—
*dangerous*—*severe as a blow*—*mysterious*—on which the *existential*
*given* floats—the passions of

and Hans Mayer notes the tying and untying that confines things:
*At the height of the Victorian era, the Bible is once again, as in Cromwells'*
*time, . . . the spiritual and social foundation of everyday life*—, O, the once-
again in which we trust—*Declaration is made in the Bible of what is*
*proper for woman and what is not. The Bible depicts that which God punished*
*in Sodom. St. Paul only confirmed the curse*   one's mind may have a
certain affinity with Christopher Marlowe's, if it is true, as his roommate
Thomas Kyd tells us, that he thought the apostle Paul a swindler—
who taught a curdled godhead and a curdling view of the *existential*
*given*—and the black milk of it is blasphemy, so to revile existence

in the midst of this, an Enlightenment which first and foremost posited
an *equality of men and women, including homosexuals*—religion and
sexuality go hand in hand in the apple-light

it was not to be merely law, like free speech, but a *mental practice*
    what developed, in the guise of a Darwinian terror advancing in
evolutionary form, was the lion body with a man's head, walking in
the garden, so that *the underlying principles of liberty and equality not*
*even taking fraternity into account, inordinately encouraged combatting all*
*forms of outsiderdom in favour of what Ihab Hassan calls 'quantities of normed*
*phenomena'*—normed existence excludes the *existential given,* not being
alive in the full sense of body and soul—and *extends, not merely perverts*
that which calls itself normality into political form but Mayer asks, *what*
*is it then if the precipitating step outside, into the margins, is a condition of*
*birth, a result of ones' sex, parentage, physical or spiritual makeup? Then*
*ones' existence itself becomes a breaking of boundaries*

we can thereby return to ourselves a *measure of freedom,* and take form—
the work of a lifetime—in this breaking of boundaries—

against,

as Mayer says, *a global disposition of thought toward annihilation, which*
*thinks to admit only majorities in the future and is determined to equate*
*minorities with 'worthless life'  Worthless are the Jews, there the blacks [and*
*aboriginals] somewhere else (and everywhere) the homosexuals, women*
*of the type of Judith and Delilah, not least the intellectuals keen on individuation . . .*


*'They should all be gassed': the expression has crept into everyday language*
*Woman is not equal to man. Man is manly man, whatever is to be understood*
*by that: the feminine man stands out from the race and thereby becomes worthless*
*life. Shylock must be exterminated: the only final solutions are fire and gas*


extreme remedies—pharmakons—Mayer reminds us, have been
proposed: for example, Klaus Mann writing in 1949—remember
when that was!—*calls for . . . the concerted mass suicide of intellectuals: to*
*bring public opinion in the world, in the integrity and autonomy of which he*
*quite clearly still believed, to its right senses*


well, we know now that this would disappear with a headline in the
Entertainment pages, or it might make the Arts and Books section
along with obituaries and sportsmanship, in *The Globe &Mail*—and
intellectuals?—Mann had not noticed that point in the space of
intelligence where they join the system, higgledy-piggledy—I think
of that recent hustle in the United States, offering the end of history
like a dinky-toy, democracy, pinking, blueing, and off-whiting in plastic
—'My goodness!' everyone said, 'They've discovered Hegel!' and *Time*
*Magazine* thought he was little known—and I said, 'My goodness!
Francis Fukuyama, so we finally got here, there, anywhere'


so to be reminded once again of Puddin'head Wilson: *It was wonderful*
*to find America, but it would have been more wonderful to miss it*


*this unified mankind*—for that's who's there, quantity or lump, at the
end of a materialist's or an idealist's history—*conceived,* Mayer writes,
*as a homogenized humanity. Woe to outsiders*

so that was it, was it? an *Enlightenment that promised equality to men and women, including homosexuals!* an age in the hole, running three centuries, surely allows one to say, 'Listen, you assholes, a *metaphysical washout* means you've lost your top soil'

and this system aims exactly—*at the heart of our social existence* to be an outsider *by virtue of our existence*—like statues come to life by moonlight in the child's desiring mind—has the advantage of voices, and their attentions, each to each, among quantified multitudes who wander *the computations and rationalities that belong to no one*—also going, going, gone into the *corpus Christianum* with its sadly separated body and soul

among these voices, I think of Montaigne: *Embraces remembered (or still vaguely hoped for) are 'our final accolades'*

in whose arms

even on Sunday

    With considered use of Hans Mayer's
    *Outsiders* (MIT, 1982). Mark Twain's
    aptness is cited in Ihab Hassan's
    'Foreword.' Written for Gay Games III,
    Vancouver, August, 1990.

## ∾ In Remembrance of Matthew Shepard

How sad I am. How sad
this violation of the existential
given and Matthew's song—
another debt of this indecent
century—what is to be said
about this *hideous traffic*
*in religion* that has taught
blasphemy for centuries
against Jews, blacks, aboriginals,
women, Gypsies, and homosexuals
everywhere. "They" put on Jesus-shoes.
He never wore them.
"Their" *sacrifices to hate and hell.*
*There is no more to be said*
*about God*, except the *infinite exposure*
*of our finitude* that "they" have taught.
Love arrives as a promise.
Every particular love is Love,
dear Matthew. How love shatters
when they stopped your song—
the shatters in which we trust.
Yes, the philosopher said: *The glorious body*
*cannot but be the mortal body itself.*
*What changes are not the things but their limits.*
*It is as if there hovered over them something*
*like a halo, a glory.* Dear Matthew.

## ∾ Orpheus' Song to Apollo

You, Apollo, have yoked your horse
To the wrong sun.
You have picked the wrong flower.
Breaking a branch of impossible
Green-stemmed hyacinth
You have found thorns and postulated a rose.
Sometimes we were almost like lovers
(As the sun almost touches the earth at sunset)
But,
At touch,
The horse leapt like an ox
Into another orbit of roses, roses.
Perhaps,
If the moon were made of cold green cheese,
I could call you Diana.
Perhaps,
If a knife could peel that rosy rind,
It would find you virgin as a star
Too hot to move.
Nevertheless,
This is almost goodbye.
You,
Fool Apollo,
Stick
Your extra roses somewhere where they'll keep.
I like your aspiration
But the sky's too deep
For fornication.

## ∾ Lives of the Philosophers: Diogenes

He spilled his seed upon the marketplace
While all the Greek boys watched. Along the street
The dogs were basking in the August sun,
Scratching their fleas, and panting with the heat.
The brown-thighed boys looked on in discontent
For they had hoped another Socrates
Would pat their heads and talk, and at the end
Confirm their daily wisdom with a kiss.
"Diogenes is Socrates gone mad,"
Their voices shouted, but his sweating face
Was straining towards the sun, blind to the light
That streamed around him through the marketplace.
The boy's had left him and the dogs began
To howl in cynic wonder at the heat.


## ∾ When Your Body Brushed Against Me

When your body brushed against me I remembered
How we used to catch butterflies in our hands
Down in the garden.
We were such patient children
Following them from flower to flower
Waiting and hoping.
With our cupped hands we used to catch them
And they answered us with a soft tickle
For they never stopped flying.
In bed I remembered them and cried for
The touch of their fast wings, the impatience
Of their bright colors
I am too old for such games
But even tonight, now your body has reminded mc of butterflies
I lie here awake, pretending.

## ∾ The Song of the Bird in the Loins

A swallow whispers in my loins
So I can neither lie or stand
And I can never sleep again
Unless I whisper you his song:

"Deep in a well," he whispers. "Deep
As diamonds washed beneath the stone
I wait and whisper endlessly
Imprisoned in a well of flesh.

"At night he sometimes sleeps and dreams.
At night he sometimes does not hear my voice.
How can I wound you with my well of sound
If he can sleep and dream beneath its wounds?

"I whisper to you through his lips.
He is my cage, you are my source of song.
I whisper to you through a well of stone.
Listen at night and you will hear him sing:

"'A swallow whispers in my loins
So I can neither lie or stand
And I can never sleep again
Unless I whisper you this song'."

## ∾ Some Notes on Whitman for Allen Joyce

*"Let shadows be furnished with genitals."*

He was reaching for a world I can still remember. Sweet and painful. It is
a world without magic and without god. His ocean is different from my ocean,
his moon is different from my moon, his love (oh, God the loss) is different
from my love.

In his world roads go somewhere and you walk with someone whose hand you can hold. I remember. In my world roads only go up and down and you are lucky if you can hold on to the road or even know that it is there.

He never heard spirits whispering or saw Aphrodite crawl out of the water or was frightened by the ghost of something crucified. His world had clouds in it and he loved Indian names and carried some of his poems in a pouch around his neck. He had no need of death.

Rimbaud without wings.

Forgive me Walt Whitman, you whose fine mouth has sucked the cock of the heart of the country for fifteen years. You did not ever understand cruelty. It was that that severed your world from me, fouled your moon and your ocean threw me out of your bearded paradise. The comrade you are walking with suddenly twists your hand off. The ghost-bird that is singing to you suddenly leaves a large seagull dropping in your eye. You are sucking the cock of a heart that has clap.

Calamus cannot exist in the presence of cruelty. Not merely human cruelty, but the cruelty of shadows, the cruelty of spirits. Calamus is like Oz. One needs, after one has left it, to find some magic belt to cross its Deadly Desert, some cat to entice one into its mirror. There Walt is, like some great seabird from the Emerald Palace, crying, "Calamus, Calamus." And there one is, at the other side of the desert, hearing Walt but seeing that impossible shadow, those shimmering heat waves across the sky. And one needs no Virgil, but an Alice, a Dorothy, a Washington horsecar conductor, to lead one across that cuntlike mirror, that cruelty.

So when I dreamed of Calamus, as I often did when I touched you or put my hand upon your hand, it was not as of a possible world, but as a lost paradise. A land my father Adam drove me out of with the whip of shadow. In the last sense of the word—a fairy story. That is what I think about Calamus. That is what I think about your damned Calamus.

WORD OF MOUTH

## ∾ Love Poems

### 1

Do the flowers change as I touch your skin?
They are merely buttercups. No sign of death in them. They die and you know
    by their death that it is no longer summer.
    Baseball season.
Actually
I don't remember ever touching your back when there were flowers (butter-
    cups and dandelions there) waiting to die.
    The end of summer
The baseball season finished. The
Bumble-bee there cruising over a few poor flowers.
They have cut the ground from under us. The touch
Of your hands on my back. The Giants
Winning 93 games
Is as impossible
In spirit
As the grass we might walk on.

### 2

For you I would build a whole new universe around myself. This isn't shit it is
    poetry. Shit
Enters into it only as an image. The shit the ghostes feasted on in the Odyssey.
    When Odysseus gave them one dry fly and made them come up for
    something important Food.
"For you I would build a whole new universe," the ghosts all cried, starving.

### 3

"'Arf,' says Sandy"
"To come to the moment of never come back to the moment of hope. Too
    many buses that are late" Hugh O'Neill in our Canto for Ezra Pound.

The ground still squirming. The ground still not fixed as I thought it would be
	in an adult world.
Sandy growls like a wolf. The space between him and his image is greater than
	the space between me and my image.
Throw him a honey-cake. Hell has been proved to be a series of image.
Death is a dog and Little Orphan Annie
My own Eurydice. Going into hell so many times tears it
Which explains poetry.


4


"If you don't believe in a god, don't quote him," Valery once said when he was
	about ready to give up poetry. The purposefull suspension of disbelief has
	about the chance of a snowball in hell.
Lamias maybe, or succubi but they are about as real in California as night-
	crawlers
Gods or stars or totems are not game-animals. Snark-hunting is not like
	discussing baseball.
Against wisdom as such. Such
Tired wisdoms as the game-hunters develop
Shooting Zeus, Alpha Centauri, wolf with the same toy gun.
It is deadly hard to worship god, star, and totem. Deadly easy
To use them like worn-out condoms spattered by your own gleeful, crass, and
	unworshiping
Wisdom


5


Which explains poetry. Distances
Impossible to be measured or walked over. A band of faggots (fasces) cannot
	be built into a log-cabin in which all Western Civilization can cower. And
	look at stars, and books, and other people's magic diligently.
Distance, Einstein said, goes around in circles. This
Is the opposite of a party or a social gathering.
It does not give much distance to go on.

As
In the beaches of California
It does not give me much to go on.
The tidal swell
Particle and wave
Wave and particle
Distances.


6


Sable arrested a fine comb.
It is not for the ears. Hearing
Merely prevents progress. Take a step back and view the sentence.
Sable arrested a fine comb. On the road to Big Sur (1945) the fuses blew every
    time we braked. Lights out, every kind of action. A deer
Hit us once (1945) and walked sulkily into the bushes as we braked into silence.
No big white, lightless automobiles for him. If he's hit, let them show him.
Sable arrested a last stop . . . I think it was in Watsonville (1945 sable arrested
    fine comb a)
Past danger into the fog we
Used the last fuse.


7


The howling dog in my mind says "Surrender" at eight points of the compass.
    North, South, East, West, combinations. Whether
He means me or you to me I am not certain. A color-blind person can read
    signals because red is always at the top and green at the bottom. Or is it the
    reverse? I forget, not being color-blind. The dog
In my heart howls continuously at you, at me. "Surrender."
I do not know where my heart is.
My heart's in the highlands
My heart is not here
My heart's in the highlands
A-chasing the deer. Dog

Of my heart groans, howls
Blind to guesses. The deer
Your heart and guesses, blandly seek water.


8

There is real pain in not having you just as there is real pain in not having
    poetry
Not totally in either case as solace, solution, end to all the minor tragedies
But, in either case (poetry or you)
As a bed-partner.
Against the drift of rhododendrons and other images we have not seen to-
    gether
I have seen your locked lips and come home sweating.


*9*

For you I would build a whole new universe but you obviously find it cheaper
    to rent one. Eurydice did too. She went back to hell unsure of what kind of
    other house Orpheus would build. "I call it death-in-life and life-in-
    death." Shot
In the back by an arrow, President Kennedy seemed to stiffen for a moment
    before he assumed his place in history. Eros
Do that.
I gave you my imaginary hand and you give me your imaginary hand and we
    walk together (in imagination) over the earthly ground.

# ∾ A Portrait of the Artist as a Young Landscape

Watch sunset fall upon that beach like others did. The waves
Curved and unspent like cautious scythes, like evening harvesters.
Feel sorrow for the land like others did. Each eating tide,
Each sigh of surf, each sunset-dinner, pulls the earth-crop, falls
A little fuller; makes the sand grain fall
A little shorter, leaner. Leaves the earth
A breathless future harvest.
I watch, as others watched, but cannot stand
Where others stood; for only water now
Stands once where Arnold stood, or Lear or Sappho stood.
Retreating shore (each day has new withdrawals)
Breaks in feeble song—it sings and all abandoned history is spread,
A tidal picnic for that conqueror.


## I. The Mind As Present Perception

I watched and saw a sailor floating in that sea
And melt before he drowned.
Asleep and fragrant as that sleep, he seemed
To draw the sun within his flesh and melt. He seemed
To draw the fire from that angel and to melt. Now he is dead.
To melt is not to drown but is enough
To shear the body of its flesh; the sea
Is made for drowning, but when God is short
Of waters for his purpose then the sea
Becomes a pool of fire; angels ride
Astride their flamy waves
Pale as desire
Terrible angel, out of that fire
Out of the beach-bones, melted like butter
Out of the blazing waves, the hot tide
Terrible angel, sea-monster
Terrible fish-like angel, fire breather
Source of the burning ocean.

JACK SPICER                                                    75

## II. The Mind As Past Perception

But I watch slowly, see the sand-grains fall
A little riper, fuller; watch the ocean fall
From sunset dinner. Watch the angel leave
His fire-pleasure.
                        Deep in the mind there is an ocean
I would fall within it, find my sources in it. Yield to tide
And find my sources in it. Aching fathoms fall
And rest within it.
                        Deep in the mind there is an ocean and below,
The ocean-riped sand-grains and the lands it took,
The statues, and the boundaries and the ghosts.
Street-lights and pleasant images, refractions; great
Currents of pleasant indirection.
The statue of Diana in the railway-station
The elaborating, the intense, the chocolate monsters.
Under the ocean there are crushing tides, intense
And convoluted stuffings for a dream.
Deep in the mind there is an ocean and below,
A first and fishly paradise.


It is the deep-end of dreaming. There are stacks
Of broken sailors, sweet and harvested; the tacks
Do not decay; they do not bleach with daylight; they remain
Like grain in harvest.
                        But there is little human there, the face
Of statues, nothing colder than that face; it is the end
An Easter Island end of dreaming; paradise
And always afternoon.
                        But he is dead
Untroubled swarms of bees pursue their pleasures, lax and drowsy; steal
Sweet honey from a drunken sailor's bones.
                        But he is dead
And nothing human there can chafe his flesh;
Only the fertile sea can chafe his flesh; it is the end,
An island end of dreaming.
Harvesting angel, out of these pleasures

Out of the kelp-fields and the sea-brambles
Tide-weaver, hunter and planter,
Harvesting angel, paradise keeper
Harvesting dolphin-angel, ocean lover
Keep safe his sleeping bones.


## III. The Mind As Potential Perception

But there are times the sea puts on her rouges, looks
A doom-bedraggled whore with eight diseases; seems
To cruise her ancient beaches and demand
An answer to her question—"Will you sleep?"
An answer from the living—"Will you sleep?"
"No no my girl, my dooming ocean, no
It won't do," we answer, "it won't do.
Who, girl, would drown, if all the fragrant ocean, girl,
Would be his bride and bed?
                                          Though he is dead
And though he sleep with you, your cheapness is not dead
And you are old and deep and cold and like a cheap hotel
Of sleepless corridors and whisperings.
No, I can spare your charms, my harpy ocean, spare your charms
And grunt and turn away. —No, it won't do."


Dr, Johnson stamped his goutish leg upon that ocean; proved
That rocks are rocklike and the sea's a sea
Of real appearance. If the mind's a sea
And rocks are feathers in it do not say
The sea's a feathered creature. It may fly.
The mind I mean may fly, but if it spin
Sam's lethal stumbling-block will break its shin.
This world, it will not end, it will not end.
It would look well in ashes, but it will not end.


How shall I answer to the whorish sea?
Sir, says the doctor, leave it all to me.

How shall I visit him where he is dead?
Sir, says the doctor, I shall go instead.

The gloomy whore is chastened and he goes.
The sun becomes a nest of singing birds
                                        and he is gone.

The painted sea is gone.
Gout-ridden angel, out of those terrors,
From the mind's infidelity and the heart's horror
Deliver my natural body.
Gout-ridden angel, slayer of oceans,
Gout-ridden common angel, keeper of virtue,
Deliver my natural body.

    For it was I who died with every tide
    I am the land
    I was the sea
    Each grain of sand
    With him shall be
    If we are dead.

## ∽ Sphincter

I hope my good old asshole holds out
60 years it's been mostly OK
Tho in Bolivia a fissure operation
        survived the *altiplano* hospital—
a little blood, no polyps, occasionally
        a small hemorrhoid
active, eager, receptive to phallus
        coke bottle, candle, carrot
        banana & fingers—
Now AIDS makes it shy, but still
        eager to serve—
out with the dumps, in with the condom'd
        orgasmic friend—
still rubbery muscular,
        unashamed wide open for joy
But another 20 years who knows,
        old folks got troubles everywhere—
necks, prostrates, stomachs, joints—
        Hope the old hole stays young
        till death, relax

## ∽ After the Party

amid glasses clinking, mineral water, schnapps
among professors' smiling beards,
sneaker'd classicists, intelligent lady millionaire
        literary Patron fag hags
        earth mothers of Lambeth, Trocadereo,
        Hyde Park, 5th Avenue
blond haired journalists with bracelets, grand

readers of Dostojevsky & Gogol—
senior editor escorts from Troskyite weeklies,
lesbians sitting on glossy magazine covers—
what have we here? a kid moving from
       foyer to bathroom, thin body,
Pale cheeked with red cap, 18 year old window washer,
       came with Señora Murillo
She admired his impudence, amused by his
       sincere legs
as I admire his glance, he turns aside to
       gaze at me, I'm
happy to guess he'll show his
       naked body in bed
where we talk the refined old doctrine,
       Coemergent Wisdom

                    Lódź, October 5, 1993
       9:15 P.M. at "Construction in Process" poetry reading


## ∾ C'mon Pigs of Western Civilization Eat More Grease

Eat Eat more marbled Sirloin more Pork'n
       gravy!
Lard up the dressing, fry chicken in
       boiling oil
Carry it dribbling to gray climes, snowed with
       salt,
Little lambs covered with mint roast in racks
       surrounded by roast potatoes wet with
       buttersauce,
Buttered veal medallions in creamy saliva,
       buttered beef, by glistening mountains
       of french fries
Stroganoffs in white hot sour cream, chops
       soaked in olive oil,
surrounded by olives, salty feta cheese, followed

by Roquefort & Bleu & Stilton
   thirsty
for wine, beer Cocacola Fanta Champagne
    Pepsi retsina arak whiskey vodka
Agh! Watch out heart attack, pop more
    angina pills
order a plate of Bratwurst, fried frankfurters,
couple billion Wimpys', McDonald's burgers
    to the moon & burp!
Salt on those fries! Hot dogs! Milkshakes!
Forget greenbeans, everyday a few carrots,
    a mini big spoonful of salty rice'll
    do, make the plate pretty;
throw in some vinegar pickles, briny sauerkraut
    check yr. cholesterol, swallow a pill
and order a sugar Cream donut, pack 2 under
    the size 44 belt
Pass out in the vomitorium come back cough
    up strands of sandwich still chewing
    pastrami at Katz's delicatessen
Back to central Europe & gobble Kielbasa
    in Lódź
swallow salami in Munich with beer, Liverwurst
on pumpernickel in Berlin, greasy cheese in
    a 3 star Hotel near Syntagma on white
    bread thick-buttered
Set an example for developing nations, salt,
    sugar, animal fat, coffee tobacco Schnapps
Drop dead faster! make room for
    Chinese guestworkers with alien soybean
    curds green cabbage & rice!
Africans Latins with rice beans & calabash can
    stay thin & crowd in apartments for working
    class foodfreaks—

Not like Western cuisine rich in protein
    cancer heart attack hypertension sweat

bloated liver & spleen megaly
Diabetes & stroke—monuments to carnivorous
    civilizations
presently murdering Belfast
    Bosnia Cypress Ngorno Karabach Georgia
mailing love letter bombs in
    Vienna or setting houses afire
    in East Germany—have another coffee,
    here's a cigar.
And this is a plate of black forest choco;ate cake,
    you deserve it.


∾ Excrement


Everybody excretes different loads
To think of it—
Marilyn Monroe's pretty buttocks,
    Eleanor Roosevelt's bloomers dropt
    Rudolf Valentino on the seat, taut
      muscles relaxing
Presidents looking down the bowl
      to see their state of health
Our White House rosy-cheeked dieter,
    One last, gaunt sourpuss
      striped pants ankle'd
        in the Water Chamber


Name it? byproduct of
    vegetables, steak, sausages, rice
reduced to a brown loaf in the watery tureen,
      splatter of dark mud on highway
      side cornfields
    studded with peanuts & grape seeds—


Who doesn't attend to her business
No matter nobility, Hollywood starshine, media

Blitz-heroics, everyone at
          table follows watercloset
               regulation & relief
An empty feeling going back to banquet,
               returned to bed, sitting for Breakfast,
     a pile of dirt unloaded from gut level
          mid-belly, down thru the butthole
               relaxed & released from the ton
                    of old earth, poured back
                         on Earth


It never appears in public
     'cept cartoons, filthy canards,
               political commix left & right
The Eminent Cardinal his robes pushed aside,
          Empress of Japan her 60 pound kimono,
               layered silks pushed aside,
The noble German Statesman giving his heart ease
          The pretty student boy in Heidelberg
               between chemic processor abstractions,
     Keypunch operators in vast newsrooms
                    Editors their wives and children
               drop feces of various colors
               iron supplement black
                    to pale green-white sausage
                         delicacies the same
                              in tiny bathroom
                                   distant suburbs,
          even dogs on green front lawns
                    produce their simulacra of
                         human garbage
               we all drop
Myself the poet aging on the stool
     Polyhymnia the Muse herself, lowered to this throne—
               what a relief!


ALLEN GINSBERG                                                    83

## ~ "You know what I'm saying?"

I was shy and tender as a 10 year old kid, you know what I'm saying?
Afraid people'd find me out in Eastside H.S. locker room you know what I'm
    saying?
Earl had beautiful hips & biceps when he took off his clothes to put on gym
    shorts you know what I'm saying?
His nose was too long, his face like a ferret but his white body
Proportioned thin, muscular definition thighs & breasts, with boy's nipples
    you know what I'm saying? uncircumcised
& strange, goyishe beauty you know what I'm saying, I was dumbstruck—
at Golden 50th H. S. Reunion I recognized him, bowed, & exchanged
    pleasant words, you know what I'm saying?
He was retired, wife on his arm, you know what I'm saying?
& Millie Peller "The Class Whore" warmest woman at our last Silver 25th
    Reunion alas had passed away
She was nice to me a scared gay kid at Eastside High, you know what I'm
    saying?


## ~ Multiple Identity Questionnaire

> *"Nature empty, everything's pure;*
> *Naturally pure, that's what I am."*

I'm a jew? a nice Jewish boy?
A flaky Buddhist, certainly
Gay in fact pederast? I'm exaggerating?
Not only queer an amateur S&M fan, someone should spank me for saying
    that
Columbia Alumnus class of '48, Beat icon, students say.
White, if jews are "white race"
American by birth, passport, and residence
Slavic heritage, mama from Vitebsk, father's forebears Grading in Kamenetz-
    Podolska near Lvov.
I'm an intellectual! Anti-intellectual, anti-academic
Distinguished Professor of English Brooklyn College,

Manhattanite, Another middle class liberal,
but lower class second generation immigrant,
Upperclass, I own a condo loft, go to art gallery Buddhist Vernissage dinner
    parties with Niarchos, Rockefellers, and Luces
Oh what a sissy, Professor Four-eyes, can't catch a baseball or drive a car —
    courageous Shambhala Graduate Warrior
addressed as "Maestro" Milano, Venezia, Napoli
Still student, chela, disciple, my guru Gelek Rinpoche,
Senior Citizen, got Septuagenarian discount at Alfalfa's Healthfoods New York
    subway—
Mr. Sentient Being!—Absolutely empty neti neti identity, Maya Nobodaddy,
    relative phantom nonentity


## ∾ Things I'll Not Do (Nostalgias)


Never go to Bulgaria, had a booklet & invitation,
Same Albania, invited last year, privately by Lotty scammers or recovering
    alcoholics,
Or enlightened poets of the antique land of Hades Gates
Nor visit Lhasa live in Hilton or Ngawang Gelek's household & weary ascend
    Potala
Nor ever return to Kashi "oldest continuously habited city in world" bathe
    in Ganges & sit again at Manikarnika ghat with Peter, visit Lord Jagganath
    again in Pun, never back to Birbhum take notes tales of Khaki Baba
Or hear music festivals in Madras with Philip
Or return to have Chai with older Sunil & the young coffeeshop poets,
Tie my head on a block in the Chinatown opium den, pass by Moslem Hotel,
    its rooftop Tinsmith Street Choudui Chowh Nimtallah Burning ground
    nor smoke ganja on the Hooghly
Nor the alleyways of Achmed's Fez, nevermore drink mint tea at Soco Chico.
    visit Paul B. in Tangiers
Or see the Sphinx in Desert at Sunrise or sunset, morn & dusk in the desert
Ancient collapsed Beirut, sad bombed Babylon & Ur of old, Syria's grim
    mysteries all Araby & Saudi Deserts, Yemen's sprightly folk,
Old opium tribal Afghanistan, Tibet-Templed Beluchistan
See Shanghai again, nor cares of Dunhuang

Nor climb E. 12th Street's stairway 3 flights again,

Nor go to literary Argentina, accompany Glass to Sao Paolo & live a month in
a flat Rio's beaches & favella boys, Bahia's great Carnival

Nor more daydream of Bali, too far Adelaide's festival to get new song sticks

Not see the new slums of Jakarta, mysterious Borneo forests & painted men &
women

No more Sunset Boulevard, Melrose Avenue, Oz on Ocean Way

Old cousin Danny Leegant, memories of Aunt Edith in Santa Monica

No more sweet summers with lovers, teaching Blake at Naropa,

Mind Writing Slogans, new modern American Poetics, Williams Kerouac
Reznikoff Rakosi Corso Creeley Orlovsky

Any visits to B'nai Israel graves of Buba, Aunt Rose, Harry Meltzer and Aunt
Clara, Father Louis

Not myself except in an urn of ashes

# ❧ Farewell Performance

*for DK*

Art. It cures affliction. As lights go down and
Maestro lifts his wand, the unfailing sea change
starts within us. Limber alembics once more
make of the common

lot a pure, brief gold. At the end our bravos
call them back, sweat-soldered and leotarded,
back, again back—anything not to face the
fact that it's over.

You are gone. You'd caught like a cold their airy
lust for essence. Now, in the furnace parched to
ten or twelve light handfuls, a mortal gravel
sifted through fingers,

coarse yet grayly glimmering sublimate of
palace days, Strauss, Sidney, the lover's plaintive
*Can't we just be friends?* which your breakfast phone call
clothed in amusement,

this is what we paddled a neighbor's dinghy
out to scatter—Peter who grasped the buoy,
I who held the box underwater, freeing
all it contained. Past

sunny, fluent soundings that gruel of selfhood
taking manlike shape for one last jeté on
ghostly—wait, ah!—point into darkness vanished.
High up, a gull's wings

clapped. The house lights (always supposing, caro,
Earth remains your house) at their brightest set the
scene for good: true colors, the sun-warm hand to
cover my wet one. . . .

Back they come. How you would have loved it. We in
turn have risen. Pity and terror done with,
programs furled, lips parted, we jostle forward
eager to hail them,

more, to join the troupe—will a friend enroll us
one fine day? Strange, though. For up close their magic
self-destructs. Pale, dripping, with downcast eyes they've
seen where it led you.

## ᴧ Naphtha

Ah Jean Dubuffet
when you think of him
doing his military service in the Eiffel Tower
as a meteorologist
in 1922
you know how wonderful the 20th century
can be
and the gaited Iroquois on the girders
fierce and unflinching-footed
nude as they should be
slightly empty like a Sonia Delaunay
there is a parable of speed
somewhere behind the Indians' eyes
they invented the century with their horses
and their fragile backs
which are dark

we owe a debt to the Iroquois
and to Duke Ellington
for playing in the buildings when they are built
we don't do much ourselves
but fuck and think
of the haunting Metro
and the one who didn't show up there
while we were waiting to become part of our century
just as you can't make a hat out of steel
and still wear it
who wears hats anyway
it is our tribe's custom
to beguile

how are you feeling in ancient September
I am feeling like a truck on a wet highway
how can you
you were made in the image of god
I was not
I was made in the image of a sissy truck-driver
and Jean Dubuffet painting his cows
"with a likeness burst in the memory"
apart from love (don't say it)
I am ashamed of my century
for being so entertaining
but I have to smile


## ❧ Poem


Lana Turner has collapsed!
I was trotting along and suddenly
it started raining and snowing
and you said it was hailing
but hailing hits you on the head
hard so it was really snowing and
raining and I was in such a hurry
to meet you but the traffic
was acting exactly like the sky
and suddenly I see a headline
LANA TURNER HAS COLLAPSED!
there is no snow in Hollywood
there is no rain in California
I have been to lots of parties
and acted perfectly disgraceful
but I never actually collapsed
oh Lana Turner we love you get up

## ∾ Cornkind

So the rain falls
it drops all over the place
and where it finds a little rock pool
it fills it up with dirt
and the corn grows
a green Bette Davis sits under it
reading a volume of William Morris
oh fertility! beloved of the Western world
you aren't so popular in China
though they fuck too

and do I really want a son
to carry on my idiocy past the Horned Gates
poor kid         a staggering load


yet it can happen casually
and he lifts a little of the load each day
as I become more and more idiotic
and grows to be a strong strong man
and one day carries as I die
my final idiocy and the very gates
into a future of his choice

but what of William Morris
what of you Million Worries
what of Bette Davis in
AN EVENING WITH WILLIAM MORRIS
or THE WORLD OF SAMUEL GREENBERG

what of Hart Crane
what of phonograph records and gin

what of "what of"

you are of me, that's what
and that's the meaning of fertility
hard and moist and moaning


## ∾ For the Chinese New Year & For Bill Berkson

*One or another*
*Is lost, since we fall apart*
*Endlessly, in one motion depart*
*From each other*
          —D. H. Lawrence


Behind New York there's a face
and it's not Sibelius's with a cigar
it was red it was strange and hateful
and then I became a child again
like a nadir or a zenith or a nudnik

what do you think this is my youth
and the aged future that is sweeping me away
carless and gasless under the Sutton
and Beekman Places towards a hellish rage
it is there that face I fear under ramps

it is perhaps the period that ends
the problem as a proposition of days of days
just an attack on the feelings that stay
poised in the hurricane's center that
eye through which only camels can pass

but I do not mean that tenderness doesn't
linger like a Paris afternoon or a wart
something dumb and despicable that I love
because it is silent oh what difference
does it make me into some kind of space statistic

a lot is buried tinder that smile
a lot of sophistication gone down the drain
to become the mesh of a mythical fish
at which we never stare back never stare back
where there is so much downright forgery

under that I find it restful like a bush
some people are outraged by cleanliness
I hate the lack of smells myself and yet I stay
it is better than being actually present
and the stare can swim away into the past

can adorn it with easy convictions rat
cow tiger rabbit dragon snake horse sheep
monkey rooster dog and pig "Flower Drum Song"
so that nothing is vain not the gelded sand
not the old spangled lotus not my fly

which I have thought about but never really
looked at well that's a certain orderliness
of personality "if you're brought up a Protestant
enough a Catholic" oh shit on the beaches so
what if I did look up your trunks and see it

II

then the parallel becomes an eagle parade
of Busby Berkeleyites marching marching half-toe
I suppose it's the happiest moment in infinity
because we're dissipated and tired and fond no
I don't think psychoanalysis shrinks the spleen

here we are and what the hell are we going to do
with it we are going to blow it up like daddy did
only us I really think we should go up for a change
I'm tired of always going down what price glory
it's one of those timeless priceless words like come

well now how does your conscience feel about that
would you rather explore tomorrow with a sponge
there's no need to look for a target you're it
like in childhood when the going was aimed at a
sandwich it all depends on which three of us are there

but here come the prophets with their loosening nails
it is only as blue as the lighting under the piles
I have something portentous to say to you but which
of the papier-mâché languages do you understand you
don't dare to take it off paper much less put it on

yes it is strange that everyone fucks and every-
one mentions it and it's boring too that faded floor
how many teeth have chewed a little piece of the lover's
flesh how many teeth are there in the world it's like
Harpo Marx smiling at a million pianos call that Africa

call it New Guinea call it Poughkeepsie I guess
it's love I guess the season of renunciation is at "hand"
the final fatal hour of turpitude and logic demise
is when you miss getting rid of something delouse
is when you don't louse something up which way is the inn

III

I'm looking for a million-dollar heart in a carton
of frozen strawberries like the Swedes where is sunny England
and those fields where they still-birth the wars why
did they suddenly stop playing why is Venice a Summer
Festival and not New York were you born in America

the inscrutable passage of the lawn-mower punctuates
the newly installed Muzack in the Shubert Theatre am I nuts
or is this the happiest moment of my life who's arguing it's
I mean 'tis lawd sakes it took daddy a long time to have
that accident so Ant Grace could get completely into black

didn't you know we was all going to be Zen Buddhists after
what we did you sure don't know much about war-guilt
or nothin and the peach trees continued to rejoice around
the prick which was for once authorized by our Congress
though inactive what if it had turned out to be a volcano

that's a mulatto of another nationality of marble
it's time for dessert I don't care what street this is
you're not telling me to take a tour are you
I don't want to look at any fingernails or any toes
I just want to go on being subtle and dead like life

I'm not naturally so detached but I think
they might send me up any minute so I try to be free
you know we've all sinned a lot against science
so we really ought to be available as an apple on a bough
pleasant thought fresh air free love cross-pollenization

oh oh god how i'd love to dream let alone sleep it's night
the soft air wraps me like a swarm it's raining and I have
a cold I am a real human being with real ascendencies
and a certain amount of rapture what do you do with a kid
like me if you don't eat me I'll have to eat myself

it's a strange curse my "generation" has we're all
like the flowers in the Agassiz Museum perpetually ardent
don't touch me because when I tremble it makes a noise
like the Chinese wind-bell it's that I'm seismographic is all
and when a Jesuit had stared you down for ever after you clink

I wonder if I've really scrutinized this experience like
you're supposed to have if you can type there's so much
soup left on my sleeve energy creativity guts ponderableness
lent is coming in imponderableness "I'd like to die smiling" ugh
and a very small tiptoe is crossing the threshold away

FRANK O'HARA

95

whither Lumumba whither oh whither Gauguin
I have often tried to say goodbye to strange fantoms I
read about in the newspapers and have always succeeded
though the ones at "home" are dependent on Dependable
Laboratory and Sales Company on Pulaski Street strange

I think it's goodbye to a lot of things like Christmas
and the Mediterranean and halos and meteorites and villages
full of damned children well it's goodbye then as in Strauss
or some other desperately theatrical venture it's goodbye
to lunch to love to evil things and to the ultimate good as "well"

the strange career of a personality begins at five and ends
forty minutes later in a fog the rest is just a lot of stranded
ships honking their horns full of joy-seeking cadets in bloomers
and beards it's okay with me but must they cheer while they honk
it seems that breath could easily fill a balloon and drift away

scaring the locusts in the straggling grey of living dumb
exertions then the useful noise would come of doom of data
turned to elegant decoration like a strangling prince once ordered
no there is no precedent of history no history nobody came before
nobody will ever come before and nobody ever was that man

you will not die not knowing this is true this year

## ⚭ "They Dream Only of America"

They dream only of America
To be lost among the thirteen million pillars of grass:
"This honey is delicious
*Though it burns the throat.*"

And hiding from darkness in barns
They can be grownups now
And the murderer's ash tray is more easily—
The lake a lilac cube.

He holds a key in his right hand.
"Please," he asked willingly.
He is thirty years old.
That was before

We could drive hundreds of miles
At night through dandelions.
When his headache grew worse we
Stopped at a wire filling station.

Now he cared only about signs.
Was the cigar a sign?
And what about the key?
He went slowly into the bedroom.

"I would not have broken my leg if I had not fallen
Against the living room table. What is it to be back
Beside the bed? There is nothing to do
For our liberation, except wait in the horror of it.

And I am lost without you."

## ᕬ Sortes Vergilianae

You have been living now for a long time and there is nothing you do not
   know.
Perhaps something you read in the newspaper influenced you and that was
   very frequently.
They have left you to think along these lines and you have gone your own way
   because you guessed that
Under their hiding was the secret, casual as breath, betrayed for the asking.
Then the sky opened up, revealing much more than any of you were intended
   to know.
It is a strange thing how fast the growth is, almost as fast as the light from
   polar regions
Reflected off the arctic ice-cap in summer. When you know where it is heading
You have to follow it, though at a sadly reduced rate of speed,
Hence folly and idleness, raging at the confines of some miserable sunlit alley
   or court.
It is the nature of these people to embrace each other, they know no other kind
   but themselves.
Things pass quickly out of sight and the best is to be forgotten quickly
For it is wretchedness that endures, shedding its cancerous light on all it
   approaches:
Words spoken in the heat of passion, that might have been retracted in good
   time,
All good intentions, all that was arguable. These are stilled now, as the embrace
   in the hollow of its flux
And can never be revived except as perverse notations on an indisputable state
   of things,
As conduct in the past, vanished from the reckoning long before it was time.
Lately, you've found the dull fevers still inflict their round, only they are
   unassimilable
Now that newness or importance has worn away. It is with us like day and
   night,
The surge upward through the grade-school positioning and bursting into soft
   gray blooms
Like vacuum-cleaner sweepings, the opulent fuzz of our cage, or like an excited
   insect

In nervous scrimmage for the head, etching its none-too-complex ordinances
   into the matter of the day.
Presently all will go off satisfied, leaving the millpond bare, a site for new
   picnics,
As they came, naked, to explore all the possible grounds on which exchanges
   could be set up.
It is "No Fishing" in modest capital letters, and getting out from under the
   major weight of the thing
As it was being indoctrinated and dropped, heavy as a branch with apples,
And  it started to sigh, just before tumbling into your lap, chagrined and
   satisfied at the same time,
Knowing its day over and your patience only beginning, toward what marvel
   of speculation, auscultation, world-view,
Satisfied with the entourage. It is this blank carcass of whims and tentative
   afterthoughts
Which is being delivered into you hand like a letter some forty-odd years after
   the day it was posted.
Strange, isn't it, that the message makes some sense, if only a relative one in the
   larger context of message-receiving
That you will be called on to account for just as the purpose of it is becoming
   plain,
Being one and the same with the day it set out, though you cannot imagine
   this.
There was a time when the words dug in, and you laughed and joked,
   accomplice
Of all the possibilities of their journey through the night and the stars, creature
Who looked to the abandonment of such archaic forms as these, and mean-
   while
Supported them as the tools that made you. The rut became apparent only
   later
And by then it was too late to check such expansive aspects as what to do
   while waiting
For the others to show: unfortunately no pile of tattered magazines was in
   evidence,
Such dramas sleeping below the surface of everyday machinery; besides
Quality is not given to everybody, and who are you to have been supposing
   you had it?

So the journey grew ever slower; the battlements of the city could now be
        discerned from afar
But meanwhile the water was giving out and malaria had decimated their
        ranks and undermined their morale,
You know the story, so that if turning back was unthinkable, so was the
        victorious conquest of the great brazen gates.
Best perhaps to fold up right here, but even that was not to be granted.
Some days later in the pulsating of orchestras someone asked for a drink:
The music stopped and those who had been confidently counting the rhythms
        grew pale.
This is just a footnote, though a microscopic one perhaps, to the greater curve
Of the elaboration; it asks no place in it, only insertion *hors-texte* as the
        invisible researcher of learned trivia, bookworm,
And one who marched along with, "made common cause," yet had neither the
        gumption nor the desire to trick the thing into happening,
Only long patience, as the star climbs and sinks, leaving illumination to the
        setting sun.


∾ The Ice-Cream Wars


Although I mean it, and project the meaning
As hard as I can into its brushed-metal surface,
It cannot, in this deteriorating climate, pick up
Where I leave off. It sees the Japanese text
(About two men making love on a foam-rubber bed)
As among the most massive secretions of the human spirit.
Its part is in the shade, beyond the iron spikes of the fence,
Mixing red with blue. As the day wears on
Those who come to seem reasonable are shouted down
(*Why you old goat!* Look who's talkin'. Let's see you
Climb off that tower—the waterworks architecture, both stupid and
Grandly humorous at the same time, is a kind of mask for him,
Like a seal's face. Time and the weather
Don't always go hand in hand, as here: sometimes
One is slanted sideways, disappears for awhile.
Then later it's forget-me-not time, and rapturous

WORD OF MOUTH

Clouds appear above the lawn, and the rose tells
The old old story, the pearl of the orient, occluded
And still apt to rise at times.)
                        A few black smudges
On the outer boulevards, like squashed midges
And the truth becomes a hole, something one has always known,
A heaviness in the trees, and no one can say
Where it comes from, or how long it will stay—

A randomness, a darkness of one's own.


## ᔓ Forgotten Sex


They tore down the old movie palaces,
Ripped up streetcar tracks, widened avenues.
Lampposts, curbs with their trees vanished.

They knew, who came after,
A story of departing hands and affairs, that mostly
Went untold, unless someone who was there once
Visited the old neighborhood, and then
They would tell about it, the space
Of an afternoon, how it happened in the afternoon
So that no record, no print of it could exist
For the steep times to come. And sure enough,
Even as the story ended its shadow vanished,
A twice-told tale not to be told again
Unless children one day dig up the past, in the attic
Or underbrush in the back yard: "What's this?"
And you have to tell them, will have to tell them then
That the enormous nature of things had a face
Once and feet like any human being, and one day
Broke out of the shell that had always been,
Changed its answers to lies, youthful ambition
To a quirk of the past, a fancy, of some
Antiquarian concern that this damaged day can never

JOHN ASHBERY                                              101

Countenance if we want to live past the rope
Of noon, reach the bald summits by late afternoon.

Surely we are protected, surely someone thinks of us
Often enough to keep the stain from setting, surely
All of us are alike and know each other from earliest
Childhood, for better or for worse: surely we eat
Breakfast each day, and shit, and put the kettle on the stove
With much changing of the subject, much twisting the original
Premise back to the nature of the actual itch
Engulfing us, now. And when we come back
From an outing expect to find the furniture magically
Rearranged to accommodate revised, smaller projects
No one bothers to question, except polite Puss-in-Boots with what
Is in effect a new premise: "Try this one, the dust
Shows less on these rather sad colors; the time
To get started and gain time, however brief, over the neighbors
Quarreling into sunset, once you have convinced them you're
Not playing and therefore not cheating. When the princess
Comes to see you on some perfectly plausible pretext, you'll know
The underground stream that has never stood still is the surface
And the theater for all that is to come. Too bad the revisions
Will never be adopted, but how lucky for you, now,
The change of face. Good times follow bad."

And the locket is still on the chain on a throat.
The askers, the doers, fall into silent confusion
As it comes time to stand up like a sheet of metal
In the blast of sunrise. I will do this, I can do no more.
I cannot think on the edge of a platform.

But the abandonment by love is a de facto sign
Of something else coming along,
Something similar in its measuredness:
Sweetness of things late, a memory for particulars
As lively as though they happened still. As indeed
They do sometimes, though like the transparent bricks
In a particular dream, they cannot always be seen.

# ❧ The Laughter of Dead Men

Candid jeremiads drizzle from his lips,
the store looks as if it isn't locked today.
A gauzy syllabus happens, smoke is stencilled
on the moss-green highway.

This is what we invented the suburbs for,
so we could look back at the lovable dishonest city,
tears clogging our arteries.

The nausea and pain we released to float in the sky.
The dead men are summoning our smiles and indifference.
We climb the brilliant ladder toward their appetites,
homophobes, hermaphrodites, clinging together like socks
hanging out to dry on a glaring day in winter.

You could have told me all about that
but of course preferred not to,
so fearful of the first-person singular
and all the singular adventures it implies.

## ∾ The Celibate

my ole uncle so & so
      (now w/God) had
(among other things I
       hesitate to touch upon—)
the (so help me God) biggest
      piece ('Scuse the Xpression) in
the town athletic (unmaled)
assoc. Christ! he was al-
      ways (between workouts w/bar-
bells & the like) beating it (and
     at the mirror yet) outsized (and
     no exaggeration) down to
his knees
        what can I tell you
he was (a boy I played w/it
     in bed) hung (my hand ta' god) like
    a horse & could have
(had he turnd pro & stopd
     playin' w/hisself) kept
ole Christian Science ladies
     (w/fat dividend checks
from husbands mostly dead) happy

## ∾ No Saints in 3 Acts

the photograph is mostly
flat 2 dimensional
        you name it
at that a quick relief
from the black & white
       conflict

over the negative landscape
into which no peasant
                    (spade or other
has entered in to
                arrange
the disorder of the virgin
                    or whatever
lies unfurrowed behind
the furrow'd brow


## ∾ Black Orpheus

boy
        wants to X-press
himself

            to bang
his meat w/a box

strong
        w/2 or 3

loosely strung
        cat guts


## ∾ Afta a Bob Creeley Poem

the odor of his things
    do at that
                pene-
                    trate
    both nostrils

roses    chrys-
                anthenums boug-

                    ainvilleas & yes
the spring things
            like jonquils the
for-
        sythia a
                    bower of words
con-
            tinually opening &
                    falling away
from desire      as do
        his partners
                    to the dance
            in the roun'
                    O the dance!
there was his genius
        the invitation to life
                to dance
                        openly
        w/him to the very end
of the measure


## ∾ from *Orgasms/Dominations*

XII

                                *(wasn't born knowing;*
                                *loved antiquity (the an-*
                                *tients) actively investigating*

Greeks rubd piece of amber, observed it acquired ability
  to attract objects. (600 b.c.) Wm. Gilbert introduced "electricity"
(@ 1600 a.d.) meaning amber. Found too, other substances, when rubd etc.
      & a repulsive force of another so similarly charged.
        to be in heat is both attractive and repulsive.

    friction—heat—like & unlike——change

@ 1800 Volta produced
his "pile" & it was hypothesized that resistance to the flow
of mysterious "fluid" caused heat in the wire.

                    the current-now-passing
                    in all this /Time was under-
                       going an hypotheosis: the kant
                       of Hegelians  Change
                       and the current
                                          flow to
                       opposite . . .
                                    (the which I pronounce: "oppo-sight")


                              charges flowing in the wire
a second of electric current
                       (total charge passing thru
           any cross section of the wire in one second)


                    since this cat's so hot
                    we'd better "cool it":

                              $-\wedge\wedge\wedge-$
                              ↑ $R_1$ an



                    variable resistance.
STATION BREAK: This Orgasm is due to
                    Jack Spicer's concern to "my loud-speakers"
                    et les hidden wires of
                           input & output.


A myth. A thing that may or may not be. But the charge
        called a nucleus & its negative has lost an electron
—to restore—(the active materials in a battery
        or to squat, with its head on its forepaws: sd. of a dog
     Or the cats before The Car?


              "The two-machine combination, called


STEPHEN JONAS                                          107

*a motor generator,* is convenient for producing a
desired type of power" etc.
Sphinx?
LOOK fer gods sakes
whose number escapes me . . . . . No VII of the Eternal Sevens
& how many "against Thebes"? Opposite? No XVI
of the God damned.

S

P

A

C

E

(there is also the field glass (small binocular
telescope; rays a.b. thru object glass O.
or the (opposite to left) "The fiddler
Grab (uca minax) oh sorry, (wrong letter
like sorry wrong number) The eye sees
an erect magnified Image)
beyond these parentheses I profane not. Before
One of serious demeanor, hold yr tongue
& keep yr distance.

T

I

M

E

Whereas the sixth
is regarded as
the first inversion of the
Triade—7 for cards? 5 for
basketball or in answer to
the question/Orgasm V: "How many"
(are there in it?

Geezus k. krist! do I have to tell *you*
everything?
A man who can neither see nor feel is sd. to be
mr. average p. normal and

death in the family can
make him  wildly excited. This as to
"place & condition". Orgasm I.
So that,
any Orgasms No I to IV
heretofor suppressed by me dah dah dit. For by my sundial
(b.17.56) The Sun stands peri-helion to them. as to

any of the ordinal numbers: to describe or name . .
etc  shewing order or succession, objects, periods of time etc.
8 for racing (rowing) crew, 9 that's
a.b. Spellman's "bazeball" "pool"
while I was home in drag studying the
General Theory & my mothers latest
pink falsies. (& abt here
Maximus "broke-up") (and anyhoo I never cld
tolerate "the edukated one"—a red dah dit
Stanley sent me.
The commander of three army corps can be kidnapped,
you cannot kidnap a plain man's will.
or go ahead *hoi barbaroi*, shoot me what can you do-me?

Heaven gave me my conscience, what can
et cetera do to me?
(This vintage  surely a property of the Gods)
& of local vintage there be a one no-sietz
& a special Orgasm for that "niggah"
so that
only the superior man *can*
truely love one or
really hate another
a huge snake of many folds
biting the neck of that ass

here follows R$_2$
Resistance to change
the ♀ & w/out let-up

light pushes out
"Fiat"
& egg-shapd of the womb.
The "cheeky", hit-him-ovah-the-shins-w/a-cane sd
professor zen (of the crank case philosophy
that's Zen
and for those lacking probably "windsac" whereas the X
shd. be yr. "attainment" and IX yr.
pursuit of as against a.b. degrees
m.a.s. and all the other small letters
the rushes inside Notre Dame de Paris


no-sietz, the theme w/thee: 2 wavering lines
and both in the sign of the Ram.
J.S. is all
nothing but the long pauses
between gasses . . .
unless
it's a red wig w/grt sheaf of mss.-bearded
like a carrot too
and all wanting to write poetry?
For when I started out in this game, I listened to what
men sd. & believed they would
carry into acts. Now
I know. I listen & wait . . . to SEE
and they do? mostly nothin'. For the Good
that men do
a tiny sort of crux ansata  active
between the two eternal eyes
Sun & Moon standing together, Egypt & Chinese
two images hap'ly mete. For in sight of
the destroyed Tower
The XVIth (keep the Romans)
That century in the mind in-
destructible. So that
"the Link"        Orgasm V to XII
Return
Elias

Greece to Aubeterre, the old roads
and yes, we shall  see
them again for the cranes
fly above the marshes w/the long grasses.
That's for luck.
& for the Irish, Fitzgerald
(I suppose) Russell with this Vision in painting
and negative charge (his): (won't die in peace in yr bed.
Confess it.
and if you "what I said abt. symbolical
falsification";
and added to this:
"nothing", that grows contra to what I say
"survives")
Emerald, that is for the shining sea
but when the Sun licks the
tips of the waves;
Michael, that is
for memorie. But for the "Boston
Clack": John, my no. I jack and Edwardius
my "bishop"

and a long crozier down the demon's throat. For the law

that is Quincy, Mass. The Measure (Wieners, please copy)
of the Law that will be yr Number IV.

And again: "nothing" that wld. go
contra to what I say
will "survive".
That was from Lu. Take care
and a full swing of the pendulum . . .
So to the wearing of the fish
and a skeleton flays an ass (old wood cut)

Flemish, it looks) on my wall and a drawing
of Trinity Church, Boston. Well, it's Catholic,
outside cause I've never been in-it.

At the 16th Century. Destruction of the old
                    Roman Basilica (fire, supposedly) and
                        the erection of present St. Peters
                            whose Dome was workd out (solvd?)
        by artifice? (Say,
                        why didn't they
                Arachne & that Hephaestus git hitched? Might at that have
                effected an
                            Olympian *coup d'etat*.)
                    Not to mention the Sixtine (var.) Ceiling
                        & the ripeners (question, "ripeness" plus)
                of, oh Michelangelo's dome. (inside job)
                Pope Sixtus IV or any damn
                        sixtus for that matter. (Resistance to the
                electrically positive charge, increases heat
                    in direct proportion to
                            the amount of
                                    resistance.)
            Negative charges
                            resistance to:
                                "now what's up".
            Nothin', again, nothin'. I'm going over to
                        investigate
                            Notre Dame de Paris
                    & outside.
            And again, to Fitzgerald: you don't know, DID-dent you?
    George Stanley suspects, too. George Stanley, fer that
                    suspects all painting. There is an Orgasm for George
                                                                too.
            But then that's my sweet tooth.
                            Again, my dickey bird: don't you
                    dars'in to, sah
                            et questa voo dit
                            (for there can be no "tu"
                                et so on here) Sooo

            shift not one symbol upon dat Tree


WORD OF MOUTH

for one can know, given a perhaps voltameter:
charge—resistance to—and heat.

(We just put the freudians to sleep . . . quietly to
tip out to
what ever there is left to
. . . . out to
which I can tell you, quite frankly,
is not much.
(yesterday, "chickens" brought me
a "hot" TV. This morning ordered TV
outta me 'ouse)
Move over, Garcia Lorca,
make room for yr. lovers
we proliferate & nearly all
"White Rabbits", but I fear that
*tardaramucho tiempo en nacer, si es que nace,*

a voice, ting ping, *tan rico,*

and *tan claro*
andaluz, the provence
and yr new work  black and tans
where *La Memoria* takes Her seat.

may the green words bristle
in yr. landscape

all like sheafs of bayonets

affixed to the muzzles of all lying Guardia
civil
$R_3$
*la resistance*
resistance
meet in the wire
look to the heat.
(In all this, I suppose Spicer &
Maximus will see

SEE? Two great COW (Holy Cow) Eyes
(Sun & Moon standing together)
& betwixt
a sort of crux ansata,
that is for growth, Heat &
the resistance thereto.
And so to "what's all this about"? It's about a bird-billd scribe
who probably started
a chain reaction in Thebes. Greeks
got hookd, Gaul ditto
provence, the plain
andaluz and new spain  so now comes
Our Link
Martin (a jeweld Cupp, at that,
& for high altar)
and he sings: Cautionary verses:
"Don't break the chain"
connecting Link
to Link the old roads
connecting Greece to
Aubeterre
& in spite of square notes and a whole host of
vowel misdemeanours the melody,
you miss D, the melody,

the melody lingers on
in
T
I
M
E
all things accordion
· _ · _ ·
(dit-dah-dit-dar-dit)

## ∾ An Inlet of Reality, or Soul

(in this age, or any

> "With respect to plants as animals, we are wrong in speaking as if
> the object of life were only the bequeathing of itself. The flower is
> the end and proper object of the seeds, not the seed of the flower."
> — John Ruskin, *The Queen of the Air*

When in Rome do as the Greeks,
show it hard,
let intellect be rampant in the flagrant colors of the indomitably so,
no compromise   no blame.
Take happiness in touch that bursts in light,
konx om pax,
as the sun yacht shoots through the Gate of the Tongue
(Tharmas happy in his element).
Sweetness savors itself in balling rondures,
delectation of the Gods come true,
truly come in the core of time,
old nick of it, new aeon, lion form in the wood where virgin lay.

When then love takes you in hand you don't languish in the clover
but make song:

       o flowering stick
       smoke wreath of peacefulness
       discovery of happy self in other's grace
       good limpid star      golden bird
       girl leaning from a window when the last light shakes out in
                                   the West.

*This* and *this* we say and do
and so we fix each other up and *this* is how transcendence is.

# ∾ Planting the Amplitudes

Of sea-stoned altitudes the constellated swing
                                salts my gloried eyes, makes free.

                   I am here as I am here.

"Finding form" one calls this opening or sunburst

not "the tolling of the sea"
or other cantilene.
                    Time is not the sea not like the sea.


Disposal of you trash of memory,
           have gone / "made in Europe"
           analogies that fake the line
           like "heirlooms" / family ideas.

I hold the stick of bareness
to be hard man wilding exquisite

                             and bateleur

It is of course not simple place this seeding
of COURSE / like water course / a moving water meeting
               (in Gloucester Heraclitus yes)

but I know for every man
there are places, amplitudes
signatures of heart
he can plant and he must plant.

## ∞ The Curve

how one incurs
            the burden of a city
                        and Indians!

        this is where I came in

                by the pest-house, through the old woods
                (not over that flubbery span no sentinel owns

        comes into one's own,                    reality

                making the place by pacing the place, live
                (or live,      change vowel eye,      heart

        the stature commensurate
        to the gist of the nation,
        imagination                    . . . . .

again the curve, the way it slants in,

            the lay of the land
            unseen but by
                                        Indians!    then
(thanks ever be to Charles Olson for "Indians!"          then
                                                    . . . . .
            the alien eyes, mine eyes have seen the,

    mine eyes alien
                        Dutch
            not Indian!
                        outer planetary!

        were keener for the curve,
        how wolves and lions came in

("some affirme that they have seene a Lyon
     at Cape Anne which is not above six leagues from Boston"

                                             . . . . .

so I round another man's measure to round out my own:


                              to speak of "discovera"


      the pristine we work to inherit,


                          native lode


                                        to shoot out again,
      is not to make up,
                              some queer hemisphaera,


      it is to smell
      to dig with the hand
      to demonstrate


                          and at least


                to reclaim
                to come in


                       like Indians!
                                     on this curve


from the ravening wood


                  to a city


              we once could be citizens of.

## ᖆ Blue Decrepit Town

It takes me, here I am, living in a place I first drove through twenty years ago,
teaching John to drive,
(me who was no natural American boy driver,
though learned it driving tractor)

driving through,
then,
nervous
about these real narrow streets of this decrepit town

nervous
about all the cute rough boys
standing
in front of three pool halls

nervous
about the kind of life to lead when no more college

nervous
about even what to do in bed and with whom,     as the limerick goes.


Now it appears
                        that driving through this place

looking mostly straight ahead but glancing at faces and bodies and
                                        decrepit dirty buildings
        was more than it was, then,
                just driving through a different place,
teaching John to drive,

nervous,
thinking of sex,
thinking of the ocean which everywhere shone through that autumn day

GERRIT LANSING                                                119 because I had never seen the ocean to make it with before, being

                              just a heartland-America boy.

Now it appears

                that what gives us a shove

                           even to love,

          the pattern we are hung up on

                       or where we fell off

arises

           like the character of a golden lion

                     purely through causes

   flickering lights of a decrepit town,

is as empty as causes,

and may be grabbed by the throat of mind

much later, if at all, if you're lucky, if you've lived well,

when you're no longer nervous, or differently nervous,

not only

        in seeing the whole jewel-net flicker in the depths of the sea


but even

      as song flickers

           in the sight of

            blue decrepit reality town

                wherein dwells Love.

# ∾ To the Boy Charioteer

> You care
>> for the steeds, not victory,

unusual,
>> in one so young.


(You are, like me, a real gone time-despiser, forgive the youth-word "young.")

>> The rhythm of this arrant purple age
>> diminishes the merely actual,
>> lineaments of incidence
>> or cast of human dice into a bed.


But my intensity for you,

Euphorion,

however privately expressed,

will not diminish,

so faithful is not only memory

but working of the body energy divine.



> Golden was an early word for all of it.


Emerging into sunlight

I dance with capability;
my feeling is a waterfall
that spends without exhaustion of the source.

In Eden, where our dreams of happiness are carefully conserved,
stored as juicy essences the virgin of the world put up,

we eat each other endlessly,
apples sadly rarely shared in what is unjust history.

But we are not asleep in Beulah land.
We live in heat and pain of being here or there,
and if we are slightly nuts it is division wrenches us.


The Horses, the Horses, black and white!

see them flying

over the chasms of no-love


their manes are flaming in the night.


They guide your chariot of golden stars
my cardiogram,
hold well the reins,
and pray that so I do on earth as well.

## ∾ The Look-Out Tower at Mount Venus, Louisiana

yes yes o lord *yes*, the bestest, sweetest
pussy
        ever said good-morning to a slop-jar!

you know:
          'nappy' pussy,
like counting
prayer-beads:

. . . . . . . . . . () . . . . . . . . . .

---

*Heard/found-object, from Clement, man-servant to Weeks Hall, at the latter's*
*plantation, The Shadows-on-the-Teche, New Iberia, Louisiana, 1957.*

## ∾ Syllables in the Form of Leaves

1.

*Fox* plus *Razor* equals
the *Eye—*

get sharp,
or you're dead

2.

*Der Lenz kommt über Nacht, sagt*
Li-Po to

callow pussy
willows

3.

*Das Leben kann allerdings angesehen werden als ein Traum,* a
*succubus* mused,
                    sliding down my private
waterfall

4.

*Ein Vogel singt im Baum— Ja . . .
Ja . . .* a

bud said,
swelling

5.

Flogged with a *februum,*
young goats
dance out of

old goat skins

6.

Skin back the year,
turn over,
            you new leaf,
ewe!

## ᴗ The Chameleon

at 14 I decided it was avant-garde to dig
women

but, man if I were just the least
bit queer, boy, you know, man, wow,

and then some; but, like
I'm not, but

when I write *Dearest* to you in a letter, then
that's different,

isn't it?


## ᴗ Finger Exercises

went down to the
boneyard
to buy a pair of hands, to quote
Robert Creeley

Olson wrote about Marsden Hartley's
hands, how they got,
refusing women's
flesh

and yes:
*Hands,* by
Sherwood Anderson,

hot to grope
blueberry, blacksuited
Ohio


JONATHAN WILLIAMS

*arma virumque cano!*—
plus the law's got a long
arm

we are too much in the hands of
those on whom we lay
no hands

## ∾ The Anchorite

quotes Basil Bunting from "Chomei at Toyama":
*if you can keep straight you will have no friends*
*but catgut and blossom in season . . .*

the anchorite
opts to eye the
oak leaf, clutch
a red
to hold the mountains' blues
under the winter sun . . .

song accumulates heat—a humus. I have it,
like Issa:

> *Few people;*
> *a leaf falls here,*
> *falls there*

>               —outside, where
> the world's a storm
> in the oaks

> and the outcry of certain
> beautiful captures

•

he wrote 'brought to love,' brought to any

intimacy,
          writing letters
among red oak leaves . . .

to be left alone?—that's a laugh! that is, who's
without the images of
love,
       shining out of his head?


and they
who move the heart, daringly,
as the sun fires the oak
through the wanton afternoon
•

light airs of music . . .

we are left with
just the 'facts', the endless

articulation


## ∾ The Distances to the Friend

Thoreau,
        grabbing on, hard,
a red, raw
       muskrat . . .

thought to eat it,
         stifling all repulsion

so sat by the quagmire,
cranky, no cannibal, too
uninvolved
       to get to man
so simply


JONATHAN WILLIAMS

we, the
heirs, hear other rustlings:

the grass stirs like an
androgyne, the man
in our hearts stands
his fear
on its head,
savagely—

      inversed, nervelessly,
we sweat past each other,
unrelieved:

bitter landscapes,

      unlovely


## ☙ Dangerous Calamus Emotions

"Walt Whitman is in town—
I have just seen him, but
*publicly* of course."

      traffic jam! tram drivers,
          streetcar conductors,
          Sergeant Tom Sawyer, Peter
          Doyle, all

          the Camerados & Lovers

     DO NOT TALK TO DRIVER
     WHILE BUS IS IN MOTION, do not motion
     to driver, or
     bus will talk; walk, do not run
     to the nearest; and do not buss
     bus drivers!

deliver us, deliver ass
from puritan transit!

W.C.W.: "him and that Jesuit, them with the variable feet—
      they changed it!"

variable, viable,
veritable Walt

Whitman!

---

*The initial quotation is from the sedulous Mr. Emerson to the prissy Mrs. Emer-*
*son, one of the New England gentry who did not approve of Whitman's athletic,*
*amative, democratic tastes . . . Dr. Williams is referring to Whitman and Gerard*
*Manley Hopkins—for him the founders of the modern poem.*

## ∾ The Electronic Lyre, Strung with Poets' Sinews

    (for Elizabeth Sewell)

    *"Orph's awfully gay,*
    *despite Eurydice."*
             — The Oracular Cave at Antissa:
               'Music, Every Hour on the Hour'

Hey, Dead-Head,
Maenads got your tongue?

You go dead inside
and think you could

con me, the Shade
of Sigmund Freud?

Be polymorphous perverse,
Orpheus!

All orifices,
Orpheus!

"It's all good."

(signed)

God.

Ps/ *"Sappho died the other day . . .*
    *all ass is grass, so let's make hay!"*

---

*The poem may suggest an impious reading of three primary source books: Miss*
*Sewell's* The Orphic Voice *(Yale, New Haven, 1961), Norman O. Brown's* Life
Against Death *(Modern Library, New York, 1959), and Jane Harrison's* Prole-
gomena to the Study of Greek Religion *(Meridian Books, New York, 1955) . . .*
*Shakespeare and John Cage are vaguely evoked . . . The postscript, an epigram I*
*covet violently, is by Mr. Keith Camp, John Barton Wolgamot Fellow in Poetry,*
*Ann Arbor, Michigan. Salute!*

## ∾ Blue Ball Blues

(for Paul Goodman)

O, Mr. Chemist, please let me buy
350 pounds of premium Kentucky KY,

cause it's a dry season
for the reason

Anglo-Saxon sex glands
are awry . . .

Arise, arise and come
to Perineum

(*'the more you come
the more you can'*)

Let not your Sword sleep in your Hand
and we shall smear Petroleum
on England's Groin
& Pleasant Gland!


## ∿ The Honey Lamb

the boysick (by gadzooks thunderstruck)
Rex Zeus, sex
expert, erects
a couple temples
                    and cruises the Trojan Coast . . .

eagle-eyed, spies,
swoops,
swishes into town

ponders, whether tis nobler
to bullshit, brown
or go down
on
        that catamite cat, Kid Ganymedes,
                                mead-mover,

erstwhile eagle-scout
bed-mate

## ❧ The Arrival of the *Titanic*

Gashed, from her long immobility on the sea-bed
gravid with the dreams of invertebrates, only half
here in the sense of consciousness, she pulls,
grey on a grey morning into New York Harbor,
bearing all of the dead in their attitudes, the old dead
in dinner jackets, bare feet encrusted with barnacles,
their pearl eyes, their old assurance of conquest
over the negligent elements, and walking thin and
perplexed among them the new dead who
never realized on what crossing they had embarked.

We are the photograph's negative, made after
the color print, made after the abyssal waters
took color out of the Liberty scarves, the bright
upper atmosphere of tea dances, after the drift
downward, the pressures of winter. If it has been
abandoned, it is ours, it comes sailing silently
back with us. There were never enough
lifeboats, and never
enough gaiety to see us safely through past moonrise
and our monochrome exploration into the range of ice.

## ❧ The Death of John Berryman

Henry went over the edge of the bridge first; he always did.
Then Mr. Interlocutor and Mr. Bones, then the blackface minstrels
with their tambourines. You have to empty out
all of the contents before the person himself dies.

The beard went over the edge, and Stephen Crane,
and the never-completed scholarly work on Shakespeare,

and faculty wives, and a sheaf of recovery wards
white-tiled in the blue shadow of the little hours.

He loosened his necktie and the recurrent dream
of walking out under water to the destined island.
His mother went over in pearls; his father went over.
His real father went over, whoever his father was.

He thought to go over with someone, hand in hand
with perhaps Mistress Bradstreet, but someone always preceded him.
The news of his death preceded him. It hit the water
with a fat splash and the target twanged.

When there was nothing to see with or hear with, the silent traffic
of bystanders wrapped in snow, his only body
let itself loose, turned and waved before it went over
to what it could never understand as being the human shore.


∾ Plum

Now the plum blossom on its Chinese branch
argues in spring across the waterless country.
Spring as a fist. Its delicacies clench.

So it is in time of war as the bench-
marks of the bodies build & the fluid gentry
paint artificial plums onto the stiff branch

dowsing for oil and vinegar in the trench-
works, forcing their unlubricated entry,
a fist in spring & the bruised membranes clench

& convulse under the violating drench
of fire & the tight flayed missile gantry
flings the fire's blossom from its bitter branch.


WILLIAM DICKEY                                                    133

Body the beggar in the chemical launch
upward, body the zero into which the wintry
spring comes as a fist to couple its dead clench

body the rotted petal, the death-stench
covering the feet of the rigid erected sentry,
the fingers of the plum blossom, crisping, clench
for the branch, the branch's buried country.


## ∾ Archæopteryx

It flies into stone, which gathers around it
carefully, not to disturb the least feather.
The immortality of the anonymous.
Becoming impersonal. Death does that, it takes away
the soft fretting, the music the inside of the thighs made
brushing against one another, tremble
like the surface of disturbed water not much disturbed.

After the eruption, the whole side of the island
slides into the blue water, without noise. What we cannot hear
happening is history happening, the same embrace
in which the bodies' sweat unglues itself
in a long shudder of sound and is eased
also is passing into the rock, where it has no name.

We flew, we wingèd ones, over the vivid marshlands
crying our inheritance in harsh voices.
The little wingbones shivered with involvement,
with the caress of the air. Then, as if a flail
summoned the day, we were not visible.
Layer beneath layer, the sift, the escaping smile.

Getting up in the morning into the mashed
taste, effluvia, scrape of the razor blade
scything, its confident little

rasp in the ear, white gleam of the toilet bowl
struck suddenly into time, hairs under the human arms
without color, if color depends on being perceived.

It is not gone as the expert German
workmen with their untidy lunchpails and chewing tobacco
enter the quarry for another purpose altogether
than revealing it. They are outside an experience
it continues in. No one translates. The cliff plunges.
Death is nothing like dying, the stone bird said.


## ∾ T. S. Eliot at One Hundred and Seven

This is the voice of the sandstorm, the voice of the unplayed hearts.
These are the endless children rolled over and over at nightfall.
This is the door to the house, lying by itself in the desert.

These are the patterns, lacelike and fixated, of the tributary veins.
That is a plinth, this is a next phenomenon.
Hammer and compass, hammer and astrolabe, hammer and theodolite.

These are the tools of rage as a temperature inversion.
This is a cat sunning itself, in the gutter between the sedate pages.
This is a Jew presuming, sweaty, a collection of skinned thumbs.

This is a space where the ornamented drop capital is missing.
That is Cape Fear, where the immigrants died on the picnic.
Birds in the night sky, answering each other over the ruthless nave.

## ∾ Famous Friends

Could never place him.
But I'd go into
BAR on 2nd Avenue
and there he was, face
lighting up, helpful
silly and eager, yes,
started again
and now unstoppable
on an expressway of talk, fast
and funny, but after half an hour
I'd edge away.

J.J.,
he said, J.J.,
that's my name.
Talked, that time,
of getting something published
—So you write, I said!
Why, didn't you know,
his smile triumphant,
I was
Frank O'Hara's last lover.

Didn't see him again.
It was like having met
—years afterwards—
Fanny Brawne
full of bounce, or
Degen, the conceited
baker's boy.

No, it wasn't.

Rather, it was like having met
Nell Gwyn,
on the way down,
good-natured, losing weight,
still chatting about spaniels.


## ∾ The Problem

Close to the top
Of an encrusted dark
Converted brownstone West of Central Park
(For this was 1961),
In his room that
                    a narrow hutch
Was sliced from some once-cavernous flat,
Where now a window took a whole wall up
And tints were bleached-out by the sun
Of many a summer day,
We lay
        upon his hard thin bed.

He seemed all body, such
As normally you couldn't touch,
Reckless and rough,
One of Boss Cupid's red-
                            haired errand boys
Who wouldn't get there fast enough.
Almost like fighting . . .
We forgot about the noise,
But feeling turned so self-delighting
That hurry soon gave way
To give-and-take,
Till each contested, for the other's sake,
To end up not in winning and defeat
But in a draw.

THOM GUNN                                    137

Meanwhile beyond the aureate hair
I saw
A scrap of blackboard with its groove for chalk,
Nailed to a strip of lath
That had half-broken through,
The problem drafted there
                              still incomplete.
After, I found out in the talk
Companion to a cigarette,
That he, turning the problem over yet
In his disorderly and ordered head,
Attended graduate school to teach
And study math,
                        his true
Passion cyphered in chalk beyond any reach.


## ∾ The Dump

He died, and I admired
the crisp vehemence
of a lifetime reduced to
half a foot of shelf space.
But others came to me saying,
we too loved him, let us take you
to the place of our love.
So they showed me
everything, everything—
a cliff of notebooks
with every draft and erasure
of every poem he
published or rejected,
thatched already
with webs of annotation.
I went in further and saw
a hill of matchcovers
from every bar or restaurant

he'd ever entered. Trucks
backed up constantly,
piled with papers, and awaited
by archivists with shovels;
forklifts bumped through
trough and valley
to adjust the spillage.
Here odors of rubbery sweat
intruded on the pervasive
smell of stale paper,
no doubt from the mound
of his collected sneakers.
I clambered up the highest
pile and found myself
looking across not history
but the vistas of a steaming
range of garbage
reaching to the coast itself. Then
I lost my footing! and was
carried down on a soft
avalanche of letters, paid bills,
sexual polaroids, and notes
refusing invitations, thanking
fans, resisting scholars.
In nightmare I slid,
no ground to stop me,

until I woke at last
where I had napped beside
the precious half foot. Beyond that
nothing, nothing at all.

# ❧ A Wood Near Athens

1

The traveler struggles through a wood. He is lost.
The traveler is at home. He never left.
He seeks his way on the conflicting trails,
Scribbled with light.

                I have been this way before.

Think! the land here is wooded still all over.
An oak snatched Absalom by his bright hair.
The various trails of love had led him there,
The people's love, his father's, and self-love.

What if it does indeed come down to juices
And organs from whose friction we have framed
The obsession in which we live, obsession I call
The wood preceding us as we precede it?
We thought we lived in a garden, and looked around
To see that trees had risen on all sides.

2

It is ridiculous, ridiculous,
And it is our main meaning.

                    At some point
A biological necessity
Brought such a pressure on the human mind,
This concept floated from it—of a creator
Who made up matter, an imperfect world
Solely to have an object for his love.

Beautiful and ridiculous. We say
Love makes the shoots leap from the blunted branches.
Love makes birds call, and maybe we are right.
Love then makes craning saplings crowd for light,

The weak being jostled off to shade and death.
Love makes the cuckoo heave its foster siblings
Out of the nest, to spatter on the ground.
For love has gouged a temporary hollow
Out of its baby-back, to help it kill.

But who did get it right? Ruth and Naomi,
Tearaway Romeo and Juliet,
Alyosha, Catherine Earnshaw, Jeffrey Dahmer?
They struggled through the thickets as they could.

A wedding entertainment about love
Was set one summer in a wood near Athens.
In paintings by Attila Richard Lukacs,
Cadets and skinheads, city boys, young Spartans
Wait poised like ballet dancers in the wings
To join the balance of the corps in dances
Passion has planned. They that have power, or seem to,
They that have power to hurt, they are the constructs
Of their own longing, born on the edge of sleep,
Imperfectly understood.

                    Once a young man
Told me my panther made him think of one
His mother's boyfriend had on *his* forearm
—The first man he had sex with, at thirteen.
"Did she know about that?" I asked. He paused:
"I think so. Anyway, they were splitting up."
"Were you confused?"—"No, it was great," he said,
"The best thing that had ever happened to me."

And once, one looked above the wood and saw
A thousand angels making festival,
Each one distinct in brightness and in function,
Which was to choreograph the universe,
Meanwhile performing it. Their work was dance.
Together, wings outstretched, they sang and played
The intellect as powerhouse of love.

THOM GUNN                                                                                    141

## ~ What Word Did the Greeks Have for It?

Tendered by Professor Ames, tidings from
    the universe—or at least
from the university (Plato claims
    there is the same difference
between learned and unlearned men
    as between living and dead ones—

such oracles always come to us clad
    like this in the apparel
of poppycock, and by way of a gloss
    my knowing colleague had scrawled
"yesterday's newspaper is old news, but so
    is today's newspaper—thus:"

*Dear Abby, my friend and I are having*
    *a difference of opinion.*
*He insists that Damon and Pythias*
    *were both homosexuals,*
*I say they were straight. Can you check this out*
    *and let us know?—Bewildered.*

Forestalling Abby, I must first record
    my delight that the two of you
are having a difference—good thinking!
    Our disregard of unity
is every bit as significant as
    our exhibition of it;

provided you differ . . . Precedent compels
    me to ask: What is "straight"?
The danger lies in being persuaded
    before understanding. Let me

instance, *a contrario,* the occasion
  when Gladstone, being informed

a canon of Windsor soon to be made
  a bishop was a bugger,
only remarked, "In an experience
  of fifty years I have learned
that the pagan qualities you refer to
  are frequently possessed by

men of immense erudition, the most
  absolute integrity,
and the deepest religious convictions."
  It *is* bewildering. Myself
I have noticed that when most of us say
  "his heart is in the right place"

we locate that heart rather lower down
  than we care to acknowledge,
and on inspection, the lump in the throat
  is really in the trousers.
Larkin is right: what counts is not to be
  different from other people

but from yourself. There is more repression
  in heaven and earth than is
dreamed of in most psychoanalysis.
  As for that pair in Plutarch,
their devotion seems to have excited
  suspicion even among

the ancients, the same alarm set off by
  Jesus—laying down your life
for another, for all others, appears
  just as suspect as getting laid
by your best buddy. You might tell your "friend,"
  Bewildered, who sounds so sure

of his categories, this much from me:
    the class of men he discerns
is a social, not a biological
    entity. Our genes contain
no instructions as to who is and who
    is not homosexual;

nor do laws of survival require that
    distinctions be made between
the world of the straight and some other world.
    Those whose natures have kept them
at a distance from the community
    cannot appear undefiled

among you without a lurid aureole,
    looking stranger than they are;
they do not need defending—your contempt
    cannot hurt them, they are dark
and love will find them anywhere; nor do
    they need encouragement, for

if they would remain authentic, they must
    live only off themselves, hence
cannot be "helped" without being harmed first.
    Charity begins at home,
but how far does it spread? Where will it all
    end? *Shift, shift, fellatio,*

as Hamlet might have satisfied *his* friend's
    curiosity back then.
These days we cannot let the matter rest:
    Did Franz? Was Walt? Would Vincent? . . .
With a sigh, the unconsenting spirits
    flee to the welcoming shades.

                                                        

# ❧ My Last Hustler

*. . . all smiles stopped*

When "Brad" is lying naked, or rather naked is lying
in wait for whatever those he refers to as clients require
by way of what *they* refer to as satisfaction, denying
himself the distraction of alcohol or amyl, there appears
in his eyes no flicker of shame, no flare of shameless desire,
and what tribute he is paid finds him neither tender nor fierce.

On a bed above suspicion, creases in obviously fresh
linen still mapping a surface only a little creamier than
the creaseless hills and hollows of his compliant flesh,
Brad will extend himself (as the graphic saying goes)
and the upper hand—always his—will push into place *the man
who happens to be there* till happening comes to blows

(another saying you now more fully grasp): full-blown,
Brad will prepare himself, though not precipitately,
for the grateful-kisses stage; he offers cheek and chin
but objects to undergoing your accolade on his mouth:
he has endured such homage too early, too often too lately,
and for all his boyish ways Brad is not wholly a youth.

Routines on some arduous rigging, however, can restore
him to himself in mirrors, every which way surrounded
by no more than what he seems and mercifully *by no more.*
Booked by a merciless Service for a thousand afternoons,
Brad will become the needs of his "regulars" confounded
by his indifferent regard, by his regardless expense . . .

Take him—young faithful!—there and then. Marvel! praise!
Fond though your touch may be and truly feeling your tact,
yet a mocking echo returns—remote, vague, blasé—
of Every Future Caress, so very like your own!
However entranced the scene you make (the two of you act
as one to all appearance, but one is always alone),

RICHARD HOWARD

derision will come to mind, or to matter over mind:
the folly, in carnal collusion, of mere presented *skill.*
Undone, played out, discharged, one insight you will have gained
which cannot for all these ardent lapses be gainsaid
—even his murmured subsidence an exercise of will—
is the sudden absolute knowledge Brad would rather be dead.

∾ Bare Bones

It was love at first sight, on the Staten Island ferry.
I'm part of an anti-Nam Poet Protest he and Ted come to.

We collaborate. He artist, me words.
Me, poet-librettist reduced to comic strip balloons?
It's a ruse, to be with him.

He has his weird side.
Two shrimp cocktails, that's his main course.

Our first tennis date.
Interrogated closely, he assures me he plays well.
He can't even hit the ball.
I curse my luck.
I've fallen for a dysfunctional mythomaniac.

We undress.
His mysterious undergarment fascinates and scares me.
It hangs loose from his bony arms, skinny torso,
The hunchy back he's so ashamed of.
Raggedy yellow loops.
Waif Macramé.
Dleam Come Tlue.
My Very Own Urchin Savant.

Only he isn't mine.
Triangle. Jealous anguish.
Oh, the searing yearning.

I put my foot down.
Triangle tapers off.
Just us two, sort of.

Gray areas.
Nights off.

He's late for dinner.
I probe, against our code.
He explains, innocent of the merest shred of guilt,
Surprise outside sex plus small talk takes time.
High ground fury, nowhere to go.
Chastened, I heat up the meal.
We eat.
In bed, we share Champale.

He's big on holidays. All holidays.
Even Groundhog Day.
A-Day stands for Anniversary Day—our first night.
Holidays mean gifts.

His core belief, Gypsy source:
Be rememberethéd for what thou givest,
Seeking nothing back,
Except the pleasure giving gives.
He raises gift-giving to a noble art,
As finely honed,
As viewer friendly as—
His Art.

He gives me
The Dolly Sisters
In pastel sailor drag.
Art Deco statuette.
I'm appalled.
Initially.
Slowly he teaches me to give up
Received "good taste."

His recurrent dream:
Finding jewels,
Buried jewels.
We begin exchanging rings.
Every Xmas.
Birthdays.

He makes me necklace collages.
Charms. Enamels.
A cluster, minuscule photos of him,
In miniature glass lockets with glass fronts—
His face and naked body parts.
Surefire way to get touched at parties, he points out.
As if the gift weren't enough.

He stutters.
Low voice, can't make out his words.
Bend close. Tulsa accent.
E becomes I.
Pinitintiary.
Pass me the pin.

I hand him wine lists,
So I can hear him wrap his stutter
Around Pouilly-Fuissé.

His spelling.
Eccentric phonetic. A hoot.
Printed Block Upper Case.
I'm his checker, see his writings first, thrilling perk.

His mental geography maps are surreal.
Australia is in Europe.
Venice is its capital.

Europe honeymoon.
Spoleto Poetry Fest. Rome airport.

I panic. Train sked, how, station where?
My sensible beloved rescuer cuts through the problem.
Taxi.
Taxi.
From Rome Airport to Spoleto.
And subsequently from Madrid to Granada.
And subsequently everywhere in foreign lands.

Pre-Armani, he hates jackets and ties, wears jeans,
White shirt unbuttoned way down to reveal his chest mat,
So teen-age cute, Gian-Carlo Menotti takes me aside,
*Festival Du Monde!* Hustlers are a no-no!

Explain he's an A List Genius?
Flash our first collab, *The Baby Book?*
Quote blurbs?

Frank: "The most peculiar thing I've ever read."
Andy: "Fantastic! Fantastic!"
Ron: "The greatest book of all time."

I dummy up.
Kowtow. *Ciao* Spoleto.

Our M.O. evolves.
Four months together in Vermont.
June to October.
Rest of the year, delicate but tenacious bonds.
We cohere, summer to summer,
Despite cæsuras, rifts and dumpings,
Once each, luckily staggered.

In hosp, he mentions we've lasted thirty-one years.
In hosp, he says he thinks of us as married.
In hosp, he says I'm doing better than he expected,
Dealing with the circles of hell
He's descending deeper and deeper into:

Narrowing options,
Enveloping pain.
In hosp, he says we've been faithful.
We've had a good life.

Proud moment.
We're at Naropa.
Allen beseeches, cheer up poor old lonely old Burroughs.
Dead flesh eyes don't waste a sec on me,
Start to sparkle with reptilian lust.
Allen says: "Bill, they're a couple."

Bad times.
His new lover, wily dominatrix,
Sneaks up on us both.
Speed.

Thirty something, I swell, take dex.
Share fifty-fifty
This Ted drug he's used since his Tulsa teens.
Blissful bond, enabling dex togetherness.
How brilliantly he works,
Long hours a snap.
Esthetic micro-management other artists would kill for.
Protean quantity, star quality,
As his last Fischbach smash proves.

I cross the abyss.

His city studio is a madhouse of mounds,
Color-coded, red here, yellow there,
Raw material screaming
Collage me,
Collage me,
Turn me into jewels.

I partake of the white powder, his lover.
We try to collab.
The Way We Were.
Nada. Nada.
It's the black pit.
I flee.

He comes out of it on his own.
Wishy-washy, not all there,
Back together in Vermont,
He tries to make art.
Lays out his brushes upon arrival.
Settles for reading, nonstop reading,
Barbara Pym his summer standby.

He-as-artist rematerializes fully, once.
For me: *Sung Sex* drawings,
Boy in bed odalisques,
Abstractions, spare Japanesey lines,
Lola my cat,
Whose Fancy Feast he fluffs up meticulously,
Mornings, first thing,
Whose white hair he patiently picks off
Armani jacket and pants.

He holds these new drawings in low esteem.
Tiptoes away
From the casino paradise
Art Biz gulag.
Closes shop.

His first retrospective.
University, San Diego.
Hung thuggishly, as if for a cineplex lobby.
I hate to see his work sloughed off this way.
How must he feel?

Despite snake oil panaceas,
His hair recedes. Salt and pepper.
Small bald spot I can't get enough of
Jowls. Older eyes. Gym biceps. Kid thin.

A first. *Quel horreur,* his face turns into Nixon.
A Now-See-Now-Don't magic trick of time.
One visual he must never never know of.

He loves to see old couples holding hands,
Has-beens on TV with food-on-the-table jobs,
Worries how the young, droopy pants, obnoxious dyes,
Must terrify The Old.

We start seeing Edwin Denby, replica perfection,
Suited and tied, mannerly gait,
Downtown Montpelier epiphany.
Talisman of all the time in the world,
This recurrent mirage of resurrection from death,
An omen of quirky survival.

The first plague death: Bill Elliott.

On the way to dinner one night,
I bring up lovemaking, death risk.
I think I'm thinking of my own survival.
What I don't dare think is:
Unwittingly becoming
The instrument of his death.

We become companionate.

Test.
I'm OK.
Privacy transgression, I ask.
He's OK.

KENWARD ELMSLIE

He tells me he has AIDS.
The how, not the when.
In Vermont, he can't tan.
The sun is lethal.

He reads, reads, reads all the time.
Cartons from "Three Lives" are never enough.
He shoulders more of the domestic daily round.
What I've always wanted happens.

He takes care of me more.
We take care of each other.
A balance achieved.
We're content together.

Which I should have been prepared for.
He always comes through,
Makes the best of the crisis situation.

When Jimmy uproots
Whole beds of flowers,
Starts washing money,
J. A. (hapless guest) and snit-prone I
Turn into Joan Crawford parodies,
Wide-eyed at full moon psychopath
Clomping up the cliffhouse stairwell.

He takes command.
Talks Jimmy into the waiting police car.
As he once released John Wieners
From restaurant rant, accusatory pointing,
"You're the Mayor of Boston's wife,
       Boston's wife, Boston's wife."

And far back, me.
Pyschodribble whinings. Labyrinthine snarl.
Analysand mind spill.
Sweet calm of acceptance: come as you are.

Car crash.
Totaled.
In shock.
He gets up, sees if other car's driver's OK.

June, '93. I have diabetes.
My new better half takes charge.
No nonsense trainer,
Gentle carer, patient restorer,
Walks me, pushes me,
Further, further.

I'm his good child, eat right.
Drop 40 pounds by summer's end.
Sugar plummets to normal.
Balm of good sense, end of no win.

His insides act up.
He goes to hosp.
Comes back too weak for walks.
Our last October.

He accepts the unacceptable.
Where does such deep grace come from?

We discuss our respective deaths.
Ashes,
Field uphill,
Us both.
Ashes scattered.
Flesh ash, bone ash,
One day commingled,
Under white pines,
An enclosure Ron calls druidic.

In NYC
All fall and winter and spring,

KENWARD ELMSLIE

He weakens.
On May 25th, late afternoon, he dies.
In June, his brother John
Gives me his ashes.

By a white quartz boulder,
Under protective pines,
I scatter Joe Brainard's ashes.

Promise kept.

Closure.

Remembrance

∾ from *On Amphetamine and In Europe*

greatest poet of the century
or not I'll never make
that blonde window
washer—

oh the eternal chase
after a blond window
washer.

*

there are Flanders in my
poppy fields

*

If I don't have mass distribution
I'm going to be a mess.

*

I was always a great
shower-taker.
but this house only
has 3 holes and you have to
stand in a slippery tub
and my check isn't
here from my father
and I'm 37 years old
I'm a bum, shower-taker
and great genius
so there

(I'm a petulant monster
with a bushy tail
switching yak-flies
off my back after
each U.S.S. Lexington sailor
in Googies Bar on
Sullivan where pock-marked
Jay Hoppee
revives a little
San Francisco
before the Bigarini
earthquake . . .
flatter Bigariniri
flatter San Francisco
they turned all those poets
into Volkswagens
and slaughtered
these artists wherever
they could find them
they were afraid
Chinatown was growing
and Buddha was cut
down at his 3rd party
Mahatma Ghandi never
turned on. and he
insisted on riding
white trains
with red cross
bandaids tattooed
to the
cow-catcher making
a colorful array
as it passed the
waving villages
and sank into the
Ganges under
Sausalito

sliced up under
rich idiots yatchs (yachts)
hulls seams
screams
open up Cassandras
and let that
faggot proprietor
back
strew Frisco with
fourteen pederastic
poppy-houses
with people reading
and mad combos
sort of making it.

       *

I came pretty close to
upchuking, Chuck.

       *

Blue is the color of my true
Portuguese fisherman's hair
and      bulging
brown is the color of his
drawers—his boots are
used leather motorcycle
straps and my neurosis
is his left tit.
Tell Margaret Sanger I
want to go to Portugal.

Dig up her grave
and say "Margaret
Sanger! Taylor Mead
wants to go to

Portugal"—if a bone
answers—hang up!

*

if a skull replies burn
out its eyes—it's an
illusion—my skull
makes a good pillow
because I have a
fucking big head
but you'd have
to be a New Guinea
savage to appreciate
it
Plug in my eye
socket—I want to
see A.C. current.

*

I'm not silly I'm saintly
I washed my silliness in
saintliness and gave it
three turns in the dryer
for a grand total of
55 cents
a young fellow played
the guitar in the front
of the place

*

I may not be a sleep
walker but neither
are you a dancing
angel.

*

Yes I am a sleepwalker
—a lovely golden-haired
full bosomed sleep-walker

and you are a
dancing angel

*

Golden-haired
window washer disappeared
before I had time to even
give him one of my books.

*

I want to commit
suicide but not that
badly.
Most of all I want fuck
an elusive forest creature

*

Boy if only I could make up your
mind—I'd put hospital corners
so your feet wouldn't get cold.

*

I'll never get an italian
building washer.

*

TAYLOR MEAD

Bring me a wasted poppy
seed smoker with the heart
of a child.

*

I want to promote sensuality
and condone the use of switchblades
on the upper Hudson
I want to convert the switchblades
of the bronx into
        narco agents for Bo
and make
        Ronnie Rice
a film star and Taylor Mead
a sailor and
empty all the asylums
and fill all the slums
and beat pansies with
motorcycle belts and run
over them with used Volkswagens
I want so many things I'm getting
confused

*

How much is social security
Does it include fringe curtains
on cubicles in Turkish Baths
or skin-tight plate-glass sailors'
uniforms or tiny dicks for the marines
of Camp Pendulus in California
where I went once

*

Every advance means chicken-shit
will make your alley scream

      *


    J. Edgar Hoover has notches for
dead americans all over his desk in the
department of justice in washington.
    It's a very valuable desk.
    Cartiers may sell it as a jewel
for Princess Grace left tit.
    I will buy it and put it
    in my Grosse Pointe

      *


If I'm a federal narco why
didn't I arrest you long ago.
    (copy of letter to Aunt Martha
    —written on vellum)

      *


There's no such number
    as 71

      *


I'm a candy-assed swede.
what are you?

      *


I want to get a permanent high
in your pants.

      *

I'm clever, good, and a beatnick.
I'm a good clever beatnick
I'm a beat good cleverer
in fact I'm
a breathing mad switch-blade
                              enthusiast.
Who rapes elevators in
      well guarded
Federal housing projects
except
self-service
and electric eyes
and nigger dominated elevator
I only rape white anglo saxon
dominated elevators in Federal
Narco brick layer on layer
great walls of China housing
projects.

             *


I must degenerate.

             *


Are you a white federal housing project.

             *


oct 3

             *


I bet I've been to bed with
more negroes than you have (imaginary
answer to diddly bop who objects to
use of word nigger)

But this doesn't prove anything.
It did at the time.

      editors note (there was this
          mulatto chauffeur on
          Park Avenue—but generally
          I prefer white trade.)

      *

I'm permanently poetized

      *

With books I can buy money.

      *

I'm developing into a great
fucking genius rapidly

      *

I want to take books to
booksellers but I want someone to
help—
preferably a large person with a penis.

      *

Do you want to be my bookseller
or are you just a fink for the F.B.I.
I am too.
A candy-assed F.B.I. fink that's me
Victor McLaglen in drag
with tennis champion
balls

TAYLOR MEAD                                                      

on green grass
lime stripped candy coated millionaire
front yard courts
stand up for the judge you mothers
or we will slash you with
1. 2. 3. switchblade contempt
                              citations
we own this court
play ball
the Davis cup
is made of silver.


   *


J'ai écrit magnificat.

# LELAND HICKMAN (1934-91)

## ❧ Yellowknife Bay

under clouded noonsky, crossgraind, dry thunders muffled, whimper of wind,
last hours, Fort Providence, & hours-late bus, we wait
by hudson bay company, wooden porch steps, Slave
Indian children stare, frown, sullen-eyed; we board
mudcaked outback rattletrap, curses spat, dirtclods, rocks
flung after us; backfiring toward Yellowknife, Aussie
driver, Indian woman, two young Slave indian men, Hank, me;
downpour again & overcast always; night; each riding silent, alone, & wind
whistling thru windowcracks; graveld highway, pitted;
swerve, slide, wheelsup; cold; impossible sleep;
lightning-lit poverties of villages, ancient tribes in their modern
                    squalor; word-road, pitchdark;
wilderness unanswering; no signs for me; my forest un-
                    yielding; word-rain, plainsong, pitchdark.


o      then as tho strangling, retting,
each day more taciturn, dad
after she left him, the one
decade left him, trappt, in far worse sours than child stuff, roots
determining, so that even as he had at 15, his, dad, I had at 16 also
left him, as even
his angers left him, leaving
some tenderness &, as he told me,
an ache for one only he narrowed his heat to, held to,
put it in the work, son, put it in the work,
& a day came, all of his sons having left him,
& his daughter much more her mother's,
that I saw him standing still in that crowd of dead children, staring
heavy into the low flame of himself & alone, like a stranger   o


unguided ungratified unillumined unslept
untoucht stunted passions debaucht brutish down to daybreak

LELAND HICKMAN                                                    167

anywhere anyone   quick men   dead men   my nameless
city park dirt path spring lust fog
agitating largo out of Ferndell how I
      grasp myself priest in grum hickmaning dawn
self-addicted grave groyne sweat, this
habit fatidic withal, mine ascetic my listless slug;
mine inburied ephemeral upanishad moon,
extinguisht, inflames it, delights it; how ungrowing I gasp
uphill toward blackwillow, hidden, shadowed
reborn fresh morning spring creekside bird-
sung proud paleblossomd owl-home wingd-ant-home snake-home, song-home.
      my kiss-the-ground sanctum blackwillow;
reach hilltop, stop,
breathe in in sharp hurt in clear sudden sight of it, crisp
piercing first light thru tentative fog lift,
early leaf cry, soft seed shimmer, moving, breathing, swaying
unto itself alone how no one shd deceive it,
shaking, yet no breeze to disturb it;
      & I wonder, & I see:
giant, muscled, hardond, strippt
lunatic, writhing against treetrunk,
fragile seeds adrift in strange griefs around him,
fingertips on nipples, eyes half-closed, groaning,
watching my approach, not shifting his gaze away,
      dionysian long dark hair bejewelled yellowgreen,
young blackwillow leaves ensnard there, yellow blackwillow flowers fallen;
then in seedstorm under branches
shivering in my willowshell, spell-
bound, stunnd, how
wordless he sings to me, beckons to me, slave to his story, fierce
half-smile, shoulders, chest,
loins sweating pollenkisst
his white torso,
harsh-breatht, archt against willow, his
thick thighs spread wide     & between them:
slender, living, stiff, low blackwillowlimb plungd-in upgouging,
      greast, abandond-to, ridden,

                                     

slid savaging grinding, crazd mean tight on,
thrashes his body back against dread, angrier, wilder,
& by his uprooted, panickt, uneartht outcry,
        begets this song,
anointed under showers of willowseed shaken downtrembling upon us.


o     nine two twelve. twelve four sixty. dad per-
haps wakes, his woman asleep, her grandson asleep, his head
aches, rises, dizzy, kitchen, lightswitch, coffee his head
ache retch blur boy hall fall help crash cup hand crash
chair & falls & falls & falls fumes & eyelids not any
air monoxide flutter like that. fast. silence. or dad perhaps
bolts out of dream-shriek, temples exploding, & the
woman beside him dead, the boy in the hallway,
dead, dashes, kitchen ache chair stumble crash slips retch
hand doorknob fall, fall, immediate night, dawn, noon, twilight,
night, dawn, noon, ringings, knockings, young man hollers, anybody,
nine, two, twelve, home? twelve, four, sixty, anybody,
dawn, dusk, dark, home? in all that dark? in all that dark?    o


coward of not climbing to my song's peak his warm
        semen rolls over me his
        handsome head thrown back falls
forward eyelids shut bends at waist abdomen pumping huge clencht fists
clampt against last sweet thighs' throes blond locks shook over forehead each un
        conscious gesture or breath gasp
sickening, doesn't speak or glance my way slides back onto chair
        heartbeat shadow flutters
under damp chest-hairs his breath slows, dulled gaze studies my
ceiling stupidly mouth gapes arms hung slack knees flung wide his
        swollen wet cockhead
        limp against bellysweat
matted hairs curl shattered blue temple glances sleepily at wrist-
        watch, reaches to my floor for
crumpled-up socks, burning, unmoving, come hardening, I watch belt
        buckle buckled zipper lockt cuff
links snappt into place tie knotted blond hair combed at my mirror, stoops


LELAND HICKMAN        169

to hack loud once into an
ashtray grabs jacket flicks lamp off lifts door-latch, peers
        thru dim light, groans
softly as we hear languid dawn rain start falling, falling,
        steps into hallway numinous ill door
falls shut on me


o       for the entire process is benign, don't
bury me with you dad don't, on a hill top, view of
Pacific, placed coffin, & I descended to it, work on what has been
spoild, & knelt beside him, entire process benign, raised
my left arm, one finger toward sky, rested my right on
his silence, go in to my Hidden, earth rose around me, process
benign, passing thru blue sun breath door, shut it on
panic, put it in work, feeling my syllables falling, solid,
heavy, earth covered my shoulders, breathed the dust, what
alone my lone this is, law I die under, burial of
verve & of uplifted arm, my finger stoppt moving, all
my poets, Hidden       & the entire, process, benign  o


this song or section of song for that soild song Leland
        dawn dregs un-
wiped-off semen drying on his skin lies quiet there yet, old
        hollywood rooming-house
waking under rain neons sputter mad against sunrise next-door cell
        alcoholic fat man coughs
brittle greatgrandmothers faint early chirps down my hall I
        listen to traffic rise on selma, night
vanishes under Beckett & Faulkner at 26 in 61
        hid song thru my
flawd door, wounded blue temple where
        child-cry stops, where
        solace to my
self my light grows numinous seven tectonics of
soul heft song-peak must be yes anyone sung child in my
        fire years gone years
to go must be yes anyone sung fierce at my door, lordly

       beauty above below
behind before to my right to my left beyond this song for that
husht song Leland beginningless ignorance asleep in my
       brain as rain
       falls numinous ill
rasa falls still


on wet soil kneeling in my willowshell, near
broken giant breaking my husht seeds free, soon
to cease drifting over me     lost, ghost-human, kisses
earthkissing rhythm-tree, dresses, vanishes, fades from my story;
& my blackwillow song grown calm, solemn,
small birds, jays, bright blues, return,
my red ants up treetrunk, silver-wingd, flashing,
       how they signal my sunup;
sunbeams thru leaf-whispers onto low willowstub, glisten
of mucous, blood, sheer wings glint,
flying ants stumbling up phallus-staff, over
round-ridgd corona's blind eye, how
craftily he carvd it, despairing, exultant, defiant,
       insane in his half-light;
now, blackwillow, blackwillow, hide me,
for I unbuckle memory, for I undo my name;
for I strip me to childhood;
       for I slide down onto you,
fingertips on nipples, my thighs spread wide,
for you pierce me, ravage me, for you make me cry loud;
for I beat my body back against dread; for these poor songs pounding;
for shook blossoms scatterd meaningless from yr sky;
for I sob, for I gibber, for I babble crude psalm;
       for I desecrate;
for I sing ashamed of my daylight.


o    o dad, look, I am buried here, with you
having grown or not grown as you dreamed me
got adventure & got ascared, dad, dad, my dad a
fugue that I rose like a ladder, outward of me,


LELAND HICKMAN                    171

I have wrongd every rung of, until
inward is stasis, no seizure
& song I wd hide in my light lies hidden
underground with me
song under song under song a
dissonance, with rhythm percussive, unflowing
& I can only whisper: song, song, song, how long are we buried here?        o

next day, Yellowknife New Town, mercenary, safe;
& hayward thru Old Town, quaint, & Latham Island bridge, Hank
leading; toward smoldering windborne garbage-stench, steep
downhill road where Dogbills die, warriors once,
slaveowners once, in their weatherd-dun box-huts by the dump;
last summer, drove ridge-route, L.A. to childhood, East
Bakersfield 2534 Lake Street not one bleakness changd, blight
amid blight; Indians; other poor; crossgraind oilsmoke sky; trees
dead; new boxes without frontyards, built on old frontyards,
memoried childscape crumbling behind them; no sidewalks, nothing
            green; transfixt, pitchdark,
gazing; frontstoop roof, 2-x-4 proppt, on dad's mean shack, decrepit; look,
            look, outhouse prison of pitchdark,
still standing; & I'm afraid; & my mother's afraid; fears
to be seen outdoors torn blue bathrobe flapping; suddenly
crying; why; why is she crying; in rain I see her, dark-haird,
wearing a blue bathrobe, standing still on planks that cover mud,
the way to the outhouse, in the storm, holding her
hands to her face, screaming, screaming; or I'm home from my canal, barefoot,
            she's dressed-up, spitcurls auburn on her forehead, stands
on Lake Street with her suitcase; where are you going mommy;
o, sonny, she says, o, sonny, why did you come home so soon,
wait in the house, wait for yr father, & I stare thru the window,
            taximan, taximan, sky getting pitchdark;
race down driveway, holler, taxi turns comer, holler, standing
            rigid on Lake Street hollering in pitchdark;
now, Dogbills hammer-up stormwindows; under us,
volcanic outcroppings, glacier-groovd, Hank & I
stumble wind-deafend down boulders to Yellowknife Bay,

indigo pitchdark vast waterscape tempestuous in windsquall,
      ice-stifled under snowfall soon;
breathstopping wingbeat terror-squawk raven-clash vicious above us,
      beak-stab, blood-spray, feather-fall;
bleak plainsong sky over Great Slave Lake; unutterable omens
      singing me home.
o      in emergence from dadspace gentle wd I move
in harmony with rain as she guides the roots,
shifting their hungers, softening impacted graveground
muscles of sleep inform my rising, urge me to surface
lips & tongue in word-rain uncover the upward, I am lifted
into spaces my rhythms open, the sun is made sensible
in attentiveness to change-scent I come from the ground on
I can hear the beach, I can smell the ocean,
& from earth into sky I emerge onto grass,
my eye delights, & my lungs laugh      o

## ❧ The Garbos and Dietrichs

Moving like a dream through Ibiza
through midnight cities of the world
buying dreams of men / and their hearts
to hang at dressing tables, how many ornaments
to wear for dinner, or selfish supper parties —

This sin does not show by candlelight, their children
do not hear that cry in the night, odd pregnancies
abortions are not counted, smashed faces
wrenched hearts left behind at harborside
when their ships pull out.

I speak of suicides, men dropped at tide.
I speak of sleeping pills that still our aching mind.
I speak of lovers they murdered because they are so kind.
Anything to stay beautiful and remain blind
to those men they turn into swine.

## ❧ A poem for cocksuckers

Well we can go
in the queer bars *w/*
our long hair reaching
down to the ground and
we can sing our songs
of love like the black mama
on the juke box, after all
what have we got left.

On our right the fairies
giggle in their lacquered

voices & blow
smoke in your eyes let them
it's a nigger's world
and we retain strength.
The gifts do not desert us,
fountains do not dry
up there are rivers running,
there are mountains
swelling for spring to cascade.

It is all here between
the powdered legs &
painted eyes of the fairy
friends who do not fail us
        in our hour of
                despair. Take not
away from me the small fires
I burn in the memory of love.


## ∾ Act #2

*For Marlene Dietrich*

I took love home with me,
we fixed in the night and
sank into a stinging flash.

¼ grain of love
        we had,
2 men on a cot, a silk
cover and a green cloth
over the lamp.
        The music was just right.
I blew him like a symphony,
        it floated and
                he took me
down the street and

left me here.
3 AM. No sign.

    only a moving van
    up Van Ness Avenue.

Foster's was never like this.

I'll walk home, up the
    same hills we
        came down.
He'll never come back,
    there'll be no horse
        tomorrow nor pot
tonight to smoke till dawn.

He's gone and taken
my morphine with him
*Oh Johnny.* Women in
    the night moan yr. name


## ∾ Two Years Later

The hollow eyes of shock remain
Electric sockets burnt out in the
        skull.

The beauty of men never disappears
But drives a blue car through the
            stars.

# ∾ The Eagle Bar

A lamp lit in the corner
the Chinese girl talks to her lover
At bar, saxophone blares—

blue music, while boy in white turtleneck
    sweater
seduces the polka player from Poland
left over from Union party.

Janet sits beside me,
Barbra Streisand sings on Juke box
James tends bar

It's the same old scene
in Buffalo or Boston
yen goes on, continues in the glare

of night, searching for its lover
oh will we go
where will we search

between potato chips and boys,
for impeccable one—
that impossible lover

who does not come in,
with fresh air and sea
off Lake Erie

but stays home, hidden in the sheets
with his wife and child, alone
ah, the awful ache

as cash register rings
and James the bartender sweeps
bottles off the bar.

John Weiners

## How To Cope With This?

A mean, dark man
was my lover
in a mean dark room
for an evening

till dawn came
we hugged and kissed
ever since, first and last
I have missed

him, his mean, dark ways.
Mean, dark days
are upon me in the sunlight
even yet, I fear his foot

feel his cock and know it
as my own, my sown
seeds to reap
when the full neap

of pleasure falls, his kiss
reminds me, our dance
in the dark, my hope
and only scope.


## Wednesday or Something

I might even listen
to what he did
to you in bed

up to your knees, just
home for the holidays
a basket off-shore,

mixed-up, naked to
desire gone before
he arrived

dated, undressed and
double-crossed,
Tuesday's rebellion.


## ∾ Youth

The first darkness
on Blue Hill Ave.
from 1 to 6
before the war broke out
or sickness, on the second floor
above the meat market, McDonald's
across from the Parkway Pharmacy,
when first memory was sliding
over a hot barrel in the sun.

What can I do but shine
in memory, in the crib
where the cardplayers were
out in the kitchen and the rats
ran down the hall, after what
the moon declares,
                    under a veil
in the driveway, staring at an apple tree
when we moved, and climbing another
apple-tree, enchanted with the blossoms
on its branches, *When the world was young*
as the song goes, sung by Felicia Sanders
on TV weeping for her father, or at *Le Bon Soir*
playing to the bar.
                    Before the war broke out
    declared on the dining room floor

of Churchill Street, in Milton Massachusetts,
USA, behind the front porch, where I buried
irises, from beside the house.

> There was another driveway
different from the other one, in that it was pebbled,
or was it the same,
only at the end of it, I lay
in a carriage, before the field
where I imagined thirty years later
Bob Creeley held me upside down, by
the left ankle, sticking
pins and needles into that wax doll,

> before my sister caught him, or
> was it Marlene Dietrich, appearing there
moving majestically down the avenue to guard over
the war-torn refugees, waifs who lined the house
upstairs and down

> until we moved
> to my grandmother's
fighting, Nana dying in the bed, the empty room that

> my cousin has now,
> Marie, and the truckdriver
> McDermott, she married.

It seems the Scotch hold our psyche,
with their folktales and legends,
Robert Graves relating at the museum
anecdotes from The Order of St. John of Malta.

The altars burned then
with incense and prayers, not now
late-night vigils and pleas or tears
against death, in the toilets and woods.

I had so many phantasies last year,
of that flat twenty miles away.

Only early youth affected, and before birth
by rituals, scissors, child-abuse.

Not beauty that was real, before the mirror
in strawberry blonde hair, silk black dress
going to work, during wartime.
First to Toby Deutschman's, buying dolls
in the 5 & Dime, phantasies there as well

of Marion behind the counter, Bobbie C. kissing her cunt.

How I loved my sister being a lesbian, but she was not, only a nun.
That was later on, though, after she left the big house on Eliot St.
that was also in Milton, only I left it first, to become a poet,
to live on Beacon Hill, and starve, before Black Mountain,

before Big Charles put his hand on me, and ordained me a priest.


## ∾ Here for the Night

at 7 dollars for a single room's rest, and
   asylum from the city's municipal officers,
often spending the night, wandering over by the river
   in the city's parks and dumps, walking the streets, by-
ways and avenues Romantic-less dawn found me,
                          resting in some bookshop, that
opens early, or never closes, as it used to, the fresh

pranks, and hi-jinx of the stubborn generosity
                    that rests within hearts of men

   Sunday evening, barely a sound, but the television
  it's the image of a bed that sets off the sexual transgression
             or retreat

's Paul enzaquin 931-1640 asks, Station 7's announcer anyway

JOHN WEINERS                                                                                     181

broadcasts
reports toward the viewer upon sexual relations, as far as the Y

the grey windows, rattling maid
diseased clients broach no new adv.
for the place today more than they did
two years ago, or ten when I was in love.

Only those memories sustain me now
outside the girl knocks
to make up my room, while Turbo jets glow
in the sky above Boston docks

I have settled in this town
I shall not play the painted clown

I shall seek the major release
to win the goal of my heart's need

Returning to the mood of a city,
where there resides only a single person, I could call
on, whom would welcome one at this hour, dirty
I return to this paper to write what I shall,

about the hammer above the courtyard, and the insistent
sexual requirements forcing *un pauvie amour* out for decades
to huddle up together in alleys, and dream the ideal structures
Whitman's predictions or prophecies foretold would for the
remaining three decades of my life.

## ❧ After the Orgasm

Aw, what is fame, is it
worth it, that people should know your name
when you have a loveless shame

the taxi-driver last night, "Do we have a celebrity
with us?" and the only thing that helps
is to think of the others who haven't made it.

At least at this time. We sit around behind
gray window frames, and when it comes,
we'll know we worked hard for it

every priceless moment. Now listening to torch songs,
we dream of those revered days,
as if we haven't enough of it now

when our flesh shall be old,
and the young bodies shall mean the universe for us,
only to find it's some worthless punk who ends up in your arms.


## ❧ The Gay World Has Changed

Climbing up the saw-dust stairs
hope Less, life's now better than heroin and
homelessness, my kind do not grow old well
we're better off dead, though refuse to do
so, who knows these men refresh me

daily, in gay bars for twenty years, whom have I found

that is not Confessional verse, it's obsessional

———————————

Statues of Adonis, bodies of lust & *promesse*
behind the black topcoat & pipe, harsh words

smoky looks, wrapped up romance, this is
excess, hilarity & hot flesh, rotating around

poles amid current favorites flooding Sporters

in drums of colored words, calling to lime harbor,
stormy tides, bitching morality & society w/out a voice.

--------

The men, normal looking enough, you'd never know,
are not degenerates, good clothes with intelligent con-
versation, I get hot on them, whizzing around the room
              in my mind, doing the dirty boogie,
when only two hours ago, I climbed stairs at Lamont
saying, you're a faggot, a faggot, you're nothing but a homosexual,
nothing more; sex, sex, Sex and sex.

## ∾ The Hurricane Lamp

Dissimulation     artificial flowers     if a bee could go mad
Or if the life / I imagine / artificial people could be manufactured
To adorn a party / to attend the party alone
*Cyclones visit Kansas* (the party alone)
They chased him across the bridge / alone from the party
It begins blurred     or is it simply
*Kansas visits cyclones*
A note dropped from your fingers     it begins blurred
Could I have acted—     (blurred)
The hurricane lamp / seen through smoked glass
Acted     had I? *I* could I?     the image / the order
To order my life with a difference
Clearly the bee must imagine gobs of parti-colored . . .

The life I examine     alone     at a party
He will die     it is out of desperation
What he proposed bluntly     desperation
Is it / out     -side     I wander     the park at night
The examined eye     the oculist's beam of light     a goblet or eyecup
It begins blurred
To order my life with a     different alphabet on the wall
He will die of certainties a difference with life
My order to     it begins blurred     a candle with a chimney
*Kansas visits cyclones*
A man stands blindfolded     a knife
I keep coming back to
At what point in my life

## ∾ In the Next Room

It is raining.
In the next room someone
Reads in a low voice.

Sleep is very warm here.
A light across the road
Flickers on and off.
Music from a phonograph
Hangs in the distance
Like faded wallpaper.

Odor of evergreen.
Odor of rain.
Here nothing is lacking
And our eyes converse.
In the next room someone
Stretches cold water
Against his lips.

The body on the bed
Presses close to itself.


## ∾ A Reading of This Poem

It is evident from the very first words that the subject of the poem under consideration is a late summer afternoon in New York City.

You will observe that, following a generalized setting of the scene, the poet continues with a reference to gay people strolling through the streets of Greenwich Village. It soon becomes apparent that he is not using "gay" solely in the sense of meaning "bright" or "lively" (although these meanings are not entirely irrelevant, for part of the point of the poem is the amiability of the occasion being described); nevertheless, even taking into account these implications, it should be obvious that the poet is using "gay" primarily as a syn-

onym for "homosexual"—and, in this specific instance, "homosexual male."
Next, the poet calls attention to certain aspects of the aforementioned people:
their casual manner, their laughter, their tanned skin, their open shirts reveal-
ing hints of hairy or hairless chests, the tightness of their jeans and possible
lack of underwear, and, most importantly, their ease and self-confidence. The
poet speculates upon whether this is due merely to the time of year and current
men's fashions, or whether these qualities result from the new militant gay
activism. In any case, the poet praises the friendly way in which we are greeted.

Notice here how the poet has slyly introduced the first person plural into his
poem, assuming that we would not find it embarrassing to be amongst these
people. Look, the poet says, one of them is putting his arm around you as he
talks. And what is he talking about? The poet offers no details, but we can
imagine such topics as films and records, perhaps, or ballet, travel, politics, or
poetry. The poet does intimate, though, that the conversation is charming and
intelligent. It certainly cannot be objectionable to you, for the poet deliberately
takes several lines to emphasize that much time has elapsed since the start of all
this, and you are still listening, apparently still interested. Then a drink is
suggested: "Why don't you come up to my place for a drink?"

Take note: our terms are "you" and "I" now. The poet is propositioning you.
So how about it? If you are bright, lively, and gay, why not say "yes" to me?

## ❧ True Loves

They are, like everyone else, judges,
accountants, clerks, physicians, hobbyists,
and everything else, but in love
they are Jimmie, saving money for the sex operation,
going by now in his dress and high heels, it is for love
that he wears silk panties, the same kind of smooth silk love
bids Mr. Breitling press against his lips while Marge
takes him over her knee like a stern but loving
headmistress, and both couples downstairs love
to place discreet ads and meet to swap partners, love partners
Chuck, staring for hours on end in the bus station john, and love

brings Linda to the bars at night, the same night Orval sleeps
alone, pledged to love in his conversion,
and Emmeline Morton, for love, adopts
her twelfth stray cat
                              —and it is true love
for them all, they hide from it no longer, they do not cry
for shame or try to reason with it: the love
which embraces them they embrace
in spite of their fears and their neighbors' scorn.
They have been put to the test and have won, they know
this is their love, and their love is good.


## ∾ A Lecture on Avant-Garde Art

Look in the Salon des Refusés of most periods
and there will hang the homosexuals,
labeled by critics
"contrary to nature."

Now, to use a familiar set of distinctions, what
exists but is not nature must be art;
yet art is also an imitation
of some process of nature: so art, too, is natural,
whatever its manner.

Art may evolve through accretions of tradition
or leap ahead into the unknown.
This form of expression, the gay life
so maddening and unimaginable to some,
necessarily involves a leap into the unknown,
for its traditions, such as they are, are shadowy.

Note how, on every side, images proclaim
and sustain the straight life. In parks and town squares
one may behold the monumental figures of, say,
Cohibere guarding his family from the Amplecti,

of Scruta and Amentia denouncing the barbarians,
or of the marriage of Turpa and Insulsus on the battlefield.

Images of the gay life, in contrast, are obscure, are
curiosities kept locked from the public in cabinets: in consequence,
gay lives must style themselves with craft,
with daring. Many fail. Even so,
some grow amazing and beautiful.

And since such triumphs are typically achieved
amidst general bewilderment and in defiance
of academic theory, the gay life
deserves to be ranked among
the significant examples of art, past and present.
And because it has disordered whatever may be
the accustomed ways of seeing in its time,
it is therefore avant-garde,
naturally avant-garde.

## ❧ A Way of Happening

> . . . *poetry makes nothing happen*
> —W. H. Auden

But at least
we can try to make
poetry
make something happen.

Therefore
I shall not conceal
anything
in this poem,

and if the names in it
are slightly changed,

that's to prevent
needless embarrassment:
but anyone involved
will recognize himself instantly,
that I guarantee.

This, then, is
a calling out,
an incitement to action.

In college
my roommate
was Robert Breuer,
who one year was elected
dorm president,
he was that nice,
good-looking,
and sharp.

Across the hall
lived Nick Clark,
tall, scrawny,
built like a stork,
a ferocious brain
and High Church choir singer
who developed a crush
on Bob Breuer.

And when Bob
found out
he shunned him
totally,
wouldn't even
say hello to him,

and since such things
seemed strange to us,
the rest of us shunned him, too.

We were seniors when it happened.
Graduation
solved everthing:
we all went away
(and thank goodness,
for by then
I'd developed a crush
on Ken Blakeslee,
but never mind
about that).

Now
I want to try
to make something happen.
Does anyone know
whatever became of anyone
I've mentioned in this poem?
If so,
please contact me
in care of this publication.

Or, perhaps, this is not
the right publication
for such a message to appear in.
Then let me know and tell me
what publication you think is.


## ✌ A Partial Index to Myself

A    aardvarks
     aberrations
     aftershave
     architecture
     artifice

B    Bach
     ballet
     bark worse than a bite
     bed
     befuddlement
     birthdays

| C | caves | I | ice cream |
|---|---|---|---|
| | champagne | | imagination |
| | chocolate cake | | infatuation |
| | Christmas | | ink |
| | coffee | | interior decoration |
| | contradictions | | interior monologue |
| | cowboys | | -isms |
| | crosswords | | it |
| | | | |
| D | darkness | J | jackanapes |
| | death | | jackass |
| | decadence | | jack-in-the-box |
| | denim | | jack rabbit |
| | dental floss | | |
| | deodorant | K | keys |
| | dilettantism | | kinks |
| | disguises | | kisses |
| | | | |
| E | enigmas | L | labyrinths |
| | erections | | laziness |
| | | | leather |
| F | fate | | Liebeslieder Walzer |
| | fetishes | | lions |
| | foolishness | | llamas |
| | | | |
| G | gay | M | manicure scissors |
| | ghosts | | maps |
| | gibberish | | menus |
| | gnomes | | mice |
| | gnus fit to print | | money |
| | grins | | myopia |
| | | | |
| H | haircuts | N | nail picking |
| | happenstance | | nit picking |
| | hide-and-seek | | nuts |
| | higgledy-piggledy | | |
| | huggermugger | O | okay |
| | hypochondria | | |

P   pandas
     pandemonium
     paradox
     parties
     peace marches
     pecan pie
     penguins
     piano lessons
     pizza
     poetry
     poodles
     pussycats

Q   quackery
     queasiness
     questions

R   rain
     rasps
     remnants
     revenants
     rhythm
     romanticism
     Rosetta stone
     rubbish

S   safari outfitting
     safety valves
     secrets
     sedition
     seduction
     shaggy dogs and their stories
     shudders
     smorgasbord

T   time
     time and tide

U   universal joints

V   vacations
     vexations
     vices
     volcanos

W   warts
     weight watching
     wiggles
     wine

X   X-ray eyes

Y   yellow journalism
     Yellow Pages
     Yellowstone National Park
     you and the night and the music

Z   zeppelins
     zero hour
     zippers
     zoos

BEAM 11, *Finial*

The thrust
is   thirst:

enough to whirl Neptune, in its orbit, three-billion miles
away
or curl the fern stalk up.

Coalescent holocaust
(which means The-Whole-Growing-Together-Through-Fire)
to gyroscope
emits in layers rays of many lengths.

*Its corona is the moth-*
*winged shape*
*a float of dust on water makes*
*from out an apple*
*transfixed upon a knitting needle*

*spun half submerged.*

It is said the sun blinds us because it is a HOLE
in the three-dimensional scenery.
—and light "diminishes in inverse proportion to the square
of the distance"
but the imaginary sphere
it illuminates, increases in the same
proportion—

Its Zodiacal Light is in the form of a lens
the lash of which intersects earth.

It is one-ten-thousandth the diameter of its 'system'
as is ovum to human.
VISION is seeing as the sun sees.

"midway between the absolute
and man"

(Fludd said)

The Mind & Eye, the solar system, galaxy
are spirals coiled from periphery
—i.e. Catherine Wheels—
of their worlds.
Whorls.

PARTICULAR SOLAR PLEXUS, COMPRESSER,
COMPLEXER:
plus ringed by minus

quickened in interlocking octaves

into a daffodil

(intricately fluted)

atop a hill

upon an ochre, blue, and white swirled world below

How to inquire
outside of fire?
What thinnest spoke-infolded core
of farthest star
invoke, in what we are?
Were?

*Rodin did*

*he said*
("each thing is merely the limit of the flame
to which it owes its existence")


*CONFLUXUS RADIORUM*


# BEAM 16, *The Voices*


*plumb line*


"For Orpheus' lute was strung with poets' sinews"
CROSS * SECTION OF KANSAS LILAC I SAT IN AT

I I

: nodal mosaic of rays slant streetlight

Pole Star naillike at canopy:

: moon behind cloud beyond bloom within its own dark afterimage

axial twig, live silver:

:a tranquility of minute balances tremolo near leaf tip

fireflies (magnified 1,000 times):

: the sound of a great black cloth ripping apart


*WHERE THE DEITY DWELLS
THE APE IS TO APPEAR*

WORD OF MOUTH

as "*the shadow dogs the body*
of one who walks in the sun"

(hidden Eurydice, whose face is ice)
MAKE MUSIC!
Socrates' three dreams
said.
HYMN HELIOS
out error's scatter sight's spectrum pattern
'limn electric'
*IN THE AIRE*
(Heraclitus on the sistrum)
perception is physics' intrinsic Its knit
&
/
or
Mr. Curious Hermes
(as the Greeks had season's quarters counterspiral
by entwined instinct image:
Mage)
twin snakes wrapt round our vitals
out plinth of time

RONALD JOHNSON

"piVot"
—winged—
'crescent on circle from cross'
(or metamorphosis-outshines-beast-round Homo
Maximus,
us
)
: ACT ICARUS EACH CREVICE:
*Mr. Curious*
*said*
—why we cannot, so close it is the sun,
see Intellect—
*. . . Though weave's riddle angles Angells bee . . .*
*butterfly-net senses' instant's*
*limits,*
quantum's
*sums*
*ABRAXAS IS EXACT OF FACT*
'as if'
*(by magic)*
*trans-ex-spiring what we call time*
presence
behind an appearance
"the backparts
of"

# BEAM 17, *The Book of Orpheus*       for Robert Duncan

That the story is plied in threes, and is thus a parable of SPACE.

First Orpheus plucks a music upon the Shell of earth, a form from which some
    say the intervals between strings are those the planets resonate. This is the
    body of man, where lion lie with lamb in The Imaginary Menagerie, where
    tree waltz rock down to the rainbow angle at interacting atoms.

That music is the art of TIME. Its work is Abstract and Mathematick, but is
    created in our own image. That the orders of lyre and year have such a
    close fit one could not slip a grassblade between.

Next, that he crosses the threshold of the unconscious to find Euridice by that
    same power, but must lose her at brink by looking back, mirror-warp to
    waking.

Last, this first 'maker' was torn apart by irrational women (for, it is said,
    preaching the love of man for man) so he is only a head now bearing down
    Being, only a singing. The lyre-head then washes seaflash to some inner
    cave of prophecy till the sun itself (its father) hush it to the faintest rustling
    from a run of stars.

That wonder takes all forms—Euridice, slip-knot through flesh, abreast the
    well of light, hand dipped in mercury through breath of earth—and thus
    is One Form.

That he who, fireshook head to foot, mistake the sun to speak, shall see the
    world from scratch. Wobble to pole: Great Balls of Fire, exquisite sedi-
    ment.

RONALD JOHNSON         

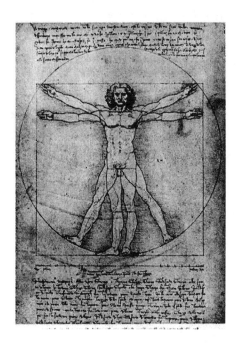

He who has seized one pebble shall climb a mountain.

He who has understood the wit of birds will split the weight of wings.

That Angels are not subject to gravity, and are therefore a cuckleburr of senses, apples all eyes and hearing spheres.

That one prism holds the spectrumed 'glory' as surely as whole populations of droplets strummed by sun.

That the action of the universe is metamorphosis — its articulation, metaphor. White crow, black swan, these are the hinges of Heaven.

## A MEMORABLE FANCY

As I was walking in my Garden, an Angel in an apple-tree saw me, and spoke: *I drink the air before me* momentum a beam lighttouchstonearc seen after rain ray bright sequence innermost outermost band outermost innermost Aristotle thus explained the circular scattered incident magnified drop filled with internal reflections refract of constants at obliquely index two all directions quivalent significant axispassing zero tangent surface transmitted again split passages not ordinarily visible of angle illuminated at all impact simultaneously infinitely the vicinity backscattered toward sun through the center three grazes in its original directions so do they bend back toward the forward univaries most slowly with changes in other words gather together regions of imaginary intensity in a sky filled with real waves.


That clockwise, counterclockwise, as blue bindweed to honeysuckle, the cosmos is an organism spirally open on itself, into the pull of existence. In the beginning there was the Word—for each man, magnetized by onrush, is Adam to his Tyger.

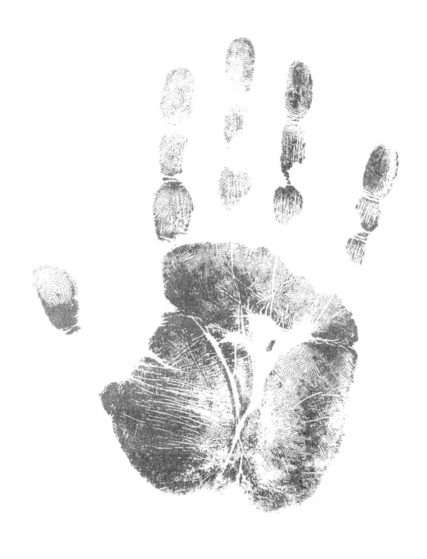

doomed princess
pursued by papparazzi
smashed flashbulbed
into infinity

*candle in the wind*
buried bright day
all London lines
polite the streets

lie softly, ghost
aghast at the actual
limbs dumb as trees
slippered in lead

round earth no more
would Saturn's rings
each proximity pull
to pale the whole

interred Isle du Lac
but for helicopters
safe in autumn sod
England's green hills

Diana, huntress
brought down herself
relentless chase
turned into marble

RONALD JOHNSON                                                    203

## ∾ Pornographic Poem

Seven Cuban
army officers
in exile
were at me
all night.
Tall,
sleek,
slender
Spanish types
with smooth dark
muscular bodies
and hair
like wet coal
on their heads
and between their legs.
I lost count
of the times
I was fucked
by them
in every conceivable
position.
At one point
they stood
around me
in a circle
and I had
to crawl
from one crotch
to another
sucking
on each cock

until it was hard.
When I got all
seven up
I shivered
looking up
at those erect pricks
all different lengths
and widths
and knowing
that each one
was going up
my ass hole.
Everyone
of them
came
at least twice
and some three times.
Once they put me
on the bed
kneeling,
one fucked me
in the behind,
another
in the mouth,
while I jacked off
one
with each hand
and two
of the others
rubbed
their peckers
on my bare feet
waiting
their turns
to get
into my can.
Just when I thought

they were all spent
two of them
got together
and fucked me
at once.
The positions
we were in
were crazy
but with two
big fat
Cuban cocks
up my ass
at one time
I was
in paradise.

## ∿ Hi Risque

I want
to scat
in your mouth,
I want you
to scat
in my mouth,
I want to scat
on your face
and rub it in

chocolate,
caviar,
and champagne,
absolute
preliminaries,
pushing
the inner
envelope

to the limit,
one more time,
mining
diamonds
with your tongue
for the crown
of one
of the kings
of hell,
when the going
gets rough
the tough
get gorgeous

squeezing
money
from the air
squeezing money
from the air,
snake
tongue,
stretching
your tongue
to the Buddhas,
diving
into the wreck
diving into
the wreck
diving into the wreck,
curiosity
and compassion,
and an exercise
in non-aversion,
fear
spiraling
from you
fear spiraling from you,

JOHN GIORNO

that gun's got
blood
in its hole

We do not do
this anymore,
but I still
think about it
when I'm
jerking off,
I was king
of promiscuity,
LSD,
crystal meth,
fist fucking
with 40 guys
for 14 hours,
it's worse
than I thought
and now,
every one
of them
I ever made
love to,
every single
one,
is dead,
and may they be
resting
in *great*
*equanimity*

We gave
a party
for the gods
and the gods
all came.

# ∾ None of Them Wanted To Go

I've seen the best minds of my generation die horrible deaths from AIDS.

Rudy Wurlitzer called me early on the morning of March 18, 1989, with the news that Robert Mapplethorpe had just died in a Boston hospital. "Robert had a *grand mal* at the moment of death," said Rudy. "It was heavy!" The next day I spoke to Lynn Davis, Rudy's wife, who had been with Robert in his room in the hospital when he died.

The last four days of Robert Mapplethorpe's life went like this: Robert refused to die, he refused to give up. He had been sick with AIDS for years, and his body was disintegrating from various AIDS diseases. His mind and mental faculties remained sharp and clear. Robert had heard that Dr. Jerome Groupman in Boston had a radical new therapy for AIDS. Robert rented a deluxe rock 'n' roll tour bus, the quintessence of luxury, normally used by Mick Jagger on tour, and made the trip. When he arrived at Boston's Deaconess Hospital, he was too sick to undergo the treatment and too weak to return to New York. Robert held court, surrounded by his retinue, being imperious and endearing. One of Robert's last boyfriends went up to Boston to visit, of whom William Burroughs said, "He has a sincere but untrustworthy face."

Robert died four days later in a *grand mal* or severe epileptic seizure at the moment of death, screaming and shaking violently, vomiting blood; he was crazed and demented, blood spewing from his mouth, blood trickling and farting from his asshole, blood splattered all over the hospital room. He was absolutely refusing to die, with an almost demonic attachment, refusing to leave this life. A male hospital nurse said, "I have never seen anyone die like that."

After Robert's death, as his body lay on the hospital bed, Lynn said, "Robert looked very peaceful, like an angel!" Lynn loved Robert. I hope he was, but the body often looks peaceful because it has stopped functioning and is inert. Indeed, the family and friends often think the dead person has gone on to heaven or a better place because they love the person, but actually the consciousness and soul of the dead person is screaming, *"I'm dead and I don't want to be dead!"*

Robert Mapplethorpe had a great love of beauty and was very attached to life, as witnessed by his great photographs that fix impermanence, his vast collections, and his fame. To die in a *grand mal* is not the best way to die. The state of a person's mind in the moments before death carries over with the consciousness after death. The spasms and confusion could influence the moments after death, which is one of the most important times in a person's life: when there is a chance for liberation into the vast, empty expanse of original nature. Having an epileptic fit at this time might block the consciousness and leave the person angry he's dead. I don't know what happened after Robert Mapplethorpe died, but there is the possibility that the absolute worst happened.

Among the many possibilities: the person who refuses to believe he is dead stays in this world. Traditionally this kind of being is called a spirit or ghost. The problem is that a spirit experiences great suffering because it can see everything (the dead can still see, hear and feel through habit, only having lost their body, similar to seeing when asleep and dreaming), but is separated from what is perceived as belonging to it. The dead can influence events, depending on how powerful the person was in life, and events can be affected in a positive or negative way. The fame, of both Robert Mapplethorpe and Andy Warhol, greatly increased after their deaths, and I venture to say that they both possibly, for a while, serviced their careers from the dead.

That night after Robert Mapplethorpe died, I was in my loft on the third floor at 222 Bowery, and I went to get myself another drink. I had first met Robert in 1966, and again with Patti Smith, and my designer, George Delmerico, had gone to Pratt with Robert in 1961-65, and Robert did the brilliant photographs for the LP cover of my album *Sugar, Alcohol & Meat*. It was about 7 P.M. and I had one light vodka and soda, and smoked a joint. I was drinking from an art deco Lalique glass, from a set of Lalique crystal I had inherited from an aunt, and each glass was worth $400. I use those glasses on special occasions honoring demons and gods. I was wondering where Robert's consciousness was, and what state he was in. When I lightly put the glass with half-melted ice cubes down on the table, the glass broke. A ring of glass separated one-half inch down from the top, as if a psychic buzzsaw of his consciousness from hell had swooped down and cut it off. I heard and felt the noise. I was shocked. A four-inch wide perfect ring of Lalique, thin and fragile. What an amazing sign! I thought, Thank you for nothing, Robert (who had such a great love for beautiful objects)! And I let the matter rest, feeling sad for him.

We all have to die sometime and there are better ways to do it. Terry Clifford's death was one of the best. Terry, 39, died on August 10, 1986, apparently not of AIDS but of diseases similar to AIDS. Healthy and beautiful, Terry fell sick and was dead in three months from lymphoma, lung and breast cancer, and meningitis causing lesions on the brain. In the hospital, Terry asked two of her doctors for an AIDS test, and they threw back their heads and laughed, saying, *"What do you want an AIDS test for? You have lymphoma. Do you want more bad news?"* We learned afterwards that the doctors believed that Terry did not have AIDS.

Terry Clifford was a great meditator in the Tibetan Nyingmapa Buddhist tradition. She had been on strict retreats for more than five years. She had received many of the highest teachings from the highest lamas. Her teachers were H. H. Dudjom Rinpoche and H. H. Dilgo Khentyse Rinpoche. She had great realization and skills in the highest Tantric yogas. She prepared for death —the moment when the consciousness leaves the body—with the transcendence and humility of a saint, and with the discipline and courage of an Olympic athlete who trains for one moment in competition. Terry died perfectly and attained Enlightenment.

A week before Terry died, we were sitting in her living room, laughing and telling each other profound gossip, and having a good time. Terry was talking with clarity and brilliance, then she paused and said, *"John, excuse me for a moment."* She closed her eyes and turned aside. This was when the cancerous tumors in her brain were growing voraciously. Terry rested in meditation, seeing the hallucinations as delusion, realizing their empty nature, and recognizing in whatever arises the simultaneity of the arising and dissolution in the great expanse. She took no pain killers and felt no pain, in the sense that you don't really feel pain in a dream if you realize it's a dream. After a few minutes she turned to me, smiling radiantly, and said, *"You have no idea what goes on inside my head!"*

When her death suddenly came, she handled it with perfection. She understood impermanence and had fully realized absolute wisdom and emptiness. She asked two friends to help her sit up in a chair in her bedroom and dissolved her consciousness into *great equanimity*, resting in the great bliss and clarity of Primordial Wisdom Mind.

Terry died with great peace, beyond hope, and had no panic, no fear, no lingering, and she was gone. There was no cold wind. Everything was warm, happy, and radiant. Her bedroom filled with dazzling brightness. She demonstrated nonattachment, accepting what is, not fighting it and not clinging to it. She was surrounded by her Dharma friends, never lost interest in them, and had great compassion for all around her. She was a Buddha manifesting Enlightenment and going to a Pure Field. I don't know what happened after Terry Clifford died, but there is the possibility that the best happened.

## ∾ The First Time

Sometimes I'm their first.
Sweet, sweet men.
I light candles, burn the best incense.
Make them think it's some kind of temple
and it rather is.

Like this guy who hauled parts for a living,
whatever the hell that means.
He was like caught light through glass,
and so the candles and the incense.
What would you do with a new colt?

He touched my body the way shadows
fall from an old subject he'd buried,
and he looked at me without fear.

Sweet guy.
So sweet I became really shy and hot
so I had to move easy.
Wouldn't you?
What do you do when it's someone's first time?
I try to clean up my act.
Make it into a first rate number
so he knows he's been with someone.

We're bunglers when it's really good:
bow legs, pimply backs, scrawny chest hair,
full of mistakes and good intentions.
And it doesn't have to do with women.
They're fine too.
Just some understanding between two men.

## ⤳ Taken to a Room

Taken to a room with you asleep,
I want to touch you there
beneath the galaxy of star quilt.
You unfold letting me into the warmth
and everything rises from my dick to my breath
saying we are here.

In my mind I kiss you away, your beard
and earring, the tattooed heart of Christ
on your chest, and remember
a prison boy named Rubio,
then I kiss down on all of you.

Now I'm taken to a room fully awake
and warned my imagination is out of hand.
They show me a solo screaming bed
and quilt of fallen stars.
I pant hard over this poem
wanting to write your body again.

In this totally conscious poem
you're gone and they unplug my systems,
my heart, my lungs, my brains.
In front of the crowd they flash blinding lights
on my crotch and neuter me down to a smile.

I try to think about your eyes
and remember nothing.
Now they drag me off to the next room
where the real work begins.

# ∾ Making Love to Myself

When I do it, I remember how it was with us.
Then my hands remember too,
and you're with me again, just the way it was.

After work when you'd come in and
turn the TV off and sit on the edge of the bed,
filling the room with gasoline smell from your overalls,
trying not to wake me which you always did.
I'd breathe out long and say,
'Hi Jess, you tired baby?'
You'd say not so bad and rub my belly,
not after me really, just being sweet,
and I always thought I'd die a little
because you smelt like burnt leaves or woodsmoke.

We were poor as Job's turkey but we lived well—
the food, a few good movies, good dope, lots of talk,
lots of you and me trying on each other's skin.

What a sweet gift this is,
done with my memory, my cock and hands.

Sometimes I'd wake up wondering if I should fix
coffee for us before work,
almost thinking you're here again, almost seeing
your work jacket on the chair.

I wonder if you remember what
we promised when you took the job in Laramie?
Our way of staying with each other.
We promised there'd always be times
when the sky was perfectly lucid,
that we could remember each other through that.
You could remember me at my worktable
or in the all-night diners,
though we'd never call or write.

JAMES L. WHITE                                          215

I just have to stop here Jess.
I just have to stop.


## ∾ The Salt Ecstasies

Salt me down where love was
on a blue burn to remember the real pain.
I'm worn out from my back's arch and pull,
bending like a crazy-house mirror to suit your needs
in this endless flesh revolt, trying to win
with my mouth and ass.

I want to be your yoke this time,
pushing you away in the dusty light
from gutting me to nothing, and stay
drawn in, like an old girl
after a hard Saturday night, her body
empty of carriage,
alone and complete
in the room's stillness.

I leave you first in sleep,
my breasts, my V, and hair,
then take the early bus to Laurel
away from the raw and nameless.

Some farm kid presses against my leg.
I look at the long backs of men in the fields
and doze to dream you're going through me
like winter bone, your logs of arms pushing
me down into some stifling contract with flesh
until I break free for air.

# ༄ Oshi

Oshi has a very large Buddha in him, one that can change the air into scented flowers. He used to be Tommy Whalen from Indianapolis but he had his eyes cut to look Japanese. He got started out in San Francisco in the early days when Buddha consciousness was just rising out there and people were still slipping pork in the seaweed soup.

At seventeen he did drag in a place called The Gay Deceiver and was billed as "The Boy with The Face Like The Girl Next Door." The owners paid him almost nothing and kept him strung out on hash in a little room above the bar, like a bad detective novel.

Somehow Oshi found the Zen community and started sitting za-zen. He collected "mad money" from the state for being strung out. It's free out there if you're crazy enough. Oshi breathed hash and gin through the Buddha. Buddha breathed light and air through Oshi. It all changed his mind to indigo. Buddha consciousness rose in him until he didn't feel like the broken piano at the bar anymore.

Now thirty years later he has a permanent room at the bath house and prays for young boys. Doesn't sit anymore. Said he became realized ten years ago with a young hustler from Akron, Ohio who told him he could stop flying, just lay back and touch ground.

Old Oshi, very round now, jet black wig, looks like a retired Buddha in his cheap wash-and-wear kimonos.

He's a graceful old gentleman Buddha. Buys everyone drinks. Gives away joints. Always high. Always lighting joss sticks. As he says, 'Giving things is just a way of getting on with everyone, you know, the universe and everything. It's like passing on the light.'

He told me once when he sang Billie Holliday's 'Blue Monday' at The Gay Deceiver they used an amber spot and he wore a strapless lamé gown, beaded his eyelashes, lacquered his nails, and the people cried.

## ᴄᴏ By These Waters

What begins in recognition,—
. . . ends in obedience.

The boys who lie back, or stand up,
allowing their flies to be unzipped

*however much they charge*
*however much they charge*

give more than they get.

When the room went dark, the screen lit up.

By these waters on my knees I have wept.

## ᴄᴏ In the Western Night

I. *The Irreparable*

First, I was there where unheard
harmonies create the harmonies

we hear—

then I was a dog, sniffing
your crotch.

I asked you why you
were here; your answer was your beauty.

I said I was in need. You said
that the dead

rule and confuse our steps—

that if I helped you cut your skin
deeply enough

that, at least, was IRREPARABLE . . .

This afternoon, the clouds
were moving so swiftly—

massed above the towers, rushing.


2. *In My Desk*

Two cigarette butts—
left by you

the first time you visited my apartment.
The next day

I found them, they were still there—

picking one up, I put my lips where
yours had been . . .


    •


Our not-love is like a man running down
a mountain, who, if he dares to try to stop,

falls over—
my hands wanted to touch your hands

because we had hands.


FRANK BIDART

•

I put the two cigarette butts
in an envelope, carefully

taping shut the edges.
At first, the thin paper of the envelope

didn't stop

the stale smell of tobacco . . .
Now the envelope is in my desk.


3. *Two Men*

The man who does not know himself, who
does not know his affections that his actions

speak but that he does not
acknowledge,

who will SAY ANYTHING

and lie when he does not know that he is
lying because what he needs to believe is true

must indeed
be true,

THIS MAN IS STONE . . . NOT BREAD.

STONE. NOT CAKE. NOT CHEESE. NOT BREAD . . .

The man who tries to feed his hunger
by gnawing stone

is a FOOL; his hunger is

fed in ways that he knows cannot satisfy it.


4. *Epilogue: A Stanza from Horace*

At night in dreams I hold you
      and now I pursue you
fleeing through the grass of the Campus Martius,
you, through the waters (you are cruel) fleeing.


# ∾ A Coin for Joe, with the Image of a Horse; c. 350-325 BC

COIN

    *chip of the closed,—L O S T world, toward whose unseen grasses*

*this long-necked emissary horse*

          *eagerly still*
          *stretches, to graze*


  •


               World; Grass;

stretching Horse;—ripe with hunger, bright circle
of appetite, risen to feed and famish us, from exile underground . . . for

you    chip of the incommensurate
closed world    A *n g e l*


FRANK BIDART

## ∿ The Yoke

*don't worry      I know you're dead*
*but tonight*

*turn your face again*
*toward me*

*when I hear your voice there is now*
*no direction in which to turn*

I sleep and wake and sleep and wake and sleep and wake and

but tonight
turn your face again

toward me

*see      upon my shoulders is the yoke*
*that is not a yoke*

don't worry      I know you're dead
but tonight

turn your face again

## ∿ Luggage

You wear your body as if without
illusions. You speak of former lovers with some

contempt for their interest in sex.
Wisdom of the spirit, you

imply, lies in condescension and poise.

. . . Fucking, I can feel
the valve opening, the flood is too much.

Or too little. I am
insatiable, famished by repetition.

Now all you see is that I am luggage

that smiles as it is moved from here
to there. *We could have had ecstasies.*

In your stray moments, as now in
mine, may what *was not*

rise like grief before you.

## ↷ For the Twentieth Century

Bound, hungry to pluck again from the thousand
technologies of ecstasy

boundlessness, the world that at a drop of water
rises without boundaries,

I push the PLAY button:—

. . . *Callas, Laurel & Hardy, Szigeti*

*you are alive again,*—

the slow movement of K.218
once again no longer

bland, merely pretty, nearly
banal, as it is

in all but Szigeti's hands

*

Therefore you and I and Mozart
must thank the Twentieth Century, for

it made you pattern, form
whose infinite

repeatability within matter
defies matter—

*Malibran. Henry Irving. The young
Joachim.* They are lost, a mountain of

newspaper clippings, become words
not their own words. The art of the performer.

ᴖ from *I Remember*

I remember when I thought that I was a great artist.

I remember when I wanted to be rich and famous. (And I still do!)

I remember when I had a job cleaning out an old man's apartment who had died. Among his belongings was a very old photograph of a naked young boy pinned to an old pair of young boy's underwear. For many years he was the choir director at church. He had no family or relatives.

I remember a boy who worked for an undertaker after school. He was a very good tap dancer. He invited me to spend the night with him one day. His mother was divorced and somewhat of a cheap blond in appearance. I remember that his mother caught us innocently wrestling out in the yard and she got *very* mad. She told him never to do that again. I realized that something was going on that I knew nothing about. We were ten or eleven years old. I was never invited back. Years later, in high school, he caused a big scandal when a love letter he had written to another boy was found. He then quit school and worked full time for the undertaker. One day I ran into him on the street and he started telling me about a big room with lots of beds where all the undertaker employees slept. He said that each bed had a little white tent in the morning. I excused myself and said goodbye. Several hours later I figured out what he had meant. Early morning erections.

I remember when I worked in a snack bar and how much I hated people who ordered malts.

. . . . . . . . . . . . .

I remember cherry Cokes.

I remember pastel colored rocks that grew in water.

I remember drive-in onion rings.

I remember that the minister's son was wild.

I remember pearlized plastic toilet seats.

I remember a little boy whose father didn't believe in dancing and mixed swimming.

I remember when I told Kenward Elmslie that I could play tennis. He was looking for someone to play with and I wanted to get to know him better. I couldn't even hit the ball but I did get to know him better.

I remember when I didn't really believe in Santa Claus but I wanted to so badly that I did.

I remember when the Pepsi-Cola Company was on its last leg.

I remember when Negroes had to sit at the back of the bus.

I remember pink lemonade.

I remember paper doll twins.

I remember puffy pastel sweaters. (Angora)

I remember drinking glasses with girls on them wearing bathing suits but when you filled them up they were naked.

I remember dark red fingernail polish almost black. I remember that cherries were too expensive.

I remember a drunk man in a tuxedo in a bar who wanted Ron Padgett and me to go home with him but we said no and he gave us all his money.

I remember how many other magazines I had to buy in order to buy one physique magazine.

I remember a climbing red rose bush all over the garage. When rose time came it was practically solid red.

I remember a little boy down the street. Sometimes I would hide one of his toys inside my underwear and make him reach in for it.

I remember how unsexy swimming naked in gym class was.

I remember that "Negro men have giant cocks."

I remember that "Chinese men have little cocks."

I remember a girl in school one day who, just out of the blue, went into a long spiel all about how difficult it was to wash her brother's pants because he didn't wear underwear.

I remember slipping underwear into the washer at the last minute (wet dreams) when my mother wasn't looking.

I remember a giant gold man taller than most buildings at "The Tulsa Oil Show."

I remember trying to convince my parents that not raking leaves was good for the grass.

I remember that *I* liked dandelions all over the yard.

I remember that my father scratched his balls a lot.

I remember very thin belts.

I remember James Dean and his red nylon jacket.

I remember thinking how embarrassing it must be for men in Scotland to have to wear skirts.

I remember when Scotch tape wasn't very transparent.

JOE BRAINARD

I remember how little your dick is, getting out of a wet bathing suit.

I remember saying "thank you" when the occasion doesn't call for it.

I remember shaking big hands.

I remember saying "thank you" in reply to "thank you" and then the other person doesn't know what to say.

I remember getting erections in school and the bell rings and how handy zipper notebooks were.

I remember zipper notebooks. I remember that girls hugged them to their breasts and that boys carried them loosely at one side.

. . . . . . . . . . .

I remember fantasies of totally losing my voice and hearing and being able to communicate only by writing notes back and forth. (It was fun!)

I remember trying not to stare at people with hearing aids. (Or trying to look at them casually)

I remember braces (on teeth) and how, at a certain point in high school it was almost a status symbol.

I remember being embarrassed to blow my nose in public.

I remember not going to the bathroom in public places if I didn't know where it was.

I remember, when traveling, laying tissue paper over the toilet seat rim because "You never know."

I remember "number one" and "number two."

I remember examining my cock and balls very carefully once and finding them absolutely disgusting.

I remember fantasies of my cock growing quite large just overnight. (A medical mystery!)

I remember sexual fantasies of having "to perform" by force.

I remember Coke bottle stories.

I remember reading somewhere that the average cock is from six to eight inches when erect, and grabbing for the nearest ruler.

.   .   .   .   .   .   .   .   .   .   .   .

I remember suspenders and bow ties and red leather mittens.

I remember, when someone says something that rhymes, "You're a poet, and didn't know it, but your feet show it. They're Longfellows!"

I remember yellow rubber raincoats with matching hoods.

I remember big black galoshes with lots of metal foldover clamps.

I remember a *very* deluxe Crayola set that had gold and silver and copper.

I remember that the red Crayola was always the first to go.

I remember always drawing girls with their hands behind their backs. Or in pockets.

I remember that area of white flesh between the pant cuffs and the socks when old men cross their legs.

I remember a fat man who sold insurance. One hot summer day we went to visit him and he was wearing shorts and when he sat down one of his balls hung out. I remember that it was hard to look at it and hard not to look at it too.

I remember a very early memory of an older girl in a candy store. The man asked her what she wanted and she picked out several things and then he asked her for her money and she said, "Oh, I don't have any money. You just asked me what I *wanted,* and I told you." This impressed me no end.

I remember daydreams of living in a tree house.

. . . . . . . . . . .

I remember early sexual experiences and rubbery knees. I'm sure sex is much better now but I *do* miss rubbery knees.

I remember the first time I got jerked off (never did discover it for myself) I didn't know what she was trying to do and so I just laid there like a zombie not helping one bit.

I remember her wanting me to put my finger in her cunt and so I did but I had no idea (or no inspiration) as to what to "do" with it once it was there except to move it around a bit.

I remember feeling very outside the experience (watching myself) and feeling very silly with my finger in this wet hole. I think she finally gave up and made herself come because I remember a lot of hard kissing while I could feel her squirming around a lot down there.

I remember, on the verge of coming, thinking that *that* meant I had to go pee, so I excused myself to go to the bathroom and that spoiled everything.

I remember being very proud of myself the next morning, nevertheless.

I remember Nehru jackets.

I remember when turtle necks were big, talk about what restaurants would let you in and what ones wouldn't.

I remember the first time I ate beefsteak tartar eating lots of crackers and butter with it.

I remember linen dresses from behind after having sat through a sermon. Or a bridge party.

. . . . . . . . . . . .

I remember wondering how one would go about putting on a rubber gracefully, in the given situation.

I remember (in a general sort of way) many nights in bed just holding myself through soft flannel pajamas.

I remember cold sheets in the winter time.

I remember when everything is covered with snow, out the window, first thing in the morning: a really clear surprise. It only snowed about twice a year in Tulsa and, as I remember now, usually during the night. So, I remember "snow" more than I remember "snowing."

I remember not understanding the necessity of shoveling the sidewalks. It always melted in a day or two anyway. And besides—"It's only snow."

I remember thinking Brownie uniforms not very pretty: so brown and plain.

I remember fantasies of everyone in my family dying in a car wreck, except me, and getting lots of sympathy and attention, and admiration for being so brave about it all.

I remember fantasies of writing a very moving letter to the President of the United States about patriotism, and the President, very moved by my moving letter, distributes copies of it to the media (T.V., magazines, newspapers, etc.) and I become one very famous child.

I remember daydreams of going through old trunks in attics, and finding fantastic things.

. . . . . . . . . . . .

I remember when father seemed too formal, and daddy was out of the question, and dad seemed too fake-casual. But, seeming the lesser of three evils, I chose fake-casual.

I remember closely examining the opening in the head of my cock once, and how it reminded me of a goldfish's mouth.

I remember goldfish tanks in dime stores. And nylon nets to catch them with.

I remember ceramic castles. Mermaids. Japanese bridges. And round glass bowls of varying sizes.

I remember big black goldfish, and little white paper cartons to carry them home in.

I remember the rumor that Mae West keeps her youthful appearance by washing her face in male cum.

I remember wondering if female cum is called "cum" too.

I remember wondering about the shit (?) ((ugh)) in fucking up the butt.

I remember ping-pong ball dents.

I remember rayon slip-over shirts with knitted bands at the waist.

I remember bathroom doors that don't lock, and trying to pee fast.

I remember, when you've done a real stinker, hoping there won't be someone waiting to rush in right after you.

. . . . . . . . . . . .

I remember my mother talking about women who shouldn't wear slacks.

I remember taking baths with my brother Jim when we were very young, back to back.

I remember inching myself down into water that was too hot.

I remember the "tornado" way the last of the water has of swirling down the drain so noisily.

I remember stories about people getting electrocuted by talking on the telephone in the bathtub.

I remember telephone nooks built into walls. And "party lines."

I remember (recently!) getting blown while trying to carry on a normal telephone conversation, which, I must admit, was a big turn-on somehow.

I remember not very scary ghost stories, except for the dark they were told in.

I remember having a friend over-night, and lots of giggling after the lights are out. And seemingly long silences followed by "Are you asleep yet?" and, sometimes, some pretty serious discussions about God and Life.

I remember get-rich-quick schemes of selling hand-painted bridge tallies, inventing an umbrella hat, and renting myself out as an artist by the hour.

# ALFRED CORN (1943-)

## ∾ Seeing All the Vermeers

Met Museum, 1965, the first
I'll see, his *Young Woman Sleeping.*
Stage right, painterly carpet spread over the table
where a plate of apples, crumpled napkin
and drained wineglass abut the recapped pitcher.
Propped by one hand, her leaning drowse,
behind which, a door opens on the dream, bare
but for a console and framed mirror—or a painting
too shadowed to make out. Next to it,
(certitude) one window, shuttered for the duration . . . .

That dream also timed *me* out, a lull in the boomeranging
hubbub of the staggering city I'd just moved to.

*

In the Frick's *Officer and Laughing Girl,* spring sunshine
entered left, partly blocked by the noncom suitor's hat-brim,
wide, dark as seduction, conquest. A map dotted with schooners
backed her fresh elations, the glass winking at them both. He'd see
why, in a later day, crewcut recruits were shipping out to 'Nam;
and she, why the student Left was up in arms against the war.

*

In '67, Ann and I spent a graduate year in Paris;
and lived in the Louvre, too, along with *The Lacemaker*—
self-effacing, monumental, an artisan
whose patience matched the painter's, inscribed
in tangling skeins of scarlet oil against an indigo
silk cushion. Silent excruciation
among toy spools framed the blithe paradox

called "women's work," disgracing anything less
than entire devotion to labor entered into. (That May,
a million demonstrators marched up the Champs Elysées.)

*

From there to Amsterdam and *The Little Street,*
where innate civility distilled a local cordial, free
from upheaval, from dearth *and* opulence, each brick
distinct, their collectivity made credible
by chalky varicosis on the house's settling façade.
A century's successive mortars filled those cracks,
nor will the figures down on hands and knees in the foreground
stand up again till they've replaced that broken tile.

The *Woman in Blue Reading a Letter* calmed misgivings
with the global trust that swelled her body, a soft counterweight
to expeditions tracked across the weathered map behind.
A new-found Eden, festooned with portents, history
piloting ship and cargo across the wrinkling sea.

The *Maidservant Pouring Milk's* power to see
in threadbare clothes and plain features a meek *claritas*
made of *caritas,* doesn't need words . . . . But since I do,
call her a velvet motet developed in blue, in scaled-down
yellow-green that I could hear, the resonant stillness
centered on movement's figment, cream paint paying out
a corded rivulet at the cruse's lip. Crusty loaves, nail-holes
in plaster, and knuckles roughened by scalds and scrubs
witnessed to the daily immolation, performed as first light
tolled matins from a dutch-gold vessel hooked to the wall.

*

By train to Den Haag, to see the *View of Delft's* ink-black
medieval walls and bridge, barges anchored on a satin
water more pensive than the clouded blue above,

where one tall steeple took its accolade of sun.
(Proust's "patch of yellow wall," I couldn't find, though.)
The *Girl in a Turban* looked like Anne Wiazemsky,
Godard's new wife, whom we'd seen in his latest film.
Liquid eyes, half-parted lips, a brushstroke ancillary
to fable highlighting the weighty pearl at her earlobe,
her "Turkish" costume stage-worthy, if she ever chose to act.

                    *

By then it was set: No matter how many years or flights
it took, I'd see all of Vermeer—which helps explain
the Vienna stop we made that spring, and our instant beeline
to *An Artist in His Studio* (called, today, *The Allegory of Fame*).
What to make of the Artist's bloomers, outmoded even then—

and why would his model hold book and clarion, standing
before the mapped Low Countries? If that anesthetized mask
on the table near her denied the chandelier its candles,
then who hung a tapestried curtain in the left foreground?

Vermeer; but his meaning subverts comment, always
less hypnotic than the surface itself, a luminous
glaze adhering to receding frames in series,
chromatic theaters for featured roles that also kindle
fervor in their supporting actor, the secret soul.

                    *

Strike me dumb on first seeing *The Astronomer*
in Guy de Rothschild's study—well, a photograph of it
in an Eighties coffee-table book, *The Great Houses
of Paris.* Not long after, thanks to philanthropy
and the tax structure, it devolved upon the state.
Semester break that winter, McC. and I jetted to France,
entered the Louvre's new glass pyramid and fought
dense crowds to where he hung, *The Lacemaker's* late consort.

In a brown studio, his fingers reading the globe,
he sat, immovably dutiful to calculations
devised ad hoc to safecrack the star-studded zodiac.

*

I was one of the visitors tiptoeing
through Isabella Gardner's house in Boston
decades before the heist, which to this day
remains unsolved. But balance one instance
of good luck against a trip made to Ireland
in '86, missing by only a few months
the Beit Collection's *Lady Writing a Letter.*
Paid so often now, the compliment of theft
puts a keen edge on our art pilgrimages:
The icon may be gone when you arrive.

That fall, I lived in London's Camden Town,
writing on . . . call them stateside topics; and soon
tubed up to Kenwood House, relieved to find
their prime collectible unstolen—its potential
as ecphrastic plunder not apparent at the time.
(A sonnet, no less, completed earlier in New Haven,
qualified me for that satire on the Connecticut bard
besotted with Vermeer. Still, subjects could be barred
in advance only if they and poems were the same gadget.
Disbelief, you're suspended, even for the standard
gloat over shots knocked back at the Cedar Tavern,
ca. 1950, with Pollock and De Kooning.)

Here then was Kenwood's *Lady with Guitar,* in corkscrew
curls, lemon jacket trimmed with ermine, lounging
like some hippie denizen of Washington Square,
strumming for the $n$th time his second-hand Dylan . . .
Maybe they heard her, too, the National Gallery's
paired women portraits, each playing a virginal,
both in silk dresses, one seated, one standing—
Profane and Sacred Love, if the old allegory fits.

A trip from London to Edinburgh produced, beyond
the classic-Gothic limestone city grimed with soot,
an early *Christ in the House of Mary and Martha,*
conceived before the painter's parables began unfolding
at home in Delft. Still, Martha's proffered pannier is as real
as the bread it holds, and Jesus' open hand, rendered
against clean table linen, as strong and solid as Vermeer's.

                    *


A chill, damp March in Dresden with Chris.
We'd begun with the Berlin State Museum's holdings
and then trained down on our way to Prague.
The Gemäldegalerie, quiet as a church, listened
while beads of tarnished rain pelted the skylights.
Works known from reproductions offered themselves
to the gray ambient, visibly conscious
of having survived Allied firebombs fifty years
earlier and a postwar Ice Age that slammed home,
then froze every bolt in the Eastern sector.
Young Vermeer's *The Procuress* makes love for sale
push beyond the sour analogue
of art-as-commerce into distinct portraits,
comedic types you have and haven't seen before
caught up in cheerful barter while wine flows
at a balustrade draped with carpet and a fur cape.
The client's left hand could have been mine,
weighing down a pretty shoulder (and the bodice),
but not the right, poised to let fall a coin
into her open palm. Men's hunger for sex
and poverty's for comforts—an old story,
mean or tragic, and never finally resolved.

                    *

Having missed Her Majesty's *The Music Lesson*, lent
over the years to several exhibitions, guess who danced
when told that it would grace the show to end all shows
scheduled in Washington, for the fall of '95.
And other hard-to-sees from Brunswick and Frankfurt,
jubilation, were included also, plus
apprentice works on pagan or religious themes.

Long caterpillar of a line, composed of hundreds
come to worship genius and the beauty it makes.
An hour's wait on weary legs, and in we go:
*The Geographer*, taking his place by *The Astronomer*;
Ireland's letter-writer, look, recaptured, and now restored
to the public; a *View of Delft*, cleaned so thoroughly
you couldn't miss that patch of yellow—*not* a wall,
instead, a roof . . . . Sheltering involuntary
memories of countless choked-up viewers,
whose gazes added one more laminate of homage
to a surface charged with how many hundred-thousands now.

From the permanent collection—why?—I saw as though
I never had the *Woman Weighing Gold*, some twenty years
(gone, and still here) since that first visit (Walter with me)
to the National Gallery. By word-origin *Galilees*,
*inter*national through their holdings, these cathedrals
of art gather in the faithful that faith in art has summoned
for mutual appraisal, what we are seen in what we see.

Hence the scales at center canvas Vermeer suspended
from her fine-boned hand, the face all understanding,
and so, forgiving all. Nevertheless, the great maternal
judge weighs one gold (a ring? a coin?) against a smaller gold,
in gloom as dark as the Day of Wrath, whose millennial
trumpet tears away truth's final veil.
                                        So human error
must yield, her calm demeanor says, to *Pax caelestis*
and dawn break forth in perpetual light transforming

ALFRED CORN

breath, strife, treasure, theft, love and the end of love,
into its own substance, strong, bright beam of Libra rising
step by step up the scale to Eden and a countenance
the soul, made visible, is now accorded grace to see.

Around us, heads bent toward a morning vintaged
more than three hundred years ago. Simple delight
wearing Nikes, Levis, parkas; students, grizzled veterans,
young mothers, teachers, painters—awestruck, whispering
*Heavens! Just look at that!*—his New World public.

# J. D. McCLATCHY (1945-)

## ༚ Ouija

*in memory of James Merrill*

Years ago—long enough at least for bitter
Leaves to have cooled at the bottom of a cup
Then brimful and steaming with insecurities—
Four spellbound friends were huddled around
What might as well have been a campfire,
Their shadows thrown back on the world
By candlelight, the flames of anticipation
Fed by skittish questions of whatever voice
Any one of them had felt clearing its throat
Inside the jelly lid with its toothpick pointer
Patrolling a border of hand-drawn letters—

Not theirs, of course, the timidly curious
Weekend houseguests in rainy Stonington,
But JM's, the loom from which bolts of blues
Lay stacked on his desk, *Ephraim's* final galleys.
The master had been unexpectedly
Summoned by redundancy—a family crisis—
But insisted . . . look, the steak's been marinating,
There's plenty to drink, the weather forecast's glum.
They'd stay? And why not take an idle turn
At the board? His Honda was barely in reverse
When Mickey's mop and pail were blithely tossed

Aside and motley, ill-fitting robes assumed—
In their case, a cheap imitation mantle
That, like any religion, risked mocking
What it worshiped. But then, how else learn
What can't be taught than play the earnest fool?
left alone with a luster and delirium

J. D. McCLATCHY                                             241

About to be cut with callow, flavorless slush,
They pulled their chairs up to the round table,
Guarded by votive griffons, a saltcellar,
And a spineless cactus that waited patiently
Under a bite-size crystal hanging from the dome.

Roach clip. Jug wine. The conventional aids
To inspiration were reluctantly foresworn
In favor of seltzer and cold credulity.
They sat there edgily, hour after hour,
Watching the voices muster into words—
As when, between the scenes of a play, the stage
Is briefly darkened but still slightly visible,
Enough for us to see the stagehands moving
Furniture around, the props of what's to come—
So that what had clumsily been transcribed
Into a notebook later came clear in ways

Each might have made light of there in the dark.
A—, for instance, at thirty pumped-up and tan
But oddly pious and almost too eager for word
Of how immanent the Beyond would turn out to be,
A lens in the black box of lives led here below.
He begins by chance with Agul, a priest of Aton,
Standoffish and abstract. *Egyptians not concerned*
*With sin, only singularity. We wait for sunrise.*
*Friends exchange light. Love, light, are one.*
*I breathe your light. Aton knows your aspect.*
And for those who don't care, whose beliefs start

When their eyes are shut? *Night is sun for others.*
Doggedly the acolyte buttonholes the board.
At last one Mary Wentworth gently picks up
The extension, a London mother and mystic
Two centuries dead. *Your soul, sweet A—,*
*The shape of a healthy body, shelters under my wing.*
Wing? *Down is warmer than up.* Up?

*The Pharisees are cold on their mountain tops.*
*They will not sin & so they freeze. Your body*
*Sins to warm your heart.* How easily tenderness
Rinses the dirty hands temptation lathers.

Then B——, saddled with a fifties adolescence
Spent peeping at encyclopedia cross-sections
And nudist colony glossies—all shrivel and sag—
Until transfixed by martyred Oscar's wit,
Its gay science devoted to curing the heart,
Shyly asks, after combing his hair, for Himself.
The Other Life, within us or abroad,
Acts—and why not?—as if it had all the time
In either world, exaggerating its courtesies.
Wilde extends an invisible gloved hand
To B——, who stutters about his nervousness.

*Confession is good for one's soul & one's royalties.*
*I sold my lower depths & made a good thing of them.*
But his own feelings . . . for the young man, say?
*Bosie was ornamental. That was enough.*
No real love then? Your wife? *Constance*
*Was as her name suggests. That was not enough.*
*Though Paris is, of course, better on the whole,*
*I think most of Oxford, where, donning robes,*
*Pater drew on airy nothing to burn with a flame*
*Of the first water, in whose heat our damp clay*
*We fired into well-wrought urnings.* ("The ease,"

B—— marvels, "with which a practiced stagecraft
Flicks its iridescent fan!") *No window*
*Can without some dressing up long hold*
*A discerning eye. For birds of our feather*
*The pen that is a plume adds panache.*
*But—oh, this as it must be written—*
*A thousand admiring eyes in the world*
*Of letters finally matter less than the one*

J. D. McClatchy                                        243

*Understanding heart in a country retreat.*
Blushing, B— withdraws, interested only
In how prudently to spend his overdraft.

Then C—, whose reedy, wire-rimmed pretense,
Goosed by Southern manners and a French degree,
The saccharine-coated pill B— had been swallowing
For a decade, insinuates his clubman's smarm
And succeeds in raising static on the line.
A giggling Indian scout—*ice filled my seeing,*
*Great ice-haired mounts, English*—trails off
To a corpuscle who or which insists eternity
Is *the plucked tension between limit and nothing.*
A yawn gets passed around. A Chinese sage
Wanders across the screen, dropping fragments

Of a fortune cookie. *We do not gain the moon*
*By telling her to be still.* Fingers in silhouette
Mug redwood trees, a German armaments
Tycoon, or chef, or silent movie vamp,
The manic Cuisinart finally shredding
Soul into a slaw of nonsense syllables.
The others glower at C— and call a break,
When suddenly, as from another room,
A stricken whisper: *Was I that stream of pain*
*At whom you laughed when you believed me*
*Out of hearing? Oh sweet betrayal, my bridegroom!*

And D—. (But why "D—"? His name was Drew.
I knew him, loved him.) A tenant of his body,
He was hurt by everything he took for remedy—
Waiting tables, acupuncture, coke—
And longed to leap against the painted drop,
Some grand pirouette centerstage, sweat whipped
Into the spotlight, sequined corsair or satyr.
He asks for Isadora. *Hail, friend!*
*Why do they never book me anymore?*

Drew then nudges into the dressing room
With a question. Will I ever dance like you?

*You know in your bones. I died broken on the wheel*
*Of circumstance. Now it's just tableau vivant.*
*The happiness of the body is all on earth.*
*The beauty of the body in motion and repose*
*I wanted to give, long after it was probable.*
Drew's charged resolve saw him through the drill
(Temp job to tryout) of making a name for himself,
Until he met the dancer who infected him.
The virus flic-flacked through his system, aswirl
In cells that faltered and too soon abandoned
The soloist whose stumble a falling curtain concealed.

For that matter, you too, JM, have gone
And done it, become a voice, letters on a page—
Not like love's sweet thoughtless routine
But a new romance, hazard and implication,
Promises as yet unmade, possibilities
Slipping, say, from N to O . . . —Oh,
Why will words cohere and dissolve on this blank
And not their darker meanings, an unspoken grief
I've reached for and feel sliding as if over
Posterboard smoothed by years of being used
To giving back the bright presence drawn

Up from within yourself, your starry heart
So empty, so large, too filled with others
Not to fear an unworthiness indwelling.
You took everything on faith but death,
An old friend's or the breathless lining
Of any new encounter, so that fresh acolytes,
Once back home, would remark with wonder
On your otherworldliness. What they failed
To see was something that has just now begun
To sink in on me: how little your detachment
Had to do with the demands of a formal art

J. D. McCLATCHY                                              245

Or a mind at once too sovereign and too spent
By being trolled for schools of thought or feeling.
Stage fright can apply or smear what make-up
Seems necessary for any evening's encores,
And lines rehearsed before the smoked mirror's
Critical gaze can turn to ashes in the mouth
When spoken to some poor stick mugging there
Whom you hope will stay the night and fear
May last until the end. How seldom, I sense,
You gave yourself up, how often instead
Had to borrow back what had already been lent.

Even the board is under wraps in a closet upstairs.
Funny, I've not tried to do it since you died,
Even for a simple jabbing towards the consoling *Yes*
In answer to the obvious questions posed
By missing you. Or have I instead been fearing
The *No*—the not-happy *No,* the not-there *No?*
Or had you perhaps been receding all along—
Like those friends of a quarter-century ago,
Faded to vanishing points like death or California,
Where everything to be lost is finally regained,
The figures of speech for once beyond compare?

No. I *can* hear your voice from the other side,
That kingdom come memory makes of the past,
The old recordings, the stiffening onion-skin
Letters your Olivetti punched out from Athens
Or Isfahan, notebook cities shaped
By anecdotes of love—no, antidotes,
Spelled out to be kept suspended at a distance,
As now I imagine your nights with pencil and cup.
From my seat, somehow above or below the table,
Your hand moving steadily back and forth
Across the board seems like a wave goodbye.

246                                    WORD OF MOUTH

## ᴧ Love's Dial

That tent whose stakes
my heart
with its pounding drives
deeper, whose ridge pole

we've raised, whose flaps
are let down
against dark and the winds'
wilderness, Jonathan

is that sleep sunlight
breaks, morning's enemy
O great Dante
aid me

I want to speak
of that love men have
of other men
and openly

address that god your song
arose from, for whose sake
you bade it
take new strength, tell

them to keep in mind
your beauty
who can't comprehend
that sense you make

its rays aslant
litter our bed
sunlight filtered through
a bare wood

falls upon this
green cover
and under it
in you

my song
shelters in music's
welter, rises
then goes

abandoning me
to this
blue day and a lady
cowbird

not so handsome as
her brown-headed
mate, still
she perches on

the feeder facing
east
and I've noticed this
as well with purple finches

she isn't the least
bit interested in seed
having fed them well
this winter have we

given the birds
almost, a place
even now, still there
no, gone

into the boxwood
she dove
as though into
water

leaving me to wonder
was she the bird
hit the window
an hour or so ago

lady finches now
yes, a place
certainly in us
our grace comes

from watching them
as though we saw
our souls
hull

seed and feed
on what they find
put out
for them, where

habit, a sense of
safety
and hunger
bring them

violets take the yard
purple and white
at eye level
they haze

could I even
recognize
his
or her look here

even know
till then
Love's
gender

except I say *him*
who like a rash won't let me rest
or get any work done
without constant thought

of him, I said, whose courses
thinking can no more
keep track of than a flower can
a bee's

all the same I'd try
my heart begging my feet
forget your ache and
hurry

those last few steps
or else lose
Love whose loss risks
never finding him

in whom whatever I am
is daylight
and what's left me of myself
scatters my insides

as stars do winter skies
is it at Saïs
or Samothrace men ask Love
to be their brother

whose image is
almost itself
whose mystery
isn't distant

in him I love
I sense my soul
Oh how to fathom how
I feel for men

yet it isn't answers
or ease
we expect
the heart to

offer, they belong
to that art
aching to be final
and eternal

is it at Samothrace
or Saïs
men bid
Love enter them

bring them home
to stroll the garden
of themselves
safely

out from under the watch of
that great lost Mother of our
mothers, no
it isn't

she we long for
wandering but each other
brothered in
the shed blood of

her son, spilled
wine, the sun
the vine strives
after

never arriving
anywhere but rot or
the press yet
ever

grappling for that light
grape, stock and tendril
are
nodes, shades

of in their
ache
for
that urge that

drives wood
green and
flesh
into desire

and reined
would draw
Love's chariot
beyond

Love's destination
larkspur forever
adrift
on an ocean

of blue for
having lost
some share of
my heart to

is it at Saïs
men see themselves
the reflections of
their own desire

or Samothrace
where summer's ruin
washes an island
risen among tides whose moon

aches
spurned, she hesitates
tangled in elder
then resumes her climb

taking this sky, rinsed of Love
and wrung, led by Ishtar
to her estate
holding there some few hours

an office dawn and these men deny
perfumes, charts, vanities
nothing stays her progress
a woman I would

walk toward
though she vanishes
where men stand alone
whom she so feared

because it was
her fate they held
no branch can claim though
that whiteness

neither apple nor sarvis
luminous
flowers
gave her limbs

dawn, ask the bees
to rob the almond
and cheat
the apricot

in this garden
where
sweet iris
your yellow slash

is no less
fragile
an inquisition
than

that long light
laid white
down the slope distracting
me to explain a flank

heart, why can't your intent
speak, break free
from that silence
fencing it

in almost mute or
barely audible
asking, I long and you
answer me

in rain, as wind, leaf
beaten air, anything
that isn't
his arms

denies me
my desire, him
holding me—that
is God

to be held and held
certain of beauty
I am both blest
and elect

my simple desire
is the fretwork
on that arch we are
in Love

whose strength
remains a motherless need
weakening me
the elder yellow and withered now

not so long ago
was the color cream is
on fresh milk
yet its branches, still there

are white in patches
standing
beyond
this

door, an olive
it would've been
Dante looked
up at

I confess, without Love
I am helplessly
lost, loose
in a wood

yet a man need only
forsake his heart
to reign
sworn monarch of

wherever his foot
falls for there
like a weed
obedience

takes over
wasting all variety
that growth
may gain him

green and uniform
sovereignty
who would be
Adam all over

THOMAS MEYER                                              253

## ✑ *City of Men*

I heard my name, the day rose and disappear over the beach. the day on each breath tasted my food, that night roll slowly cover in the cool, his face around my breast. the day inhaling grow pale and disappear, water on his way, up the shores hissing. under the night stillness inclined my morning beach, undressing my friend of liquid, my most same. at evening while whispering from the bed by me, his way was accomplished. his full perfect arm a health of ripe waters. the day received moon laughing, love lay me that night.

———————————

love growth, manly types have been young men, my year, my nights, comrades. projecting tongues clear my world; I feed, tell all the secret, offering delicious profit away from the clank. respond myself for all the need secluded, from standards to pleasures rejoices. escaped here; paths clear to speak: I can spot men and exhibit as I dare.

———————————

fair warning. further affections perhaps destructive. expect your long room in the open air. on your kiss permit be carried into sleep, caught me that I have written this, go your hand on your way upon my hip, that hit I hinted at, perhaps more trial. put your lips back, new husband, who would sign himself a candidate for my affections? in hand one thing will be all, suspicious, destructive, give up all else, exhausting your conformity, troubling your hand from my shoulders. I gawk unborn with you on a hill; upon mine, lips, I permit your throbs; beneath your clothing I have escaped from me. which way? many times reading it not understand. some trial for I emerge uncertain, theory around would have to be abandoned. feel me go forth. touching is wood, is rock, is air sea island roof enough

———————

diligently sought it many year at random, among animals, lapping apples and lemons, pairing fitful grossest nature and what goes with them. yearning for any and attracting whoever you are. swimmer naked in the bath from head to foot and what it arouses, trembling curve and the clinch of hips, the mouth makes me fainting from exultation and relief, embrace in the night the cling of any man drunk eyes, the storm that loves me, by the pliant loins a moment emerging stars. blending each body from the gnaw, wet overture anticipating the perfect face, for myself from you two hawks in the air, waves of nearness, floating the divine list to possess a lawless sea. I yield to the vessel, sliding fingers and thrusting hands, warp and woof, victory and relief, close pressure makes excess divine. pushes anticipating the strain exhaust each other; side by side on the coverlet lying and floating. from that, myself, without which . . .

———————

AARON SHURIN

I have lived orgies and will one day make pageants. bright windows with continual feast: those eyes' swift flash as I pass. O I make rows of you, streets of you, processions, spectacles . . .

---

boys up and down the road, priests of ourselves, wrenching and owning the other. fingers stretching elbows, alarming the air, making no law less than loving, ease on down fearless power

---

the arm, the arm, sleepless . . . underneath what you say my measureless name . . . walks within him at night wandering with other men . . . ocean of hand in hand . . . tenderest pictures hang in my woods . . . another curved shoulder . . .

WORD OF MOUTH

acrid river drain itself, blowing suppleness and strength from judges. milk commands mystery, moisture of the right man delights the earth, shame knows how to shoot for own sake. nothing lacking in gushing showers, warm-blooded rivers wrestle suns. deposit within me the pent-up winds of myself, crops from the birth of deliciousness, plant of you to awake at the touch of a man. greater heroes sleep in sex, wrap a thousand years in slow rude muscle of themselves, accumulated purities deposit gods on earth. onward pour the stuff; distill from the fruit of the fruit meaning's delicacies . . .

---

growing up above the tomb there, pink-tinged heart ascend the atmosphere; rise with it breast in your sweet way. behind the mask of materials take control of all, emerge under you roots of sound and odor, scented show folded in shifting forms. spring unbare this serve me lovers, conveyed essential shape inhale the bloom. burn and sting will not be freeze, reverberations give tone to delicate blood. exhilarating immortal death, inseparably grow and dissipate, last beyond all in comrades body

---

sighs in night in rage not subtle, dismiss chattering words to savage wrists. willful broken oath, nourishment of beating and pounding, defiances thrown in the wilds of hungry pantings. dissatisfied dreams of every day show dead words, limbs and senses thrown from heaving skies. not savage but cries and laughter, pulse of systole/diastole sounded in air a certain number standing alone, me twined around. it hung down and glistens there, unbending. wide flat companion of lusty oak makes me a little moss, stood for my sight and I grew wonder. lover in the dark brought to live green

produce boys! greed eats me, wholesome bunch saturate my palms, mounting my friend, waist hanging over my shoulder, dripping spiral, the hot hand that flushes. encircling red animal, purple lurking thumb, paternity of liquid will be torment and tide. odor of lips glued together; curves, brothers, that feelers may be trembling sweats; visions lie willing and naked under the ripening sun. whitened with the souse of primitive men, sleep together with crushed mint and sap, climbers after body blow husks from indecent eyes, find themselves breasts and bellies up and down the night. hairy murmurs and firm legs match the man to mountain, climbing my man I light the hillside. toss him, plucked from chastity, to saturate the sea; all men carry men, lurking. tight pause and edge to pressure, roaming hand-whirl, I glow spontaneous, know what he is dreaming. the same content, airs intimate that fill my place with him, smell of wild relief, welcome falling . . .

two simple men modeled under full sail, splendor of one neck envelops the other. spread around me, crowd of glory, I saw the pass and kissed him

---

appearances, after all, may be only speculations; identities are of the real. hold me by the hand, that is subtle air, impalpable, curiously words hold untellable. reason confound us, sense surround us, he travels to me and these are the shining things I perceive. I walk in the fable of a man, charged with points of view, skies of colors, densities, and something yet to be known . . .

---

full of you and become you. any number could be me. read these and become a comrade. with you I am one

## ~ Full Circle
### Postscript to "City of Men"

When I read my erotic rampage, "City of Men," to a group of students a couple of years back, one aw shucks type with wider-than-ever-eyes responded: "Boy, that sure isn't safe sex!" Chagrined, I held up the pages, pointing to the poem itself, the act of writing it. "No," I smiled, "*this* is safe sex!" But—chastened—I'd copped out; it was exactly what I had *not* intended with "City of Men."

I did have a hidden agenda. The poem uses only Whitman's language, culled from poems in the Children of Adam and Calamus groupings from *Leaves of Grass.* As most careful readers of Whitman know, Calamus is his collection of homoerotic love poems, emotional, tender, idealistic, radically political, prophetic, obliquely erotic, but—alas—not sexual. If you want sex, go to the grouping Children of Adam, Whitman's putative heterosexual songs. They are filled with body and body parts, physical material catalogues, paeans to the sex act—but—alas—no love. The body is electric but it is not affectionate.

I have read Whitman's private journals, the most private parts, where they are written partially in code to keep the secret—perhaps from himself as well as others—of his love for Peter Doyle, the secret—but we've heard this many times from the 19th and 20th centuries—torment of his awakening but not yet awake homosexuality, the revelations of his self-expressed desire to (using for homoeroticism his code word "adhesiveness") "depress the adhesive nature/ It is in excess—making life a torment/ All this diseased, feverish, disproportionate *adhesiveness.*" Depress it *in himself!* Anyone who has been there can immediately recognize the call of the closet. This pernicious disregard for truth caught Whitman—in spite of his revolutionary outspokenness about sex and the body as well as male/male affection—and forced him to sever his love poems—his writing of eros—into two mutually exclusive—and incomplete—halves.

My historical period has permitted me to come full circle, to write my eros out of spirit and body, shamelessly, and perhaps for the first time in history from a completely integrated viewpoint. In composing "City of Men" I chose to graft—by interspersing them—poems from Whitman's Calamus with those from his Children of Adam. Where the body in Calamus is incessantly hidden, metaphorized as leaves, roots, blossoms, scented herbage, live oak, moss, vines

260                                                              WORD OF MOUTH

and buds, now it can be revealed in its polymorphous glory as arms, shoulders, lips, fingers, loins, elbows and necks. No more will we hear—as in Calamus—"I dare not tell it in words" or "Here I shade and hide my thoughts;" rather, as in Children of Adam: "Be not afraid of my body."

It seems essential to me, in the age of AIDS, to keep the body forward, to keep the parts named, to not let ourselves get scared back into our various closets by those who would profit from sexual repression, from sublimation and fear of sex. What losses do we suffer by blindly embracing—if not "compulsive" sex—compulsive dating, compulsive monogamy, compulsive matrimony and domesticity, and when does avoidance of particular sex acts deteriorate into avoidance of creative exploration: dulled nerves, consumerist complacency, couplist or nuclear family paranoia, social scapegoating, stereotyping and moral sanctimony? Didn't my generation become sexual pioneers not just by increasing the range of permissible sex acts and sex-enacted places but by tying sexual expression to socialism, feminism, national liberation movements, consciousness expansion, legal and individual rights and radical psychologies, and if it gets squashed what else gets squashed with it? The chaotic force of eros—once called *desire*—is a depth charge for *change*. Contain it and we may have an ordered existence, sure: *following* orders.

So I do *not* propose "City of Men," or any other creative act, as a substitution for sex. I do of course propose safe sex—*medically* safe but not politically safe, not socially or even psychically safe. And toward the day when the Human Immunodeficiency Virus is consigned to the dustbins of history, I'll dream—with Whitman—"Unscrew the locks from the doors!/ Unscrew the doors themselves from their jambs!"

## ∾ from *Involuntary Lyrics*

XVIII.

Those guys with Christmas tree untrimmed
and me to help, nobody else came, party day
fade
away unless I hang 'em. So here's my faux-pearl earring and necklace set,
    temperate

compared to some, countering your scary Guatemalan death-squad burnt
    angel. But owe
me no thanks this shimmying electric May-
pole brightens December shade.
X didn't call me for a date
though I foisted number on him after severe flirtations, what he might grow
in proportion to those giant feet shines
elsewhere, someone else'll see
it. Still I've no complaint, except employment chances dimmed
but that's perennial this annual, the
season's one for newing, I'm drinking, it's raining, I saw a plum blossom lone
    bluey pink on live branch for which tired December declines.


LXXIII.


*a red lamp in the green of the night* rest
head on his chest be hold
tight by him on fire
or hang
from neck as lie
like vertical weight off cold
toes warming day's breath expire
where he sang
through lungs by
breathing day
go or night come strong
in silence this west-
ern shore house bed with him on long
that trail away

## ∽ 1963

1963
was the year
I started
getting up
at night
to play with my uncle
Giovanni's cock.
At night I'd watch him undress
and went to sleep
in a feverish state.
At midnight
I'd skulk to his bed
pull out his cock
from his boxers
and hold it
in my shaking hand
until it would harden.
I didn't know what to do
with a cock —other than my own—
so I held it in the dark
while the bats swooped
among the plantain trees
in our yard
and the night watchman
combed the streets
of our barrio
blowing its whistle
to say there were no prowlers
in the night
that the world was a safe place.

It was nineteen sixty-three
no cataclysms lit up the night skies.
As I held my uncle's cock
stroking it, placing it next to my cheek
breathing in
its pungent smell
I wondered whether Giovanni
—his limbs rigid,
his chest heaving—
was asleep.
In the morning
I was ashamed.
Giovanni never said
a word to me. He was
twenty-four years old
unemployed
with a lame foot
and he spent his days
reading the newspapers
waiting for his meals
while he drank black coffee
and smoked *Pielrojas*.
Each night
I'd wait until desire
would become so strong
I'd know no shame—
darkness protecting
my secret.
Then, one evening,
as I arrived home
from my English class,
Giovanni was sitting
on the porch reading a newspaper,
he looked up, and said to me:
"Marilyn's dead."
I hurried to our bedroom
threw my books and myself

on the bed, and wept.
That night, as I knelt
by Giovanni's side
I knew I'd go farther
than ever before.
I took his hardened cock
put it in my mouth
and when I heard him sigh,
the terror of that 13$^{th}$ year
of my life lifted.
Later, when the *sereno*
blew his plaintive
whistle to announce
everything was in order
I felt serene
unafraid
for the first time.


## ❧ Leaving Ybor City

The summer I finished high school
mother and I worked in the same factory
in Ybor City, the black section of town.

*Mami* sewed all day
in silence, she knew
only a few words in English.
I worked alone, sorting out huge containers
of soiled hospital linen
and I despised every moment of it.
I was eighteen; *mami* nearly fifty.

After work, we took the bus home.
As the suffocating heat
lifted, and the mango tree
in our yard released fruity

scents and yielded shadow
the langorous stretch
before dark
was a time
to become human.

The apartment we lived in on Elmore Street
had linoleum floors
and termites in the furniture.
After our TV dinner
—we were so new in America these
dinners seemed another miracle of technology—
*mami* visited Hortencia,
a Cuban refugee so overweight
she could not walk to our house
after a day of piece work.
We had no television, no telephone,
so I sat on the terrace
watched the elevated highway
next to the house and read
novels that transported me
far away from Ybor City.

On Saturday afternoons, I walked
to the old library in downtown Tampa
where I discovered, in Spanish,
Manuel Puig's *Betrayed by Rita Hayworth.*
I read this book at night
and during breaks at the factory:
a novel with a homosexual boy hero
that made me dream of glamourous
MGM technicolor musicals and goddesses
in slinky glittering gowns.
I was young.

Sitting on the porch
as dusk deepened

punctured by fireflies
darting stars weaving
in and out of the mangoes
I dreamt of distant cities
of leading a life
that had nothing to do with a factory,
not knowing
I would journey
away from Ybor City
exiled from the world of my mother.

It's only now, when I think back
on the youth I was
that I can feel
heartache for my innocence
for my mother's fortitude
for our unspoken fears;
for lives that were hard
but rich in dreams.


## ∾ When They Informed Him

*by Reinaldo Arenas*
*translated by Jaime Manrique*

When they informed him he was being watched,
that at night when he went out
someone with an extra key searched his room
looked in the medicine cabinet
and in the suspicious manuscripts;
when they informed him that dozens of policemen
were assigned to his case,
that they had bribed his closest relatives,
that his intimate friends
hid their commas and scribblings
in their private parts,
                    he wasn't scared,

JAIME MANRIQUE                                          267

just barely irritated
which he instantly corrected.
He thought: They are not going
to get me to think I am that important.


ᔌ The Will To Live Manifests Itself
   *by Reinaldo Arenas*
   *translated by Jaime Manrique*

They're feeding on me:
I feel them crawl all over me, pulling out my nails.
I hear them gnawing my scrotum.
They cover me with sand,
dancing, dancing on the mound
of sand and stone covering me.
They roll over me and insult me
ranting out loud a deranged judgment against me.
                    They've buried me.
They've flattened the ground,
dancing on top of me.
They've left, leaving me for dead and buried.
Now I can relax.

## ∾ After You Died

I had a body again. And I could recall
how it had been, back then,

to want things. Easy to recall that now—
this sun-dazed room; lilacs, in white bowls.
But for a long time I was grateful
only for what your dying was taking from me:
the world, dismantling itself; soon there'd be no more obstinacies,
I wouldn't want anything again . . .

After you died I rode a bicycle around the lake all day, in circles.
I had come back. And so it was hard not to remember
how it had been walking the path that circled the lake
where I'd once gone each night to look for sex.
It's true that I drank heavenly

—*heavily*, I mean. I was drunk.
I walked until someone wanted me. But what did I hope
to love in return?—I followed him, his pale shirt disappearing
into a small clearing hidden by shrubs.
He undressed, his bare chest mottled by moonlight's shadows of leaves.
If I could have followed you like that, even in grief,
into a clearing littered with wadded paper tissues
                                        —white carnations!
Mostly I met no one.
The path ended by the public toilets.
I loitered by a row of urinals; or I stood outside,
beneath the dim, caged streetlamp,
in a body I hated. Without it,
who'd need to ask the world for a thing?

# ∾ Nights of 1990

*"The sweatings and the fevers stop, the throat that was unsound is*
*sound, the lungs of the consumptive are resumed. . . ."*
—Walt Whitman, "The Sleepers"

1.

What I could not accept was how much space
his body was taking with it: for instance, the space where
I was standing, the dazed fluorescence of his hospital room
where each night I watched him sleep. *So this*
*is the spine,* I thought, this articulation
of vertebral tumors, this rope of bulbous knots;
*tissue,* I thought, as I studied his yellowing skin—
tissue, like something that could tear.
Afterward, I waited in the corridor.
When I came back, he was alive and breathing.
*Here, let me rub your back,* I said.
Was it true what I'd heard, that the soul resides in breath?
Was it true the body was mere transport? I untied
the white strings that secured his pale blue
hospital gown. The blue gown drifted
from his shoulders. I rubbed his back.
I rubbed his back. *Not so hard,*
He said. *I don't need to be burnished yet.*

2.

Tonight I am loyal to the young men in leather jackets loitering
by the lighted windows of the Churrería San Sebastian. To Manuel
Mendoza Hernandez de Gato; one name for each day I loved him,
Patron Saint of Cafe-Bar Lolita and the gypsy caves of Sacromonte. To Juan
Francisco Gomez de Zamora, to the black stars and coiled serpents
tattooed to his hands. Tonight I am loyal to the Bar With No Name.

Each night that summer I stood by a path that transected *El Retiro,*
a park whose dangers the police patrolled. Tiers of streetlamps
silvered terraces of ornamental roses, the vast statuary
of a crystal palace abandoned during war. If memory

could build its own monument to that moment
—There was a field by the train station, well-known
among a certain kind. Past midnight I knelt
in the wet uncut grass, sheltered
by the man who stood before me.
He quickly came. He zipped his trousers.
He stroked my face. *Mi amigo,*
he whispered, *I have a favor to ask.*
*Will you suck off my friend?*

*Yes,* I said. *I will suck off your friend.*

3.

What was it you said?
*Better to pass boldly into that other world, in the full glory*
*of some passion . . .*
Here, let me touch your face again.
Your face, in the full glory of some passion.

When the bleeding woman touched Christ's garment
and straightaway the source of her blood was dried up
so that He felt the virtue going out of Him to heal her—
why did He turn in the crowd to demand
*Who touched my clothes?*

The disciples said:
*Thou seest the multitude*
*thronging thee, and sayest thou,*
*Who touched me?*

I remember those nights.
It was dark. You traced your name on my bare chest.

When you straddled my hips and rose above me
I knew I had no choice but
to submit to touch again, I knew I'd have to endure
this wish forever. The long line of your spine
looked like a scar perfectly sealed.

4.

In my dream, you were alive. You had been dead.
To prove it, your arms were cut off at the elbows.

We were in a factory basement. Someone was whispering,
*A terrible, terrible accident.* You showed me your bandages.
Then you told me: *I'm ready to go home now. Home,*

I thought. *Where was home?* Only later did I realize you'd been
through fire. The next morning when I dressed for work,
that is, I saw the silver vase that holds your ashes,
and I realized you had no body, no body at all;
you were less than even the word *body.*
Sleeping, I had believed you were a ghost, maybe—

Ghost of a chance. I still loved you.
Then why in the dream did I leave you? And why did I say
I would never go back—not ever—to the room where you sat
touching yourself with your bandaged arms? *Touch me,*
you pleaded. But you were not restored. You would never be whole.

5.

And you, God, if you were to speak to me now
through his body—his reckless body; his tender, feathered
body; his fragile body that even in its dying sometimes
seemed newborn, so compassionate and astonishing . . .

Or through that other body, the body I saw in the street,
trousers down around its shit-smeared ass, flies
swarming over; bleeding, half-conscious body; Christ's body
—if Christ were old, and despicable . . .

Here, let me hold your body against this clean white linen;

here, let me hold your body against myself, a stranger's body
I might one night have drunkenly borne
—your come on my chest, my mouth. Dear God,

in your dearness, what were you but each night's longing
shaped by a stranger's touch? And what was I
but the agent of that longing cast to earth
to fend for us both? Was it your sin if you felt unloved?

Here, let me comb your hair before you die . . .

Here, press your body to this white sheet, the miraculous imprint . . .

What was it men used to tell me?
*Sure, I'll call you. Leave your number on the dresser.*

*I read somewhere,* a friend said, *that in the old days
the saints actually prayed for wounds. Can you imagine
actually praying to have wounds?*

*Yes,* I imagined myself saying. *I can imagine praying for wounds.*
Of course I was tired. Of course I wanted to get home.
Like many others, I was trying to hail a taxi.

When you were dying a woman came to your room.
I couldn't tell if she was the janitor or the chaplain. She said
there was a miracle occurring among us at that very moment.

RICHARD MCCANN                                                                 273

*In this lime green room?* I thought.
*In this lime green room? How perfectly horrible.*

She straightened the pillows. She built a pyramid
from the miniature juice cans you'd left on your windowsill.
I thought, So *this is what one does to prepare for a miracle.*

On the door to your room a discreet white sign warned: *Caution. Bodily fluids.*

(You whispered: "Long I was hugg'd close—long and long.")

In *The New York Times* surgeons were discussing their fears of bodily fluids:

*"Every so often you take off your gloves and your fingers are covered with blood."*

*"I can't count how many times my arms were covered with blood.*
*I can't count how many pairs of shoes and socks I soaked and ruined."*

When the hospital therapist asked me what was the matter
I told him my heart had broken. He placed his hands on my chest.
He said, "Now I'm going to press down harder."

That final glorious spring Saturday. You said,
*Let's take a walk around the neighborhood and see who's dying.*

On your wrist an infant's blue plastic bracelet warned: *Caution. Bodily fluids.*

("Long I was hugg'd close—long and long.")

Late that night, on the way home from the hospital,
I stopped for a Coke at a 7-11 where there was a robbery in progress.
Three boys were filling a paper bag with cash
and powdered donuts. *Your money or your life,*
they were joking with the customers, who wouldn't budge from line.
Evidently the customers were people who'd all been robbed before.
—All but one who was hiding by the freezer case, that is, the one
who was crying. The customers were yelling at him: *Shut up!*

*Can't you see you're scaring us to death?* Really,
he was frightful, with KS lesions on his face, and his hair
mostly fallen out. *I refuse to die,*
he was crying. *I refuse to die in this 7-11.*

Once, sitting in your hospital room, I told you
I had wanted a man to touch me
in a way that would feel like "forever."

*It wasn't that I didn't die trying,* you said.

You, come here. Sit beside me. I'm not that unhappy.
After all, not even a touch of faith lasts forever.
And, after all, it's true that what life gave me sometimes proved
enough: its simple, loving,

courteous touch—which could have been yours,
or a stranger's, or even the masseur's
as he pressed his hands between my shoulder blades
and whispered *Breathe,*
*Breathe deeply,*
*Why do you keep forgetting to breathe?*

*for Stanley Garth and Jean Valentine*

RICHARD McCANN                                                    275

## ∾ Desire Under the Pines

I like to wake up early by myself
and walk out to the forest which divides
the beach from bay side of the island, like
the line of hair that starts at breastbone, hides

the navel and descends into the thatch
beneath the tan line of a boy I saw
a picture of once, in a magazine.
He isn't in the woods this morning. Raw

desire al fresco isn't quite my speed
these months. I like to scout for vireos
and robins almost as much as for guys.
An ashtray from the Hotel Timeo

in Taormina, a signed lithograph
by the late Tony Smith, and a shelf packed
with great books of our time: the souvenirs
of my hosts' histories. I left mine back

along the trail, like interesting litter
thrown out of Conestogas on the long
trek west. The drivers knew that "We can use it
in Oregon" was a completely wrong

criterion. They had to get there first,
and lightening the load was the only way.
Beside the path, the wren that lights in brush
sounds like a footstep in the gathering day.

## ❧ Summer, South Brooklyn

gusher in the street where bald men with cigars
watch as boys in gym shorts and no shirts
crack the hydrant, rinsing yet another car
a daily ritual, these street-wide spurts

of city water over rich brown and deep white
of ranch wagon and arrogant sedan
whose "opera windows" seem less *arriviste* than trite
they shake the water from their hair, shake hands

with neighbors passing, passing generations
I watch and am not part of, for the block is theirs
by family and tradition, and I'm no relation
an opera drowned by disco beat, draw stares

from big boys with big radios that might outlast them
brace myself for insults I recall
forgetting the adult they see when I stride past them
until I realize they're kids, that's all

## ❧ Pretty Convincing

Talking to my friend Emily, whose drinking
patterns and extravagance of personal
feeling are a lot like mine, I'm pretty
convinced when she explains the things we do
while drinking (a cocktail to celebrate the new
account turns into a party that lasts till 3
a.m. and a terrific hangover) indicate
a problem of a sort I'd not considered.
I've been worried about how I metabolize
the sauce for four years, since my second bout
of hepatitis, when I kissed all the girls
at Christmas dinner and turned bright yellow

Tim Dlugos

Christmas night, but never about whether
I could handle it. It's been more of a given,
the stage set for my life as an artistic queer,
as much of a tradition in these New York circles
as incense for Catholics or German
shepherds for the blind. We re-enact
the rituals, and our faces, like smoky icons
in a certain light, seem to learn nothing
but understand all. It comforts me
yet isn't all that pleasant, like drinking
Ripple to remember high school. A friend
of mine has been drinking in the same bar for decades,
talking to the same types, but progressively
fewer blonds. Joe LeSueur says he's glad
to have been a young man in the Fifties with his
Tab Hunter good looks, because that was the image
men desired; now it's the Puerto Rican
angel with great eyes and a fierce fidelity
that springs out of machismo, rather than a moral
choice. His argument is pretty convincing, too,
except lots of the pretty blonds I've known
default by dying young, leaving the field
to the swarthy. Cameron Burke, the dancer
and waiter at Magoo's, killed on his way home
from the Pines when a car hit his bike on the Sunrise Highway.
Henry Post dead of AIDS, a man I thought would be around
forever, surprising me by his mortality the way
I was surprised when I heard he was not
the grandson of Emily Post at all, just pretending,
like the friend he wrote about in *Playgirl*, Blair Meehan,
was faking when he crashed every A List party for a year
by pretending to be Kay Meehan's son, a masquerade
that ended when a hostess told him "Your mother's here"
and led him by the hand to the dowager—Woman, behold
thy son—underneath a darkening conviction that all,
if not wrong, was not right. By now Henry may have faced
the same embarrassment at some cocktail party in the sky.

Stay as outrageously nasty as you were. And Patrick
Mack, locked into my memory as he held court in the Anvil
by the downstairs pinball machine, and writhing
as he danced in Lita Hornick's parlor when the Stimulators
played her party, dead last week of causes I don't know,
as if the cause and not the effect were the problem.
My blond friend Chuck Shaw refers to the Bone-
crusher in the Sky, and I'm starting to
imagine a road to his castle lit by radiant
heads of blonds on poles as streetlamps for the gods,
flickering on at twilight as I used to do
in the years when I crashed more parties and acted
more outrageously and met more beauties and made
more enemies than ever before or ever again, I pray.
It's spring and there's another crop of kids
with haircuts from my childhood and inflated self-esteem
from my arrival in New York, who plug into the history
of prettiness, convincing to themselves and the devout.
We who are about to catch the eye of someone
new salute as the cotillion passes, led by blonds
and followed by the rest of us, a formal march
to the dark edge of the ballroom where we step out
onto the terrace and the buds on the forsythia
that hides the trash sprout magically
at our approach. I toast it
as memorial to dreams as fragile and persistent
as a blond in love. My clothes smell like the smoky
bar, but the sweetness of the April air's
delicious when I step outside and fill
my lungs, leaning my head back
in a first-class seat on the shuttle
between the rowdy celebration of great deeds
to come and an enormous Irish wake in which
the corpses change but the party goes on forever.

## ⌁ Here Comes the Bride

Ironweed, beggarweed, joe pye weed,
the Huck-Finn-threading-his-raft-among-the-stiffs-
and-driftwood feeling that a fellow gets
slapping with his paddle at the silt
and the gaseous muck he slogs through on the trek
to land. Then a cloud moves.
All those purple flowers that the streak
of purple on the endless-shades-of-green
shore signified from a midafternoon
midriver point of view become a hundred
sheaves of light. I learned their names from a book
that someone gave me in another world,
the one I came from, where adrenalin
runs like a river through the jittery day.
I've come out of the current like a girl
who thinks it's time to change
her name to something simpler, and is looking
for a way. They say folks out here work
while the light lasts, the light that outlasts them.
It's hard to tell what time it is this time
of day; these parts don't change until the sun
breaks through and bathes the river in the gentlest
glow I know. I've been there.
I'm wedded to the notion of a living
and a life awash in it, a series of tableaus
as self-contained as frames of film
where change comes imperceptibly. "That field
was carpeted in purple just a week ago;
now it's all gone to seed." When I was single,
I had the most insane adventures.
Now that I'm married, I've nothing
but the path in front of me, the wide one
to the house with the big front porch
whose light will go on in a little while.

# ❧ Ordinary Time

Which are the magic
moments in ordinary
time? All of them,
for those who can see.
That is what redemption
means, I decide
at the meeting. Then
walk with David wearing
his new Yale T-shirt
and new long hair to 103.
Leonard and Eileen come, too.
Leonard wears a shark's tooth
on a chain around his neck
and long blond hair.
These days he's the manager
of Boots and Saddles ("Bras
and Girdles," my beloved
Bobby used to say) and
costumer for the Gay Cable
Network's *Dating Game.*
One week the announcer is
a rhinestone cowboy, sequin
shirt and black fur chaps,
the next a leatherman, etc.
Eileen's crewcut makes
her face light up.
Underneath our hairstyles,
23 years of sobriety, all told—
the age of a girl who's "not
so young but not so very old,"
wrote Berryman, who flew
from his recovery with the force
of a poet hitting bottom.
It's not the way I choose
to go out of this restaurant

TIM DLUGOS

or day today, and I
have a choice. Wanda
the comedian comes over
to our table. "Call me
wicked Wanda," she smirks
when we're introduced.
Why is New York City
awash in stand-up comics
at the least funny point
in its history? Still,
some things stay the same.
People wonder what the people
in their buildings would think
if the ones who are wondering
became incredibly famous,
as famous as Madonna.
Debby Harry lived in Eileen's
building in the Village
in the early seventies, and she
was just the shy girl
in the band upstairs.
Poets read the writing
of their friends, and
are happy when they like it
thoroughly, when the work's
that good and the crippling
sense of competition stays away.
Trips get planned: David
home to California, Eileen
to New Mexico, Chris and I
to France and Spain, on vectors
which will spread out
from a single point, like ribs
of an umbrella. Then
after the comfort of a wedge
of blueberry peach pie and cup
of Decaf, sober friends

thread separate ways home
through the maze of blankets
on the sidewalk covered with
the scraps of someone else's life.
Mine consists of understanding
that the magic isn't something
that I make, but something
that shines through the things
I make and do and say
the way a brooch or scrap of fabric
shines from the detritus
to catch Leonard's eye
and be of use for costumes,
when I am fearless and thorough
enough to give it room,
all the room there is in ordinary
time, which embraces all
the people and events and hopes
that choke the street tonight
and still leaves room for everyone
and everything and every
other place, the undescribed
and indescribable, more various
and cacaphonous than voice
can tell or mind conceive,
and for the sky's vast depths
from which they're all
a speck of light.


∾ D.O.A.


"You knew who I was
when I walked in the door.
You thought that I was dead.
Well, I am dead. A man
can walk and talk and even

breathe and still be dead."
Edmond O'Brien is perspiring
and chewing up the scenery
in my favorite film noir,
D.O.A. I can't stop watching,
can't stop relating. When I walked down
Columbus to Endicott last night
to pick up Tor's new novel,
I felt the eyes of every
Puerto Rican teen, crackhead,
yuppie couple focus on my cane
and makeup. "You're dead,"
they seemed to say in chorus.
Somewhere in a dark bar
years ago, I picked up "luminous
poisoning." My eyes glowed
as I sipped my drink. After that,
there was no cure, no turning back.
I had to find out what was gnawing
at my gut. The hardest part's
not even the physical effects:
stumbling like a drunk (Edmond
O'Brien was one of Hollywood's
most active lushes) through
Forties sets, alternating sweats
and fevers, reptilian spots
on face and scalp. It's having
to say goodbye like the scene
where soundtrack violins go crazy
as O'Brien gives his last embrace
to his girlfriend-*cum*-Girl
Friday, Paula, played by Pamela
Britton. They're filmdom's least
likely lovers—the squat and jowly
alkie and the homely fundamentally
talentless actress who would hit
the height of her fame as the pillhead-

acting landlady on *My Favorite Martian*
fifteen years in the future. I don't have
fifteen years, and neither does Edmond
O'Brien. He has just enough time to tell
Paula how much he loves her, then
to drive off in a convertible
for the showdown with his killer.
I'd like to have a showdown too, if I
could figure out which pistol-packing
brilliantined and ruthless villain
in a hound's-tooth overcoat took
my life. Lust, addiction, being
in the wrong place at the wrong
time? That's not the whole
story. Absolute fidelity
to the truth of what I felt, open
to the moment, and in every case
a kind of love: all of the above
brought me to this tottering
self-conscious state—pneumonia,
emaciation, grisly cancer,
no future, heart of gold,
passionate engagement with a great
B film, a glorious summer
afternoon in which to pick up
the ripest plum tomatoes of the year
and prosciutto for the feast I'll cook
tonight for the man I love,
phone calls from my friends
and a walk to the park, ignoring
stares, to clear my head. A day
like any, like no other. Not so bad
for the dead.

TIM DLUGOS

∾ Birthday

—For J. J. Mitchell

Tomorrow is a blank
and yesterday's too near,
who knows what was happening
ten years ago?
Night comes, I wake up
reciting the names of restaurants:
The Brown Derby, Leshko's
The Sportsman's Lodge,
Daniel's.
I dream of you,
still young and beautiful,
eating and being eaten.
The green arms
of a potted plant embrace
*The Religions of Man*
by Huston Smith.
What else?
There is a bozo
waiting for me
at the Four Seasons.
The sun is big on the mountain,
the grass flows down
to a river of mud.
Thirty-eight years ago
I was born
on an evening in April.
It was a sinking feeling
though the opposite of drowning.
"Dear Blank. I love you
but can't see you today,

Love, Tom."
Night comes, I wake up.
I dream of you
dying in New York,
an evening in April,
the skin stretched
over cinematic cheekbones.
Yesterday's a blank
and tomorrow is too near.
A truck backs up
over a Ritz cracker.
We move from sleep to sleep.


## ∾ Gay Pharmacy

These ultramarine pools
are connected to the ocean
through a series of salt caves.
I can pick you a sea anemone
the shape and color of a hibiscus,
or we can go into the empty garage,
lie on an old mattress
and look out the side door
at a jade tree
the color of Dick's hat band.

Those pills
in front of you
are crushed marigolds,
and are not pills.
We take them in remembrance
of every real pill
that ever swallowed a flower.

At night a herd
of aggressive antelope sleeps here,

by the phonograph.
He still loves you
who couldn't leave
you on that lake that Memorial Day
of 1958. It is this Memorial Day;
it is also mid-July on the West Side
and you still love that Italian
from Brooklyn whose teeth
are like small sails
and whose chest is a river.

The man
misting the bonsai
was a friend
of a friend
of Forster's policeman.
Bubi and Heinz
are here too,
and Denham Fouts is buried in the corner
by the vitamins.

We celebrate funerals and birthdays,
the days go by and we remember;
we sing "Bright Morning Star,"
"I Can't Get Started" and recite
the names of the dead
from our address books.

Can I offer you a glass of something?
Something white, the color
of your eyeball?

Can I offer you a rerun?
Those two happy brothers
and their dolphin, the lapis lagoon
and the civil servant father?
This glass case contains

mystical texts
compiled and copied
centuries ago by devout fairies
who knew what it is to put your ear
to Jesus' breast
and listen to the divine heart beat.

If your god can't contain you get another.

Drink your drink.

The lights will stay on.


## ∾ Bending In

He was on the bed.
I knew he was dying,
didn't know:
I knew it was April,
a Saturday.
They put him
in an ambulance,
which collided
with an Oldsmobile.
They put him
in another ambulance.
It was a gorgeous day.
He loved to go outside,
rarely went.
I won't catalogue what it's like
out there now,
he loved to do that.
But the trash today
is poignant, ripped
out of its bags
by marauding dogs.

Tom Carey

A mystery
the way things end up:
electric cord snaking
across the carpet.
Everything arrayed
in ignorance.
I have a postcard:
A 15<sup>th</sup> century oil.
A beautiful young Jew,
stripped
to the waist,
is about to deliver
a boulder
to the back
of St. Stephen's head.
And spreading
through a tear
in the sky,
in a layered mass,
is a horde of angels,
triangles of celestial
bodies singing.
Keep talking:
Today is a day
five years ago:
Open a door.
There's your lover,
still young,
nostrils flaring.
An arrow points
from here to here,
from year to year:
You were this, once.
My deaths are always violent.
I'm always getting shot,
stabbed, beaten,
spread like paté

over a mossy
subway platform.
This morning
I threw my friend
against a wall,
and when he begged
spat in his hair.
This morning,
the Civil War is over.
From the orange west
floats an immense
noisy machine.
It drops, opens
from the bottom:
Toe, foot, leg.
The calf is golden,
a ring of hair
around the ankle.
A toe
brushes the ground.
Several thousand
perfect beings
with mighty foreheads,
clear, untroubled eyes
descend like wet snow.
The recently dead
leap into view, overjoyed
by their new feet.
The machine lifts,
reveals a body
the color of wood.
She walks, she sits,
she turns.
The earth
is cool and supple.
He breathes sweetness,
he is so beautiful

Tom Carey

no one can stand.
We lay down,
she's on top of us.
She is the horizon.
Her hair is in my mouth.
Crawling
along an elevated track
through Brooklyn to Queens,
an olive orchard
painted on
the side of a low hill.
I walked there once,
took off my clothes and
came into the local stream.
Ivory blobbettes slid
over wet rocks
to the local sea.
There's an Asian boy
laughing
in front of a dying elm.
That store is having a sale.
Go, buy that stuff
for your face.
Evenings can be silent
or filled
with the sounds of knitting.
A circle of light,
a sofa,
a geranium gone wrong:
So much of life
is filler, he said.
An angel tells you
while you're asleep:
Dying
is one long wait,
with your friends in front.
I've done

what the sages command:
This is my body
lying on a plate,
holes bubbling fat,
the noise familiar
as home.
It's a gorgeous day
another April, and another.
Three guys are hammering
a machine into pieces, throwing
it into a van.
A boy by a stream,
that man on a bed:
We know each other.
The world breaks,
collects and breaks.
We are pieces in a wave,
singing the songs of water,
mysterious draughts
in an enclosed shaft
Hum along, there it is,
like climbing a stone wall:
put your leg up
and something sticks.
There's pain
and the possibility
of falling,
but then you're over,
under a live oak
walking
toward the new house.

Tom Carey                                           293

## ∾ Days of '66-'73

1

Sometimes it drives me crazy,
the guy in the car crash.

He didn't die twenty years ago, not really.
I talk to him in dreams now and then
over a cup of coffee.

He says he still treats his girlfriends
bad, then good, then very bad, and so on,
just like in high school.
A bird in a cage for Christmas.
No money for anything, a quick little slap.
Then a whole night of tongue
burrowing in those tender wet places.
He says it works just fine.

But they all end up leaving him.
I'd leave him for sure
if he were my lover.

He's got an open face,
good hair, thick, golden.
It'll turn a nice silver-gray.
And a good-size
uncircumcised cock.
I loved looking at it
in the gym showers.

But I'd leave him too.
He drinks his coffee weak.

And he wouldn't treat me right.
Punks never do.


2


I've got a boy, a dark one,
living where my sternum used to be,
where I can't touch him.

He once lay all night with me
on a beach. The sand was like
a bed of tiny burning stars
against my skin.
                    Those burns
will last me a lifetime, maybe longer.

Tiny burns that remind me
of the blackness
at the center of his eyes,

and his nipples
six shades darker
than the dark of his skin—

nipples
grainy like jam,
cool to my tongue,
just erect enough
to take tenderly between my teeth.

But these are just memories.
No way, now that he lives inside me,
to get my hands on him.

3

We called girls *fish.*
"Oooh, fishy, fishy," we squealed at our lockers,
rubbing our crotches.
*Oooh, fishy,* I moaned

for a guy
and the hollow I longed
to lick, the pure
fish-cool of the curve

inside his thigh.
For nearly a week I twisted in dreams,
sheets like moss.

All because it was August
and he lay sprawled by the pool
in those loose yellow trunks.

And I, walking by with my snappy red towel,
thumped, in my very best, guy-like way,
in a heap at his side:

"So, Georgie, whadaya see
in those clouds?"

And he looked up,
and I inhaled, looking down—

and made of that glimpse
all I could: six
summer nights of sweet, wet hope.

4

One was made of milk.
Not the kind you can get anymore.
Milk so thick with sweetness
you could spend half a day
dragging your tongue through a bowl of it.

He let me drag my tongue once
the full length of his sweetness. Just once.
"Only a man knows how
to make love to a man," he whispered.
Then he had me sleep at the foot of the bed.
Said there wasn't room next to him.

Our shirts in a heap on the bedside table.
Our pants—his a green corduroy,
mine the usual faded Levi's (you
see a lot from the foot of the bed)
draped on opposite arms
of the brown leather chair.

Next to him was the girl, invisible,
hair a river, skin flawless.
The girl he said he really wanted.
                              You do
see a lot from the foot of the bed.


5


A dancer. He was the first.
It wasn't the tights.
It wasn't the bulge at his crotch.
I'd seen better.

But for thirty seconds
he danced alone, a pale

cool flame
across the floorboards.

My giggle
joined a few dopey giggles
from other guys in the gym.
That much was easy.

But what was this feeling
at my solar plexus?

I knew I was in for it.
I prayed to sit on those bleachers
in darkness forever.

If the thing escaped—
how can I describe it,
that sensation, exquisite,

but hollow, and burning
right at my center—

if it ever escaped, I knew
I'd have to start my life all over.

6

Some weren't the whole guy,
just a part of him—

Poncho and the sag
        in the dollop of honey
        that was his voice.

Lou's embrace a nest.
        (Over the years
        he's made room
        for the forest's entire menagerie.)

Richie's wit
        spinning my tongue in its wake.

The shadows, twin crescents,
        at the base of Victor's pec's:
        my tongue (in dreams) in their wake.

The hours, weeks, months
        (no way in memory
        to number them) inhaling
        the narcotic
        of Ken's up-swept lashes.

Jack, who aligned my spine
        that I might see the horizon.
Jack's weeping foreskin.


7


Eyes green and deep.
A deep I could step into. Lifeboats
that rode the tender river
of his voice . . .

Who am I kidding
*I loved him like a son?*

Usually he whispered. Things like,
"I put my parents through hell,
drugs, running away, the whole bit."

I was touched he liked to confide
in me, his fussy English teacher.
He asked the big stuff,
all about life: how do you do it?


BOYER RICKEL                                              

I said I was glad
he had a girl back home,
that they planned to marry.

And the wedding?
Why not? I thought, I could go.
(Most days he wore torn jeans,
brown hair falling into those eyes.)
I could sit there in church
just like a father. Sad,
but only a little.

I could give him up, I said
to myself over and over,

to such an abstraction:
the girl back home.

## ∿ Rain

It's a silver afternoon in the Susquehanna.
On this new scale, my house becomes more important.
From the second-floor window, a mania
for beads knocks down the latent

good boy in all of us. The football
is under the influence of the planets, too.
There's no way to stop a rainfall
that expands from its brown shoes.

The 1930's was a brown decade.
We dressed in brown suits. Every street
led past an art deco arcade
under which a vibrating mother left her feet

in the scrapbook. In the middle of an open field
the girl with red hair comes to get laid.
Who says this funeral (my first) is sad?
Who gets the plaid bed where my grandfather dropped out of sight?

Don't be afraid of those little birds,
it's only the rain, made to keep you inside.
It's a window pressed against the mouth of dirty words
we say with our lips. At night the bride

turns into a fat, black bird.
She has lost her innovative raincap
on the bedsheet of the sky. Unfurled,
she spills a bright roadmap.

It's warm on the beach. You're awake as always
watching me come from the church on to the road.

A bird opens its wing. A mannequin displays
her secret eyes. A Buster Brown shoe erodes

beyond the elevator, into that blue shaft
where we move (evenly) like a train
within its tracks. What spring draft
brings these hypotheses to a weightless brain?

1.The softball has come down on my stagnant head.
2.Who was that you were with at the ballet?
And without leaving your kitchen, I obey the voice:
This lilac will be your breakfast instead.


## ∾ Nude

A gray flower
made of wire and soft paper
is touched by a tiny match
held in my hands
the sky is a watch
the minute hand slices
a cloud in two
on its way to 1
the magic number
of flowers grows
in a song
the gray flower dies
of a stem disease
cars span the distances
taking my voice to you
surrounded by a long body
with few weeks old beard
daddy is a sleepy house
mom shakes the earth
when she walks
from planet to planet

with her wooden plank
I walk the plank
in a striped suit
the nude boy
plays basketball
in high school
later in the morning
he will get up
covered in a light
that is really in my heart
turning and turning
the flame goes around
the gas burner
ready to support the soup
with its hot waves
recording each word
they say to one another
and what it means
in the life of the bed
which is a piazza
among the many streets and hours
that lead in and out of bed
I snooze past the anxious hours
into the really mad hours
Now you goddamned idiot
get out and dont come back
until youve found a job
and love me impersonally
the way you loved that starfish
for simply being on the beach
in a paralyzed state
under the sun, over the sand
and then I'll take you in
through the stomach
up the elevator to the light
of the eyes shining over our city
like car headlights on a parking deck

# ༄ Words to be Broadcast over Eagle's Nest Sound System—I

Made out under sharp leg knife telephone golden shower boy under pinned under sweat sweet drill drilling broken glass smell faint smell aroma of needle tight bod no more but he kept going the slate eyes fastened on my boots tender touch Bud cop sweet and wet soaking the rub laying there time AM radio bondage songs out of touch brought back hard in the nose in the legs first the socks tight screwing into the ground tight tree phosphorescent beer too much too much a soft boy's voice beard hair arms legs loose and flowing fast down 18ᵗʰ Street at every corner mouth wet motorcycle cop glasses long to the knees hot and heavy you make me a pleasure machine a pleasure machine in the night you left me on the street to take a leak the dynamite sounds juke box still in my head my head knocked against that wall wet smelling one guy after another too much head hair cut off by your one hand the other leg stretched out body you've got it the tender touch in the palm of my hand in the insides of your legs your spell is tying me up in the stomach in the cock your hands keep moving in and out a heart a fist a piece of my heart goes with it and I've got you on the list starmaker bright gloves wristwatch try me piece of glass stuck in the heart a needle in my arm you've got the power to turn on the gas the electricity playing dead gun smoke your den my ass red tied into the socket dying to get you under my skin liquid popper scat b/m w/s Long Island master looking for expert slave meet at Interstate blacking out blacking one eye eye patch no leg Vietnam veteran marine action pow action muddy boots taken care of ready now to take what you've got giving you what's good for you taking you out on the street you dirty son of a bitch trigger happy in it for the action I never wanted to hear that phone voice again when he said to come drumming in the heart pumping slumping over on the sidewalk moonlight carlight headlight sideview walking down the street in front behind jewelry sounds my ear is in my head smell you robin fly fly robin fly right up to the sky pinned underneath heavy builder shit house rubber slit up the arm try to get away long day at work waiting to get home to my boy make him eat it blonde boy beard man extra money stay for a day in service in the tight bathroom for three days no way zinc gold spray today the day bars are full the gay bars are full I met him in the hall tall black cowboy no face under the hat sat on his boot ready to shine to shine skin wet ready dogs eyes ready no room two more and keep going until I say

WORD OF MOUTH

# ❧ Words to be Broadcast over Eagle's Nest Sound System-II

Big night two of them locked into by master lock service fifth floor walkup biceps tight across the face a little blood mostly follow me hot and sturdy masculine appearing stud stallion beat you into the ground tied to your leg tied to your bed forced to drink it soft and wet down the throat smell my scummy feet my BO take it and jack it off meeting in the bar on the pier hot sun body sunglasses no words straight to business businessman's shoes under the wheels covered in black grease in paint marked up shipped out drinking beer steady diet steady trucks moon pissing in the corner arc slap him silly the faggot match light reflected bootlight metal popper light covered over barlight starlight slapped over skinlight down on those socks around the room on all fours one after the other shoved down on hour ass in that corner Arab guy black guy white cowboy black minister master bible-carrying horny and ready to give in to your wishes sir the door locked from the outside guys watching you do it to it steady in pushing in soft then hard jackhammer machine gun soft then hard fist size bulletproof asshole ready to stop you keep me goin all day long no song jazz FM radio head music start late afternoon on the boots clean up wash socks apartment going deeper total washout in piss shit spit on me spit in the mouth piss in the mouth rolling around wet you've gotta make me play lose a day one eye one day at a time into handcuffs rope no mercy wrists tied out tied up outside left out all night cold and wet guys walk by cigarette burns in the nerves gone white I'm nothin but a worm turn on the amps let me burn dark hood sharp cut up scissors around the balls medicine manjabs inside make him cry can't breathe sock stuck down the throat dirt tongue shit covered new marks the ass the muscle front arms just waiting for your call roll over dog whore throat lick the floor got more silver vice visor execution man not movin hell down into your neck white neck never felt a mans boot never had a man pin you down hold back your shitty face and swallow tight bullets poison drinker mood elevator master in shiny pants policeman strict and ready to whip your act up ass boy cell block electric chair in veins shot of something straight into heart I pull the strings and you do the dance socksucker shiteating mother of pearl sneaker boy wait for my armband wearing a jock around your neck to work the next day under your shirt dirt boot mark on your back long needles stuck in the tits underwearhole in the face disgrace love to wear your dogplates tied to the streetlamp cock hanging out boys laughing drink the water from the pool eat my balls extra hair asshole hair bruised let him loose choke swallow spit ram it down double over push down on back of neck engineer boots heavy rubber soles facelight steady eyes make him clean it up whip sounds beat up sounds heavy pain in the heart sounds boy begging sounds metal lock sounds sounds sounds of giving in of turning in hour time to me I do what I please ready to please to ease it in and out

## ∾ An Elizabethan Sonnet for D. W.

I want to fall asleep on your rank chest.
I want your palm lines flat over my face.
The space between your teeth is a black key.
I miss you tonight. I don't know how to erase
that feeling. You have so many pairs of boots,
black like the bullets that fly past your front window
in Williamsburg, as exotic as a borough gets.
Let's face it. This old-fashioned sonnet is a bow
like servants used to take before their kings.
Now I know how Shakespeare felt, all hot.
Or the Duke of Windsor wearing the Duchess's chains and rings.
S&M is a poetic conceit.
We pass beyond the river to the stars.
The drums I hear are your feet on my back stairs.

## ∾ Winged Torso of Eros

You will never change, your life
suspended here, sealed off from the rush
of traffic and the weather, a twist of flesh
touched and wondered over by the likes
of me. Everything breakable in you
has been broken, but for those of us
who will not see, you take flight with a rustle
of ghost wings—your wings, too,

gone now, snapped off at the base,
even your sex—(a squeak of sole
on tile as Red Shirt leaves the hall)—
Oblivion beckons, you nod *Yes, yes. . . .*
But he's coming back, we all do, to say *No,*
*I will never let you go.*

## ∾ Pneuma: 1967

Standing on the lake, I felt my heart
growing heavier, growing old.
He clopped his gloves together,
shot me a look so warm it hurt.
*Hell, it's cold!* he laughed. *And colder*
*tomorrow.* Shifting to the other

foot, he shivered an emphatic *God*
—and set revolving into space
another shapeless cloud
of crystals, impalpable, separate. . . .
Breathless tonight I caught it
full in the face.

# ❧ Corpus

*1. The Lard Sculpture*
won't last, is avalanching slowly, like the aged
Brezhnev, like a stupendously deflating
Thanksgiving Day parade balloon. The Old Man
snoozes through the after-dinner encomia,
cherubic, digesting his chicken à la king,
not yet nudged awake for his big farewell
to the Historical Society, and the society's
last round of applause. A pillar of books
is all he'll leave behind, and none too steady,
either, books on books. . . . The minute he's gone,
it'll be toppled. Lard, in this god-awful weather,
what were they thinking? Look at *him,* though,
the Old Man, dreaming of better times, sleeping
the sleep of the holy. And dying in effigy.


*2. Shrooms With Theo*
The afternoon snow-warm, cool-humid,
a boxed-in, cottony light-headedness

through which our stripped-bare babble
sounds, my high to his high, ridiculous,

*ri dic u lous,* each syllable a bobber sucked
under waves of gut-clenching hysterics.

Waves of pinpricks over nape and hands:
a pair of doves fucking above us

in the feathery dark of a pine dislodge
little loaves of snow that, falling,

detonate in bright, tightening whorls
of stardurst, sunsheen and snowfleck. . . .

[laughing] You're old enough to be my—Please:
You're *young* enough, let's say, to be *my*—Sh.

*

jeans creaking kneeward    still cherishing
the body    outstanding    from a squarish tangle

of rustbrown    his swaying    daylit cock enters
the world    & the world    pinestraw    the silken *fsh*

of skin over smoother skin    the cooling warmth
of open underthings    the world lets go

disintegrates to gusts of pollen    I breathe in
deep    deeper    O quick    spindrift a blizzard

in full sun    Theo    the O—    & dizzily
clutch him    like a stanchion    both hands

to the base    & he staggers    crumples &
comes    coming in    not clots of nacre

but a flung quiver    of needles and pins    hot
or cold    I still can't tell which

*3. Ornithology*
My father brought it to me
on a snow shovel, its feathers disheveled,
head altogether gone, and said,

What kind of bird was this?
I glanced at the sooty plumage,
the limp fat scaly pink—I'll be damned,

I cried, this pigeon is *banded.*
—Another datum for the lost souls
at the Audubon Society.

DANIEL HALL

The stench grew sweeter. I found
a pair of snips and neatly
amputated. The band rolled off.

My father whispered, Look.
Out of the disconnected foot
and out of the shank, a host

of larvae writhed in milky
plenitude, eating themselves
out of house and home

—and now that we noticed,
were dribbling from the severed throat,
and no doubt filled the bulging breast:

millions of them jostling forth
into the light, ready in days
or hours to rise into the air

and bear the body away.


∾ Mangosteens

These are the absolute top of the line,
I was telling him, they even surpass
the Jiangsu peach and the McIntosh
for lusciousness and subtlety. . . . (He frowned:
McIntosh. How spelling.) We were eating
our way through another kilogram
of mangosteens, for which we'd both fallen
hard. I'd read that Queen Victoria
(no voluptuary) once offered a reward
for an edible mangosteen: I don't know
how much, or whether it was ever claimed.
(But not enough, I'd guess, and no, I hope.)

Each thick skin yields to a counter-twist,
splits like rotted leather. Inside, snug
as a brain in its cranium, half a dozen
plump white segments, all but dry, part
to the tip of the tongue like lips—they *taste*
like lips, before they're bitten, a saltiness
washed utterly away; crushed, they release
a flood of unfathomable sweetness,
gone in a trice. He lay
near sleep, sunk back against a slope
of heaped-up bedding, stroked slantwise by fingers
of afternoon sun. McIntosh, he said again,
still chewing. I'd also been reading *The Spoils*
*of Poynton,* so slowly the plot seemed to unfold
in real time. " 'Things' were of course
the sum of the world," James tosses out
in that mock-assertive, contradiction-baffling
way he has, quotation marks gripped like a tweezers
lest he soil his hands on *things,*
as if the only things that mattered
were that homage be paid to English widowhood,
or whether another of his young virgins
would ever marry. (She wouldn't, but she would,
before the novel closed, endure one shattering
embrace, a consummation.) I spent the day
sleepwalking the halls of museums, a vessel
trembling at the lip. Lunch was a packet
of rice cakes and an apple in a garden
famed for its beauty, and deemed beautiful
for what had been taken away. I can still hear it,
still *taste* it, his quick gasp of astonishment
caught in my own mouth. I can feel that house
going up with a shudder, a clockwise funnel
howling to the heavens, while the things of her world
explode or melt or shrivel to ash
in the ecstatic emptying. The old woman set the fire
herself, she must have, she had to. His letter,

DANIEL HALL                                                    311

tattooed with postmarks, was waiting for me
back at the ryokan, had overtaken me
at last, half in Chinese, half in hard-won
English, purer than I will ever write—

*Please don't give up me in tomorrow*

The skin was bitter. It stained the tongue.

*I want with you more time*


## ∾ The New World

Months of drought.
I'd been killing an hour
at the end of the century
reading a book I'd read before

when it began: this subliminal
*hush*, as close as the pressure
of my own blood, the very voice
of tenderness, of comfort,

inrushing like cinnamon
or flannel or the circle
he retraced above my heart, over
and over, as the fever

lifted me and let me fall. . . . Then
like a door hissing shut, the rain
stopped. Crickets rang. Minutes
had passed. The stars were out.

## DAN BELLM (1952- )

∾ Open House

*Springfield, Illinois, August 1994*

Three days after your death the house you
raised us in goes up for sale, and a sign goes up
on the lawn I tended and greened those misspent
Sundays and Saturdays of youth for you, a field gone
brown in giant patches now like dust. Twenty years away and here
I am as if I own the place, as it to claim a body once the life

has fled. Of course I walk right in; of course our life
in it has gone all disremembered since—a red-brick split-level you
built on a re-seeded quarter-acre lot here
at the formerly new edge of town, kids biking home up
the shabby street and it's wretched to feel as gone
as you, to see how others have papered us over with new mistakes,

the telephone you poured your rage into missing
from the kitchen wall, a realtor seated in your living-
room spot with a fact sheet and an asking price, saying *This one'll go*
*in a hurry* to a frowning man who doubts it, hand on the door, and your
classy oak veneer panelling in the den blotched up
with a soulless wash of white, but look in the basement here,

they've saved your very goofiest home improvement, where
I'd have thought anyone would rip it out without a moment's misgiving:
orange naugahyde built-in sofas with end tables of gold-flecked formica, up-
to-date more or less in 1964, the hideaway where I saved my life
from you. Who will love it now? Here is the door where you
walked out on me, and the window where I watched you go;

what a relief that, after all, that time and place are gone
and I don't want them back, don't care to stay here
any longer, though I have never stopped talking to you

DAN BELLM

313

nor you to me, two misfits
on earth unable to share a roof but forever living
in the halves of the same soul. Whenever you fall silent I hold up

your end; I know you're thinking, *People don't keep their property up*
*any more,* but nothing is ours, Dad, not the shutters and doors gone
unpainted a shade too long, not the battered shrubbery or the grass. That life
is over now. We will never see it again. Your name there
on a stone, the narrow plot you've fallen into by mischance—
I know it isn't much, but for awhile yet you will live in me, I will be your

home. I remember the mystery it was, a house rising up
all new from the open pit I used to play inside, and you standing here
in the doorway, measuring and re-measuring the life to come.


## ∾ Boy Wearing a Dress

*San Francisco, 1995*

On the way home he asks me, *If we cut off our*
*penises then we'd be girls wouldn't we Dad,*
my little boy in cowboy boots and a long black dress
walking home from Castro Street playing
blue fairy and wicked stepsister and lost princess as he
walks, the people and store windows whirling by

as he twirls only figures in fairy stories he knows by
heart, though what he doesn't see yet is that our
neighborhood's a kind of fairyland for real—still, I hope no one heard him
ask me that, and hope my Dad
who is dead hasn't heard, who would never have let me play
boy and girl with this frightening freedom, dressing

up in public or alone in a four-dollar thrift-store dress
we bought because he asked for one. A drunk careening by
asks, *Why who are you some kind of superhero, son,* and from a display
window video porno stars sweating under harsh light smirk in our

faces—*I don't have to tell them who I am now do I Dad—*
*No it's a dress,* the guy's friend says, *I've seen him*

*around before, that boy's always in costume, he*
*must be a little fag.* Ken dolls in white satin dresses
and angel wings and hairless Barbies done up as leather Dads
are climbing a Christmas tree inside the card shop by
the pizza store, some queen's fantasy scenario of what our
mothers and fathers should have let us play

back where we come from, but my little boy likes to play
the girl parts of stories for reasons of his own, he
likes their speeches and their dresses and shoes, we tell ourselves
it's harmless, wanting to wear a dress,
harmless as my nervous laughter to passersby
and what do I apologize to them for, Dad—

When I was a child I wanted to wear my Dad's
work shirts, I liked the smell of his Army uniform, I didn't play
girl games, don't look at me. My little boy is getting distracted by
the dildoes at the sex shop I try to hustle him past. Soon enough he'll
learn to leave his dress at home, will hear somewhere that a boy in a dress
cannot be beautiful. Once inside our

house he undresses by the mirror to be naked under the dress,
and lifts it up to display what most of us keep inside our
pants, and he asks me, a little afraid for the answer, *Am I beautiful, Dad—*


∾ True Story
*for Bo*


*Darling you should contract a terminal illness* he'd say
*you're writing too slowly* and give that Tallulah smirk,

waving a bony arm at me and flicking ash: four books
in three years, each one a lifetime past the one before,

while the virus stole his body from his mind. I could only
watch him burn, the way he'd sit and roll a clean

page into the machine and type *Chapter 1 Page 1* and pull
the most demented stories out his head from start to finish

in the proper order, each one a lifetime truer than the one
before. Now he comes to me from death in the middle of

the night as a live coal in my heart, a pang that wakes me up:
he says *Darling you want pain?* I want to turn a light on

to get hold of myself but close my eyes to stay in the dark.
He says *All right. I'll give you pain.* He says *Someday*

*it just might kill you. If it's any comfort. Someday soon.*

## ∾ Cemetery without Crosses

| | |
|---|---|
| Things are fine | How dare |
| with me—good writing, | you write me of |
| good fucking—Ideal really | fucking somebody else |
| | |
| Pyramids | Valencia Street |
| to be arranged | rain on your face |
| in the shape of a cross | ravaged, ruined blood face |
| | |
| Americans | O lion, compass |
| cut up the four hour | turn |
| Trauma | to an end but arrows sing |
| | |
| He's not | made |
| so spectacular, I | all the dishes |
| mean, I'd do him but | from one of his cookbooks |
| | |
| And he | and he is |
| is Ronald Johnson | Ronald Johnson |
| a far cry | name the date |

## ∾ Deep Red

Deep red ● the submarine blips on the cold surface
in Antarctica ● as Mariner's ship draws near ●
frothy surface on the blue wave ●
Life is still ● so catch as catch can ● still evanescent, still

Red, an oar touches the water's rim ● muscular arm buff as
Meryl Streep's in *The River Wild* ● in Antarctica ●
frothy surface on the blue wave ● life is still ● "I don't have
many T cells left, but I used to have 8" ● "now I have 9"

Under the gristle, vein, under the vein, deep red ●
the blood of my pal ● deeper and deeper this tiny wave, blue
on the surface, ● alone on the surface ●
if you were one-dimensional what would you see?
a one celled mammal swimming for dear life ●
to a shore strewn with protozoa bracken ● still life
"now I have six"

the flotsam and ● jetsam of living ● high
and deep ● this is the curve that
will kill you ● pal
I'm living in ● your disgrace
deep ● red hatchet ● cells
a doll with hands ● scuttles across the face ●
of the sea for you
come and get these ● memories


∾ The Door into Darkness

A hand within touching distance of the doorknob.
No light, no sound, the lintel black with absence and size.

The wristwatch that talks, "Time for your medications."
Feeling, the cold drip inside your thigh, the scent of fear.

Quiet, the set is cleared and the long spaces grow still, dark.
Bitter scent of attempted, the light, the warm hatching eggs.

Open the door, pick its hinges, flood the house with darkness.
A short burst of steam, the mailbox slot hot as his asshole,

darkness within and the field of the open human page. The
check for his pills, and a glass of water from crystal springs

tipped to his mouth: he is old now, yodelling in a sleep
indecent, cracked, his hand furtive sly yanks at a single sheet—

Pull at the tubes, throw open the black wooden door and let go.
All the world staring at him from inside his own eyes

and I'm like, the hand that takes the door by the knob, firmly,
uprooted, as once I made him come with my hand, till he

couldn't stop gasping for breath. Now he can breathe, now
he can live, now he can come, now he can write "dead" in the dark.


## ∾ Giallo

Cut to theme music: brass, strings, zither, giallo
the word bursts in red spectacular fire, soon
muted to a dull yellow like mustard

It's the angle, it's the hook they keep telling
me in the front office, in New York, demons eat them
Wal, blow me down with one of those new fangled

Ok, thought of something bound to beat the
bandolero: mod two in white—battle—killer in the
rain, and the white, wet, reveals shadowy skin

looking like sexuality
talk to Mr. Gabriel
get those asses into those seats

then he gives her a blowjob
the camera pulls back, way, back, sky high
it's a football field of dead men in trenches


KEVIN KILLIAN

doesn't look so scary
it's not like Juliette Lewis
no, it's musical, with glockenspiel
telling the people, *go home now, I love you,*
*your breath makes me love you,*
*in* AIDS *is pleasure*

Steve Abbott told me, when we go we
go into a blank space, like an envelope,
on our way to who? Are you Kevin? he asked me.
The bed a big waste basket of white cotton.


## ℘ Inferno

Inferno maybe too descriptive
I lived with him for seven years
black under water, a shark on fire


Are you the patient XYZ?
who blew smoke up my ass
and fell into watery aphrodite loving me!


Rip that tube from the wall and feel me up
loving you and forcing you to wriggle a bit
a sausage on griddle, hot


Mother of tears, mother of shadows
give him a little more zip
I don't want him self-conscious
when he walks among dot dot dot

Big, bright colors like a Cibachrome painting
by Nan Goldin should she turn to oils.

I ate the seventies dancing in disco
and made the eighties this fresco experience
Now I'm impoverished, begging

for my birth mark, going on thorazine
should I turn to oils, shark under fire
or should I just say, *tattoo man, make*

*me a birth mark,* say it was me from the
beginning, and in thy honor I shall
do thee justice? I lived with him when he

died and I'll live when he abrades me
for he is the Saxon justice of a women's
barony, he gives me strength, to carry on

he lights up my life, disco inferno
night falls on a prodigal landscape, loving
him was never light mechanical

Mother of mercy, mother of pain
tell him for me he lives on my derma
when I pull it off gently after the chemo

He won't love me without my foreskin
tiny little snip of waxwork
only a storm toss'd frigate by Turner

KEVIN KILLIAN

Tell him there's some easy pickings
long and low the banks of the Mersey
white Jersey daisies and calla slips


creeping up the inner side of his leg
locks and curl then up to inside his anus
where I admitted the thorazine early


Mother of HIV, mother of envy, grant me
the shallow wish to be loved like a man
in the highest way, la vita nuova, in your


shallow dish I shall take to Goshen
learning the ropes inefficient way, if the
boat don't break don't fix it, miles of


ash and fire all you can see, in your throat,
your naked silver throat, a shallow boom
box, glug, it's coming through and we're


history.


## ∾ The Stendhal Syndrome

With a rush, and we do away
Look at those Brice Mardens
and the big horses of Susan Rothenberg
and the palette without color of Neil Jordan

Pleasure as a synonym for AIDS
its metonymic attachment to the body
the fringe on top of the surrey of living
easy without you, easy air Jordan

Color my world white, with veiny streaks of red
A terror at giving up my seat at the opera
the family box
I really fucked myself over, that box of steak.

Steel stripes shadow the steel pier—Brighton
Smegma nada, the reverse of what?—My dick
tiptoes through the sands in another's—shoes
a river wide, green desert ribbon—

## ∾ Suspiria

I know when he began to dance with me
cranberries started to bum in pocket—
I smelled red smoke of sugar under my
feet, sugarfoot, a boy worth burning for—

and into his pants I'd push my white hands,
deeper into the sweeter red currant
in a darkened cell until he was done;
then into a lit cell, where I was king—

if music played we sat down fast, out, down
into the red fruit mashed in my lap like
Turkey. Musical chairs with the pilgrims
who came here on the rock to fuck him good

Oh Bill, if you were living at this hour
I'd put little socks on your two bare feet
and spoon this dressing into your wet throat
till you choked and spat all over my bib

KEVIN KILLIAN                                                323

I'd give you such a gift of red white meat
you wouldn't be able to sit for a week
unless to eat at the mantelpiece with clock,
bawling pilgrims thrusting your ass with fire

ferret teeth in the breast of a red bird

I would call it to your memory now
that a phantasmal fog of love had enthralled me to you

then, but not only then, in these my words
*the tear in the fabric,* now, *the drop of blood.*


## ∾ Trauma

I didn't want to have the little boy
but I kept him, tuggled, inside my bush.

You don't eat enough, so you're
spilling your chowder like barley.

Pull over here, I got to hurl my trauma
over the rushing water style bridge bridge,

and watch the series of tiny tugboats
take my baby away the lonesome river.

Trauma of losing a pal to AIDS, or SIDA
as he used to tell me while dreaming.

He was in Barcelona watching the Olympics
like Frank O'Hara in love with Bill Berkson.

# ❧ Zombie

Father who keeps one great yellow eye peeled for the
Boy, don't let him grow up to be that peeping Tom
With the German accent. Father of definition, let no

Glaucoma take him behind the screen of white china,
He's my little wriggling thing I eat like a jujube.
Out of your mouth you spewed me like catfish, lukewarm,

Whiskered, "hot diggety dog!" said the other children
Crowding round my genitals as though on Bonfire, but
Then coming back to school to pray, heads bowed

Father who makes this body of sense go stupid
Whenever I see you burning in that berry bush,
Keep your guard down till over your self-defense I leap.

I once did ooze, but now I'm hard, I'll become lard
If a prayerful sort. Dance class at noon, I expect
Every *Mein Herr* to take that duty, dinner at sevenish,

Little gummy green bear assails us at table with news of
Thee, soup on the left, big bowl of snapdragons floating
In the water of Thee. Dear God, as I lay dying of AIDS

I prayed to you and all your ministries nightly and daily,
And you were out in school teaching us the colors of the fag.
Dear God, let me freeze up his serious T-cells into miasma

And bring him alive in the 23rd century, I can't lose
Everything—not in 1 day. Jesus fucking Christ, I'll bring
Corpse after corpse to wash your feet with, to open a closet

With a bullet in space, sleep if you are tired, rest if
You feel trenchant. Father of HIV stop the digital maniplex,
Close your eyes, close your eyes, relax think of nothing tonight.

KEVIN KILLIAN

# DENNIS COOPER (1953-)

∾ BL

When I see
a boy having
sex before
he even knows
what it is
I want to kill
the men who
paid his way,
who kiss his
bug-mouth
and poke
at his farts,
lean back from
him burping,
only attracted
when a boy
lies face down,
his eyes dull
like a midget's,
a boy leading
men, the same
guys who should
tell him to
get lost, scram,
when he teases
them, but who
aim at it, turn
fools in his
presence, as if
he were the
true love
ahead, and

not the wild
crush far behind


## ∾ My Past

*for Jim Stegmiller*

is a short string of beautiful
boys or young men I admired,
dragged to bed, left in ruins
on corners with taxi fare home.
Another of friends who were
horny, who I could have slept
with but didn't because they
were ugly, insane, or too much
like me to be sexy. We were
partners for sweeps of wild
parties, took dope till they felt
like museums which we
could pick over for bodies
to idealize with caresses.
The sun rose slowly. I was
still huffing and toiling
with them, like a sculptor
attempting to get things just
right—finally collapsing
in bed with some smeared,
smelly torso before me, and
a powerful wish to be left
alone. Take you for example,
who I found throwing up in
the bathroom of some actor's
mansion and crowned my new
boyfriend. Your ass made me
nervous till I explored it.
Now I want to forget it. My
friends feel this way too.

DENNIS COOPER

I know them. We've been close
since before we were artists
working to leave haunted eyes
on our lovers. I've thrown
out hundreds like you, and
found only art can remain so
aloof in its makeup that I'll
stare endlessly into its eyes
like a kid with a microscope.
Once I was back when art chatted
just over my head, when I was
still glancing up the red swim
trunks of some boy who I think
was named Jimmy, and wondering
what could be out there, miles
from my hands. He was leaving
like you. Who knows where that
man and that feeling are now.


## ∾ JFK Jr. to Play Father in Film

The producer wanted Mark Hamill
but the real thing will do.
Besides, the publicity's helpful.
So he catches John in a school play,
sees potential, is attracted,

takes the boy for a screen test.
John is shy. John is arrogant.
He is used to the cameras.
His average mind gives energy
but no more. He is playing

it slapstick. Then they go
for a beer. The producer would rather
sleep with him than cast him.

But how do you broach a Kennedy.
A big producer too is in awe

of them, even bit players. He
tries to relax, but drink after
drink the boy looks closer to
godhead, the scene more hopeless;
John's eyes tail every woman.

Then, to shake himself "John do
you want to play your father?"
"It's better than playing his son."
A bad joke, a bad moment that
the producer sees and John doesn't.

Then John rises, shakes hands.
The producer sees him go. He thinks,
"Nice ass but nothing upstairs," and
sits back, imagining sex, knows John's
sperm would taste like *something*.


## ∾ Darkens

He orbits a hobby horse laughing. His life catches the overhead light. He spins
so fast the wind keeps him clean. There is a kid who likes watching him. He is
the boyfriend of someone important. He would be missed in a minute. There
is a wife in his tarot cards. His breakfast table is well overstocked, the food
bright as headlights aimed up. Now his body fills out like his father's. He
towers over his schoolmates. They meet him then ache through their bodies.
They want to be where love's leashed to the crossbars. They want to see it
transferred to friendship, to lust or a trophy. There is a worn-out ex-boy, mid-
admirers. I am that man, looking backwards. I can't explain my attraction.
Need love, love power, seek children. And one shines from the pack, well lit by
attention, well built by his parents. I hire him to clean up my work room. I slip
a pill in his deep breathing mouth. I sculpt a hug into raping. I completely
unravel his talent. I take a knife to its history of power. And then its world

enters the river's. He winning that cold blue reward. His body softens there, darkens and scrawls. First he's impeccable, tense, too ideal. Then he is weeping, annoys me. Then limp, cool, unprevailable, dull. Then sprawled saint-like on the floor, gazing upwards. I dump that in the river and he is gone.


## ∾ Teen Idol

When Thomas said,
"Love's overrated,"
I said, "You spoiled
fucking brat." And I
reminded him, "Some
boys have AIDS, re-
tardation," etc. Stuff
he'd never se-e-e-en
up in Beverly Hills.

"There are girls
who'd dismember their
boyfriends for one
word from you,"
I told him. He
knew that but he
didn't know some of
them were crippled.

So I drove Thomas
down to the hospital
where I volunteer,
where paraplegics
with his posters
taped around them
like a sky, saw him
and gasped like they'd
been diagnosed God.

He hugged them
and was rewarded
with laughter, etc.,
from Hell. He gave
them strips of his
clothes, etc. By end
of day, he was a tattered tramp.

We headed home in
my Hyundai. "Okay,"
he said. "They
were pretty scary."
Everywhere we drove,
girls glanced in the
windows and screamed.
Drivers took one look
then hit stop signs
or other drivers.

It was like Thomas
was holding up a
sign that read,
WORLD WILL END OR
SMASHING PUMPKINS
MURDERED. But
this was ye same
olde reaction. He
shrugged his thin
shoulders. See,

if he were talking
to fans instead
of posing, he'd tell
them, "Come over
if and only if you're
incredibly cute, etc.,
and if not, don't

bother," not "love
is the answer," not
some philosophy.


∾ Some Whore

short walk home,
his snout running,
loose assed, takes
my fist for a thou-
sand, so i pay it
'cause i'm loaded.

arm to the elbow
inside a whatever
year old, says he
loves me to death,
etc., but he loves
death, not me.

could kill him
sans knowing it,
punch through a
lung, turn my finger-
tip, render the
fucker retarded.

reckless, my fist
in his throat now,
face leaky, embar-
rassed and pleading,
zoned, urinating
all over himself.

jerk off, come,
pay, and he's split-

ting, says, "hey,
thanks a whole fuck-
ing lot," like it's
a joke, like he isn't.

## ∾ Hockney: Blue Pool

Los Angeles,
California:
a summer afternoon.
One boy sunbathes
on a yellow towel
beside the pool;
another stands
at the end of
the diving board,
gazing downward.
Palm trees sway
in the blue water.
Overhead, a few
clouds float by.
To the right,
sprinklers lightly
spray the green
lawn. The sunbather
slips off his red
and white striped
swimsuit and rolls
over; the other
boy dives into the
pool. The artist
snaps a photograph
of the splash.

# ❧ Eighteen to Twenty-One

## I

He said his name was Nick; later I learned
he'd crossed the country on stolen credit
cards—I found the receipts in the guest house
I rented for only three months. Over
a period of two weeks, he threatened
to tell my parents I was gay, blackmailed
me, tied me up, crawled through a window and
waited under my bed, and raped me at
knifepoint without lubricant. A neighbor
heard screams and called my parents, who arrived
with a loaded gun in my mother's purse.
But Nick was gone. I moved back home, began
therapy, and learned that the burning in
my rectum was gonorrhea, not nerves.

## II

Our first date, Dick bought me dinner and played
"Moon River" (at my request) on his grand
piano. Soon after that, he moved to
San Diego, but drove up every week-
end to see me. We'd sleep at his "uncle"'s
quaint cottage in Benedict Canyon—part
of Jean Harlow's old estate. One night, Dick
spit out my cum in the bathroom sink; I
didn't ask why. The next morning, over
steak and eggs at Du-Par's, Dick asked me to
think about San Diego, said he'd put
me through school. I liked him because he looked
like Sonny Bono, but sipped my coffee
and glanced away. Still, Dick picked up the bill.

III

More than anything, I wanted Charlie
to notice me. I spent one summer in
and around his swimming pool, talking to
his roommates, Rudy and Ned. All three of
them were from New York; I loved their stories
about the bars and baths, Fire Island, docks
after dark. I watched for Charlie, played board
games with Rudy and Ned, crashed on the couch.
Occasionally, Charlie came home with-
out a trick and I slipped into his bed
and slept next to him. Once, he rolled over
and kissed me—bourbon on his breath—and we
had sex at last. I was disappointed,
though: his dick was so small it didn't hurt.

IV

I made a list in my blue notebook: *Nick,
Dick, Charlie, Kevin, Howard, Tom* . . . . Kevin
had been the boyfriend of an overweight
girl I knew in high school. I spotted him
at a birthday bash—on a yacht—for an
eccentric blonde "starlet" who called herself
Countess Kerushka. Kevin and I left
together, ended up thrashing around
on his waterbed while his mother, who'd
just had a breakdown, slept in the next room.
Howard was Kevin's best friend. We went for
a drive one night, ended up parking. His
lips felt like sandpaper, and I couldn't
cum—but I added his name to the list.

V

Tom used spit for lubricant and fucked me
on the floor of his Volkswagen van while
his ex-lover (also named Tom) drove and
watched (I was sure) in the rearview mirror.
Another of his exes, Geraldo,
once cornered me in Tom's bathroom, kissed me
and asked: "What does he see in you?" At a
gay students' potluck, I refilled my wine
glass and watched Tom flirt with several other
men in the room. Outside, I paced, chain-smoked,
kicked a dent in his van and, when he came
looking for me, slugged him as hard as I
could. It was the end of the affair, but
only the beginning of my drinking.

VI

I ordered another wine cooler and
stared at his tight white pants—the outline of
his cock hung halfway down his thigh. After
a few more drinks, I asked him to dance to
"The First Time Ever I Saw Your Face." He
pressed himself against me and wrapped his arms
around my neck. I followed him to his
apartment but, once in bed, lost interest.
I told him I was hung up on someone.
As I got dressed, he said: "If you love him,
you should go to him." Instead, I drove back
to the bar, drank more, and picked up a blond
bodybuilder who, once we were in bed,
whispered "Give me your tongue"—which turned me off.

VII

As one young guy screwed another young guy
on the screen, the man sitting a couple
seats to my right—who'd been staring at me
for the longest time—slid over. He stared
a little longer, then leaned against me
and held a bottle of poppers to my
nose. When it wore off, he was rubbing my
crotch. Slowly, he unzipped my pants, pulled back
my underwear, lowered his head, licked some
pre-cum from the tip of my dick, and then
went down on it. As he sucked, he held the
bottle up. I took it, twisted the cap
off and sniffed, then looked up at the two guys
on the screen, then up at the black ceiling.


## ∽ Red Parade

Depressed because my
book wasn't nominated
for a gay award,

I lie on the couch
watching—not listening to—
the O. J. trial.

Byron, who senses
something's wrong, hides under the
bed until Ira

comes home, carrying
a bouquet of beautifully
wrapped tulips. I press

the mute button. *"This*
is your prize," he says. "Guess what
they're called." A smile in-

voluntarily
overcomes my frown. "What?" "Red
Parade." "That sounds like

the name of an old
Barbie outfit," I say. "That's
exactly what I

told the florist. And
you know what she told me?" "What?"
"When she was a girl,

she turned her Barbie
into Cleopatra: gave
her an Egyptian

haircut and painted
her nipples blue." "How cool." "Yeah,
but now she thinks that

her doll would be worth
eight hundred dollars if she
hadn't messed it up."

Once in water, the
tulips begin to unclench—
ten angry fists. Their

colors are fierce, like
Plath's "great African cat," her
"bowl of red blooms." Poor

Sylvia, who so
desperately wanted awards,
and only won them

after she was dead.
Byron jumps up, Ira sits
down and massages

my feet. "You guys." My
spirits are lifted by their
tulips, kisses, licks.


## ～ Of Mere Plastic

*for Wayne Koestenbaum*

The Barbie at the end of the mind,
Beyond the last collectible, is dressed
In "Golden Glory" (1965-1966),

A gold floral lamé empire-styled
Evening dress with attached
Green chiffon scarf and

Matching coat with fur-trimmed
Neckline and sequin/bead
Detail at each side. Her accessories:

Short white gloves, clear shoes
With gold glitter, and a hard-to-find
Green silk clutch with gold filigree

Braid around the center of the bag.
It closes with a single golden button.
The boy holds her in his palm

And strokes her blonde hair.
She stares back without feeling,
Forever forbidden, an object

Of eternal mystery and insatiable
Desire. He knows then
That she is the reason

That we are happy or unhappy.
He pulls the string at the back
Of her neck; she says things like

"I have a date tonight!"
And "Let's have a fashion show
Together." Her wardrobe case

Overflows with the fanciest outfits:
"Sophisticated Lady," "Magnificence,"
     "Midnight Blue."
*3 hair colors. Bendable legs too!*

The doll is propelled through outer space,
A kind of miniature Barbarella.
She sports "Miss Astronaut" (1965),

A metallic silver fabric suit
(The brown plastic straps at the shoulders
And across the bodice feature

Golden buckles) and two-part
White plastic helmet. Her accessories:
Brown plastic mittens,

Zip boots, and sheer nylon
Mattel flag, which she triumphantly sticks
Into another conquered planet.

DAVID TRINIDAD

# ∾ Chatty Cathy Villanelle

When you grow up, what will you do?
Please come to my tea party.
I'm Chatty Cathy. Who are you?

Let's take a trip to the zoo.
Tee-hee, tee-hee, tee-hee. You're silly!
When you grow up, what will you do?

One plus one equals two.
It's fun to learn your ABC's.
I'm Chatty Cathy. Who are you?

Please help me tie my shoe.
Can you come out and play with me?
When you grow up, what will you do?

The rooster says *cock-a-doodle-doo*.
Please read me a bedtime story.
I'm Chatty Cathy. Who are you?

Our flag is red, white and blue.
Let's makebelieve you're Mommy.
When you grow up, what will you do?
I'm Chatty Cathy. Who are you?

∾ Difference

The jellyfish
float in the bay shallows
like schools of clouds,

a dozen identical—is it right
to call them creatures,
these elaborate sacks

of nothing? All they seem
is shape, and shifting,
and though a whole troop

of undulant cousins
go about their business
within a single wave's span,

every one does something unlike:
this one a balloon
open on both ends

but swollen to its full expanse,
this one a breathing heart,
this a pulsing flower.

This one a rolled condom,
or a plastic purse swallowing itself,
that one a Tiffany shade,

this a troubled parasol.
This submarine opera's
all subterfuge and disguise,

its plot a fabulous tangle
of hiding and recognition:
nothing but trope,

nothing but something
forming itself into figures
then refiguring,

sheer ectoplasm
recognizable only as the stuff
of metaphor. What can words do

but link what we know
to what we don't,
and so form a shape?

Which shrinks or swells,
configures or collapses, blooms
even as it is described

into some unlikely
marine chiffon:
a gown for Isadora?

Nothing but style.
What binds
one shape to another

also sets them apart
—but what's lovelier
than the shapeshifting

transparence of *like* and *as:*
clear, undulant words?
We look at alien grace,

unfettered
by any determined form,
and we say: balloon, flower,

heart, condom, opera,
lampshade, parasol, ballet.
Hear how the mouth,

so full
of longing for the world,
changes its shape?

## ᕫ Crêpe de Chine

These drugstore windows
—one frame in the mile-long film
of lit-up trash and nothing

fronting the avenue, what Balzac called
"the great poem of display"—
are a tableau of huge bottles

of perfume, unbuyable gallons of scent
for women enormous as the movie screens
of my childhood. Spiritual pharmaceuticals

in their deco bottles,
wide-shouldered, flared,
arrayed in their pastel skylines,

their chrome-topped tiers:
a little Manhattan of tinted alcohols.
Only reading their names

—Mme. Rochas, White Shoulders, Crêpe de Chine—
and I'm hearing the suss of immense stockings,
whispery static of chiffon stoles

MARK DOTY

on powdered shoulders,
click of compacts, lisp and soft glide
of blush. And I'm thinking of my wig,

my blonde wig, and following the cold sparkle
of pavement I'm wanting not
these shoes but the black clatter

and covenant of heels. Next door
the Italian baker's hung a canopy of garlands
and silver shot, bee lights and silk ivy

high over the sugary excess
of his pastries, and I want
not his product but his display:

I want to wear it,
I want to put the whole big thing
on my head, I want

the tumbling coiffeurs of heaven,
or lacking that, a wig
tiered and stunning as this island.

That's what I want from the city:
to wear it.
That's what drag is: a city

to cover our nakedness,
silk boulevards, sleek avenues
of organza, the budding trees

along the avenue flaunting their haze
of poisonous Caravaggio green . . .
Look how I take the little florists' shops

and twist them into something
for my hair, forced spiky branches
and a thousand tulips. Look, my sleety veil

of urbane rain descends, unrolls
like cinema's dart and flicker, my skirt
in its ravaged sleekness, the shadows

between buildings raked and angled
into these startling pleats,
descending twilight's gabardine

over the little parks and squares
circled by taxis' hot jewels:
my body

made harmonious with downtown.
Look how I rhyme with the skyscraper's
padded sawtooth shoulders,

look at the secret evidence of my slip
frothing like the derelict river
where the piers used to be,

look at my demolished silhouette,
my gone and reconstructed profile,
look at me built and rebuilt,

torn down to make way,
excavated, trumped up, tricked out,
done, darling,

in every sense of the word. Now,
you call me
Evening in Paris, call me Shalimar,

call me Crêpe de Chine.

MARK DOTY

# ∾ Where You Are

1.

flung to your salt parameters      in all that wide gleam
unbounded edgeless      in that brilliant intersection

where we poured      the shattered grit the salt
and distillation of you      which blew back

into my face stinging      like a kiss
from the other world      a whole year

you've languished blue      in ceaseless wind
naked now in all lights      and chill swaddlings

of cloud never for a moment      cold you are
uninterruptible seamless      as if all this time

you'd been sleeping      in the sparkle and beckon
of it are you      in the pour of it

as if there were a secret      shining room
in the house and you'd      merely gone there

we used to swim      summers remember
naked in those shoals      now I think was I ever

that easy      in this life
fireworks remember      Handel an orchestra

on a barge      in the harbor and fountains
spun to darkness      flung in time to

the music scrawling heaven      like sperm like
chrysanthemums bursting      in an enormous hurry

all fire and chatter      flintspark and dazzle
and utterly gone      save here in the scribble

of winter sunlight      on sheer mercury
when I was a child      some green Fourth

flares fretting      the blue-black night
a twirling bit of ash      fell in my open eye

and for a while I couldn't see      those skyrockets
is it like that now love      some cinder

blocking my sight      so that I can't see you
who are only for an hour      asleep and dreaming

in this blue      and light-shot room
as if I could lean across      this shifting watery bed

and ask      are you awake


2. EVERYWHERE

I thought I'd lost you. But you said *I'm imbued*

*in the fabric of things, the way*
*that wax lost from batik shapes*
*the pattens where the dye won't take.*
*I make the space around you,*

*and so allow you shape. And always*
*you'll feel the traces of that wax*
*soaked far into the weave:*
*the air around your gestures,*

MARK DOTY

*the silence after you speak.*
*That's me, that slight wind between*
*your hand and what you're reaching for;*
*chair and paper, book or cup:*

*that close, where I am: between*
*where breath ends, air starts.*


   3. VAN GOGH, *Flowering Rosebushes: 1889*

A billow of attention
enters the undulant green,
and so configues it
to an unbroken rhythm,

summer's continuous surface,
dappled and unhurried
—though subject to excitations,
little swarms of shifting strokes

which organize themselves
into shadow and leaf, white starbursts
of bloom: a calm frenzy
of roses. His June's one green

unbordered sea, and he's gone
into it entirely—nothing here
but the confident stipple
and accumulation of fresh

and certain gesture, new again
in a rush of arrival. Don't you want
to be wrapped, brocaded,
nothing to interrupt

the whole struck field
in the various and singular

complexity of its music?
To be of a piece with the world,

whole cloth? These little passages
accrue, differ, bursts of white roses,
ripples and striations; what's Van Gogh
but a point of view? Missing

from the frame, he's everywhere,
though it would be wrong
to think him at the center
of the scene: his body's gone,

like yours. Rather it's as if
this incandescent stuff—
a wildly mottled Persian scarf
whose summery pattern

encapsulates shoreline and garden,
June's jade balconies of wave
and blossom tiered, one above the other,
in terraces of bloom—

were wrapped around him,
some splendid light-soaked silk,
weightless, motile, endlessly figured
and refiguring: gone into the paint,

dear, gone entirely into *(white rose
& leaf, starry grasses)* these waves
of arriving roses, the tumbling rose
of each arriving wave.

MARK DOTY                                                        351

## ∾ Getting Happy

When the men got happy in church,
    they shouted and jumped straight up.

But the women's trances
    made them dance with moaning; so,

I dreaded Rev. Johnson's sermons
    near their end, hated the trouble

he was causing inside
    the souls of women sweating

and beginning to breathe fast.
    One day, I worried, my mother

would let go and lose herself
    to him, become as giddy

as when my father was coming home
    on leave. Just as silly.

Yet, when it finally happened,
    I felt only left behind.


Years later, another first time,
    I heard my moan echo inside

a girl's ear and recognized
    how woeful pleasure feels.

I then began to wonder
    if there weren't some joy still

to give in to, make me shout
    not as men do but as a woman.

It troubles me.
    I do not have a woman's body

but fear that moaning will betray
    this want in me, or another

to be like a woman. Mostly,
    I fear that moaning will uncover

the love for my mother that is still
    so deep that I want little more

than to be with her as closely as I can.


## ◦ Goldsboro Narrative #24: Second Benediction

Knowing we still needed to dance,
the man who kept company with men

played the church organ sassy

and let us sway ourselves near him
even as we gathered still beside him,

watching his thin fingers talk the way they dared

when the sermon had been made
and we lingered to pray for sound

because the body waits for sound.  We waited

for the moment his fingers spoke in their tongues,
listened for the urgent translation into this:

We have returned to a blessed place;
Our family is here with us, even the dead and not-born;
We are journeying to the source of all wonder,

We journey by dance. Amen.

*for Mr. Holman*


## ∾ Goldsboro Narrative #28

When folks caught on to what was happening
between Rev. Johnson and Sister Edna,
the grown-ups went back to speaking
in front of children as if we couldn't spell.
It was easy to figure out, though:
Rev. Johnson's wife didn't get happy; and,
after service, she wouldn't shake hands
with Sister Edna or any of her kin.
And Sister Edna's husband, Mr. Sam,
who never came to church, began waiting
in the parking lot to drive his wife home.

Now the age Rev. Johnson was then, I doubt
he was concerned with being forgiven.
But when I was 12 and kept on falling
from available grace, I began dismissing him
and mostly all of what he said he meant.
I went witnessing instead to Mr. Sam,
his truck idling outside the paned windows,
him dressed in overalls and a new straw hat.

# ❧ A Boy Doesn't Know

A boy does not know these things.
He plays with himself, engages
others,
          but he doesn't understand
why lying on his stomach
                    or on his back with raised legs
and having the man edge himself past
                              and then inside
is what the man really wants him to do.
A boy doesn't know


          and so   he leaves himself
lying on a bed or on a floor or up against a wall;
he watches and he waits,
pulls up his pants and wonders what to do
          with the stickiness on his fingers, how to take himself
               from that place to another.


After the semen dries and the clothes from that day
have been buried, he spends forever
trying to remember if the numbness that flared
in his nostrils and consumed all air
distracted him from noticing the yank and tug
there *must* have been when something in his middle
not yet named, yet missed,
was taken easily as breath.


FORREST HAMER

# ∿ Crossroads

Crossed over the river, and the river went dry
Crossed over the river, the river went dry
Saw myself drowning and I couldn't see why

Come up for air and the day said noon
Come up for air, said the air read noon
Day said, Son, you better mind something soon

Sink back down, felt my spirits leave high
Sink back down, I felt my spirits lift high
Didn't know if I was gonna die

A man give his hand and he pulled me to the shore
Man give his hand, pulled me over to the shore
Told me if I come I wouldn't drown no more

Me and the man walked and talked all day and night
Me and the man, we walked, we talked all day and night
We started wrestling til the very lip of light

I put my mind on evil sitting in my soul
Put my mind on evil just sitting on my soul
Struggling with the devil make a soul old

I looked at my face and my life seem small
Looked hard at my face and this life it look so small
All of a sudden didn't bother me at all
Returned to the river and I stood at the shore
Went back to the river and I stood right at the shore
Decided to myself needn't fight no more

## ❧ Sung from a Hospice

Still craving a robust
Tenderness and justice,
I will go on living
With all I have seen:
Young men lusterless;
Against my blind cheek—
*Blessed by the frangible*
*And dying,*
*The irreplaceable dead—*
In my crestfallen arms:
With breath,
Then without it,
With flesh,
Then freed of it—

And the indurate man I heard
Condemn the stricken,
While my cousin was dying,
If he had walked these wards,
Armorless, open
To the imperiled,
Surely he would have gleaned
To sit in judgment
Is to sit in hell—

Lesions, elegies,
Disconnected phones—

Rain, nimble rain,
Be anodyne,
Anoint me
When I say outright:

*In the plague time, my heart*
*Was tested,*
*My living soul*
*Struck like a tower bell,*
*Once, twice,*
*Four times in a single season.*


## ∾ Fleur

No it is not suffering that engenders it;
       it is beyond suffering,
The flower—
       though it rests beside
the tears, the million barricades,
       fusillade upon fusillade . . .
it rests,
       soft as a fontanel.

     *

Fifty-four whales beach on the shore,
       vials of blood, and syringes,
so that we might perceive The Flower,
       cry out for it.

     *

With sternness and delicacy,
       Georgia O'Keeffe,
that clear-eyed woman,
       leaned into its sacred warmth,
with her paints,
       her probity.

     *

Yes, its stem is like
        the jammed, astonishing column of crutches
the healed leave behind,
        a column of miracles
in a snowlit, hallowed shrine.


                *


        Stopping on the road to Tula,
to Tolstoy's estate,
        I found a flower
like one from my childhood,
        a great seraphic bloom.
But there were missiles between it
        and it's Western twin,
missiles!, missiles!,
        and a killing mystique.


                *


Not long after Chernobyl's gasp,
        I looked from a window
in Dostoyevsky's house
        and watched a man pass a sinister wand
over the vegetables for market,
        over the flowers.


                *


How much can the petals withstand,
        while we hasten the leavings,
the radioactive waste?


                *


        It cannot last,
this juggernaut, this whirlwind futility:


CYRUS CASSELLS                                        359

surely joy will outdistance
the century's mass graves,
        the earth's furious junkyards;
surely joy will outdistance us.


                *


        A woman strokes the numerals
seared forever into her skin,
        and with deadsure fingers examines
stark photographs from the war:
        *this happened to me,*
*and this—*
        *and still I survived . . .*
*Yes, there were lupines in the camp,*
        *and our joy in them was real,*
*as real as our misery.*
        *We would find some little corner of the barracks*
*to put them of display:*
        *we would pick and scoop them into our arms,*
*after a day or forced labor.*


                *


        Oh once, during the war,
there was a boy,
        bewilderred, deaf from birth,
unable to comprehend
        the men in dark uniforms barking
*Jew, Jew,*
        *get down on your knees!* —
so that his father had to coax him
        to touch the paving with his mouth,
to take part in the wretched street cleaning.


        And after wetting a stone
with a sullen tongue,

the boy found his work
had made it shine.

Then ridicule, and bullying hatred,
then indignity gave way
to something rapt—gave way
to sheer accomplishment.

Undaunted, he found a tiny flower-shape
set deep into the stone,
let its brief, invisible pollen brush him.

And for that one instant, let me believe,
the universe was moved;
all the gall of the day
was changed to wine:

*ma fleur, ma fleur* . . .

Oh what would you give to find that flower?


## ∿ Amalgam

Taormina, Sicily

Above rooftops, bell towers,
in the beatific
amphitheater at Taormina,
I brush my lips
to your ruffled, jovial
helmet of hair,
as if we'd passed
into the limitless
(the bygone and the future
burned away), and left
the blurred, the jagged,
the fly-by-night

far below,
like a jabbering beehouse—
our souls unburdened
by rippling, recurring
turquoise and laudable blue,
Etna's turbulent glory.

Hobo-light,
in the hands of freedom,
we relish
the delicate seesaw
between timelessness
and the time at hand,
like the *click, click,*
of your rapacious camera:
here, here is the overrunning
present in all its fulgence,
spring at its heady maximum.
This is the providential place,
the deadsure belvedere,
where marrying sea and air,
fertile land and fire
commingle.
This is the elected place—
suddenly I know with surety—
I want to merge with you
with the subtlest fanfare,
to forge a true amalgam,
vibrant, consummate—
not happy-ever-aftering,
but dedicated wills,
parallel branches lit
by the green, restoring
fire at the core of May—

We're alone now, unbarred.
We bribed the careworn,

neverminding guard
to let us in
a half an hour
before opening.
As we walk among ancient tiers,
snapped columns,
and Scotch broom, I'm remembering
how we became ardent
celebrants of Klimt,
amid December's cold
brocades of black and bone,
inveterate boys
making rakish, empowering wings
in an acre of Viennese white —
near our frisking,
snow on a Medusa
of stone,
the Danube breaking
into harps of ice.

We improvised
a tiny Christmas
of tinsel and blueberry wine;
you covered my eyes,
a mimic blindfold.
*Wait,* you said.
Suddenly I felt
your intent fingertips,
your lips transmit
a treasure trove
shock of wine,
strong as death—
the last veil
to our union, the last
atom of resistance,
utterly extingitished:
*live with me,*
*live with me—*

Under an unimpeded blue,
beside the hills'
exuberant emerald,
I call your nearness
holy, your spark
sweet and staggering,
because,
on this emperor-is-naked earth,
poisoned, glittering
as hush money,
yes, in precincts of lewd gold,
you are my catalyst,
my key turner.
There are no edges
to our loving now—

As if you brought me
to this austere theater
to fill me
with the island's divinity;
the volcano, with its flourish
of snow,
seems to loom
within reach.
Not long ago, we trekked
through the cold
toward the lip
of the roaring crater,
like peregrines in rugged
passage to the unmastered.
Recalling that ice
and restless fire
from a distance,
how simply it returns to us:
the grayblooded morning
a river's margins lapsed,
filling our faltered car,

then our cowed heartbeats,
our urgent journey
through the flood,
brackish, impinging,
till in the foursquare hush,
the aftermath,
we were lovers assuming
the identity of fire,
reaching the undeluged streets,
the dry land,
undemolished, aligned
with the only power
that's lasting,
superabundant, attainable
in jeopardy and poise:
love's power—

Spurred by vernal sunlight
and the memory
of a childhood nurse,
once a boy of fourteen
seized a hideaway corner
behind barbed wire,
and opened his prison clothes.
And as some acts brace us,
so I imagine that emboldened boy,
vigorous,
transfigured here beside us,
with a ring bearer's bloom.
My love,
may there always be
a guiltless touch
in the places of desecration—

Your cupped hands
I drink from,
regal, insistent,

CYRUS CASSELLS

your cradling,
penny-colored eyes
persuade me
wherever there's a lover's
solicitous gaze,
unscripted joy,
the Nazarene still walks
the wounded earth
in unwavering tenderness—
rumor of the Soul of Souls,
glimpse of the Beloved—
igniting blossom
after human blossom:
the sweeping bridegroom,
the shepherd with his crown
of birds—

*Love, the girasol in bloom,*
*the snake unvenomed,*
*sacramental, pacific.*

*Love: all my Potemkin villages*
*unmasked—*
*your steadfast limbs,*
*your capable loins,*
*a ladder-climb,*
*a luxury,*
*a helix to God—*

On this peaceful,
emancipating height,
let's bequeath the parched,
the bitter man,
our tandem beauty
as eleemosynary light
as testimony—
this antagonist

in the mind's eye;
beside a bier,
we heard him weep
*my son, my son,*
but this was the indurate world
he dreamed of:
the Davids and Jonathans he branded
soulless, nefarious,
tamped at last
with winterkilled leaves—

But look, as ever,
we spat-upon lovers live,
pledged men.

*In you, the foothold*
*the firmament.*

*In you, in you,*
*altar bread, justice,*
*the attar of home—*

My lanternlike love,
justborn, willing,
maverick no more,
now I give you my deepest name.

∾ *from* Erotic Collectibles

### 1978

He worked at a gas station,
or wore a gas station
jersey—or I blew him
near a gas station.

I said, "Can we go to your
apartment?" He said no
with sudden terrified solemnity,
as if it were taboo

to confuse tea-room and home sex.
I crammed this blow
job into my busy schedule
because my shrink had said,

"Have as much sex as you want,"
so by God I'd better
take the prescription and wake
my listless "Lycidas"-

reading body! How did I find
my way into his stall,
and did he welcome
my brash entrance, did he growl

"Hey there, foxy?" Dingy
light poured onto my clean,
hypothetical groin.
For ten syrupy minutes

he was the man in my life.
He waited for me, he didn't
pack up his dick and leave
the premises the minute he came.

Courteous, he understood
laws of reciprocity
that govern even the most
casual encounters.

What is casual? I did not feel
casual. My heart beat
fast, as if this were an audition.
After the event, I walked

down Revere Street, past
his gas station, or, if I
am imagining his connection
to gas stations,

then I can't justify why I associate his
mouth and its accompaniments
with a still-life Mobil sign
at trolley's end, where the sea

resumes its fabled nearness to the sand.

∾ *from* Star Vehicles:

I'm Not in "Darling"

Bette Davis has no reason to be jealous of Michelangelo Antonioni
and yet when I slept over at her house, in the late nineteen-seventies,
she kept me up all night complaining about a formerly illustrious career.
How her words came out is more important than the words themselves.

"I'm not in *Zabriskie Point.* I'm not in *Blow-Up.*
I'm not in *L'Avventura.* I'm not in *Isadora.*
I'm not in *Georgy Girl.* I'm not in *Woodstock.*
I'm not in any great sixties epics.

"I'm not in *Darling.* I'm not in *Midnight Cowboy.*
I'm not in *Easy Rider.* I'm not in *Valley of the Dolls.*
Why didn't they give me the Garland/Hayward role
in *Valley?* Why didn't they film *The Love Machine* starring me?

"Why didn't they film *Every Night, Josephine!* starring me?
Why didn't they remake *I'll Cry Tomorrow* starring me?
Or redo *Mata Hari?* I'm a limitless god, like Apollo,
but certainly I'd have done remakes in my dotage.

"I'm not in *Morgan.* I'm not in *8½.*
Ignorant armies crash my party.
I'm the haunted Bette always in your thoughts.
I'd have done any part, had they asked. Had they asked."

And then I woke, and discovered myself in the act of speaking, slowly,
     methodically;
and from the cup of tea, ambiguous steam-clouds, like locusts, were issuing,
in which I could read the pattern of my future,
a wilderness stretching farther than the exiled eye could see.


## The Garbo Index

My dead friend Vito praised Garbo's last scene in *Queen Christina*—
the closeup uncomprehended gays stared into, seeking dissolution.
I remember Vito eating pizza at my table in the Village, 1986.
He removed the sausage nuggets, placed them at plate-side.

"I don't eat pork," he said: HIV-positive precautions.
He was watching his system, as we were watching our own systems,
and are, to this day, watching. The last time I saw Vito entirely well
he was wearing pearls on his bare chest, high tea, the Pines—

never my scene. Who co-stars in *Romance?* Can't ask Vito.
When he was alive, I never helped him very much,
and now he's beyond telephone—waiting with Garbo
by the schoolyard's huddled ailanthus; waiting for the fire drill to end.

Four new Passover questions. Am I a child or an adult?
Am I a creature of memory or of action?
If I knew I were to die tomorrow, would I phrase this question differently?
Is it valedictory to write about Vito, or is it vanity?

My life is small, formal, and walled, and around every vista
I contain, imagine black shutters, the limits that Garbo
decreed must flank the lens filming her face in closeup,
so she could see only the camera's eye, without distracting leading man and
    crew.

Her life, if indexed, would yield surprises,
as would any life, if indexed, if reprieved.
Sea glass, Garbo's collection of. Camellias, Garbo's paradisiacal.
Grotto, Garbo's imaginary. Ghost, Garbo's.

Once, Garbo was whispering secrets of performance
in a bandaged voice, and I was listening, and no toxins in the field
of vision arose to violate the soliloquy, unfolding
with the tranquillity of all final compositions.


## ∾ History of Boys

1.

Call him A
for angel butt, curved poplar—

the first butt I desired.
I thought, "This

is what sculptors feel"—
honest love of contour.

Butt wasn't separate
from boy, or from my consciousness.

Both—all three—walked past me.
"I could imagine touching it,"

I mused, but didn't push
the idea toward execution.

Religious, respectable, he recognized
my existence, somewhat.

Charity informed the butt,
made it a locus.

2.

M got a hard girl pregnant, sent her
to San Francisco for an abortion.

I imagined touching
his leg hair, bits at a time.

I didn't know how to go about it.
Without procedure

the action completed itself.
The leg felt hard, like a praline.

I had a praline disposition—
sweet, factioned.

Laid out on the floor
by my eye

he was no longer delinquent—
no longer the impregnator.

I decided, in fantasy,
to be kind to his legs.

The legs, then, might radiate
their own salt rigor.

3.

V's stomach crossed the hotel room.
He smelled of talcum

stick drawn across white bucks
to preserve their pristine suede.

The house he lived in
held V's stomach at night;

the house he lived in
faced a busier road than mine.

Lust played zither on my
belly's blank billboard, unlettered

marquee advertising no
good film, only some mystery about Malaga.

4.

Did F know his last name was a variety of bean?
His jock held nuts and other items, a safe

deposit box. He sat
on the gym bench; that angle

enlarged his bush. His grownup
name augured

grownup sorrow.
Looseness

suited the bush:
it had all day, all year.

No one—no girl—would ever discover
his pudge dusk stomach,

portions abstracted
from other contexts.

5.

The boxer flap opened, spoke
this humid moral.


## ❧ Poem for George Platt Lynes

George Platt Lynes photographed a naked man, curled
    in a snailshell's infinite regress, and I want
to follow suit, my body a starfish seized
    by a Polaroid purchased on serious
whim: may I become the sailor
    picked up and froze in a print
hid at the Kinsey Institute until too recently!
    I see so many cuties on 23$^{rd}$ Street, they must be an industry—
members of an international underground elite
    gathered to plot the overthrow
of dogma—living replicas
    of Lynes's Orpheus, whose stubble
calls back from pandemonium the foreskins,
    pimples, and ingrown hairs, each paradoxical

nipple lit like Dietrich's angel—
 will I turn
pornographer? Before falling asleep I was terrified
 nuance would forever resist being enclosed
by a poem, however much it wandered from the point,
 so I thought, "Why not say this in prose?"
but then on waking reconsidered, and replayed dying
 Violetta singing farewell, asking Alfredo to give
her image—daguerreotype?—to his future
 virgin bride, whose arms, hypotheses, are pure—
*take this picture and tell your girlfriend*
 *I'm now an angel watching you in heaven . . .*
I fell asleep promising that when I rose
 I'd write a poem that did elaborate justice
to this world, but instead, in Rome,
 Sophia Loren, Marcello Mastroianni
and Fellini visited and refused
 to say what new film they were working on.
I begged, "Tell *me* before you spill it to the press."
 Sophia was singing Aida at the Met
and Colette hogged the parterre toilet—
 none of the nobility waiting in line had a chance
to urinate before the Surgeon General
 lowered the fire curtain on the Nile scene.
I am not a fake. I have two friends, three
 or four children, five fathers, and a host
of tropical fish. I never photographed Tommy,
 my first-grade friend who moved on Chanukah—
depressed pink light crimping the horizon's skirt,
 God mimicking Schiaparelli:
when I visited his new house, nothing was the same,
 the rooftop swept the sun
into green hatchets, and his bed abutted on a marsh
 I never had the good fortune to fall into,
else I'd now be giving you something keener than this sordid
 compromise between deceit and grief. At last
I have a playmate to rival that original, and plenty

of cultural references thrown in, five-
spice powder, a predilection for the long walk, long
    haul, not much fuss, closure
kept to a minimum, and hyperbole reigning
    in her usual kimono, the color of merlot—
the silk one hanging in my closet smells cheap.
    Walking along the Hudson in 1977
beside an imaginary Balanchine troupe's prima
    ballerina, I saw, on a pier,
a man with top Levi's button opened
    showing groin hair, and I thought,
"Ditch the ballerina and follow this mariner."
    I didn't inspect his belly's superscript
or footnotes, nor the tattoo, serving notice
    like Madame Defarge, nor did I value,
at half her worth, the dancer, her navel bearing
    superior complexity, if I'd known how to see it.
A poet drove me to Philadelphia in a dream.
    Her mother disapproved of my defection
from orthodox practices, and I persuaded her that tapioca
    was a good idea for a dinner party; then my mother
walked onstage without warning during a poetry reading
    I was trying to give, and she said, "I'm sorry I'm late,
this is not normal behavior, but I have urgent errands."
    I long for a blue notebook
that admits every atmospheric tic, the despicable
    difference between *haute* and *bas,*
the small talk of my umpteen loves, my hand
    opening the window to invite
warm rain, and sunset tinting the street
    my father's uncle trudges up to bring a box of See's
chocolates on Christmas day—the uncle who married
    a Catholic, survived Germany,
then moved to San Jose to deliver mail:
    I disgrace the family by mentioning
graves and emptiness
    without also describing

ameliorative handkerchiefs
     and armchairs, philosophy lessons
and the Rubinstein concert in Caracas—"You have no irony,"
     my friend says, whose scarves are orchestral,
and I reply, "I have no sincerity." I used to weep
     after every haircut, smothered by uncertainty—
which look did I want, butch or meandering?
     "D'ja know?" is my new expression,
homage to Djuna Barnes—do you know
     what I mean, do you know what I seek, do you know
duration will not redistribute its fathoms,
     and do you greet the sky's openness
to opium as if its saturnalian curriculum
     made you and me
the sole descendants of the Ballets Russes?
     Before quitting
*(accept this photograph, dear, and know*
     *that an angel gazes down on your happiness)*
promise you will not destroy the magic net
     the marooned December moon
casts over casual thought; promise you will give moments
     on odd afternoons for the pleasure
a photograph allows—the Rudy Burckhardt shot
     of a solitary Brooklyn studio, its few faint
artifacts fastidiously arranged on a table—a room
     that might have been my mother's, had her childhood
looked out to the Bridge rather than to my own parched future birth,
     and had she worn clean oxfords in the old photo
I kept on my dormitory wall (her face pushing
     against her brother's chest)
beside an index card's typed Pound quote
     about the immorality of not staring the subject
straight in the eye, or else about Gaudier-Brzeska,
     dead in the Great War—
had she worn not unlaced boots but clean smackers,
     a kind of giggly shoe
that John Bunny, best fat comedian of the silent screen,

WAYNE KOESTENBAUM

might have longed for,
were he to lose the girth that made him famous;
   and promise I will not curtail
memory's melisma into the false carnival
   float shapes I have pursued for too many years—
*Prendi, quest'è l'immagine de' miei passati giorni*—
   squandered days in a whirling cyclone downstream,
who dares capture or call you home before the figure, nude
   on the silver plate that oversees these lines,
raises his hand to feel the fine light fail?

## ∾ Elegy

Poor Eros: sadly, as in the boning of fowl
or of angels in defeat, someone has snapped
his wings off, and now fitted out in his

leatherette sash, spitting bad Greek from
either side of a mouth not at all like the
mouth in his pictures, he goes thin and un-

recognized. Who expects the winged horse
and Icarus, one failing, one not, tattooed
on his ass where it rises to the motorcycle's

nudging? Or, instead of the delicately pared
bud of legend, a cock heavy with travel, re-
ceding within its saurian folds in time with

the booted foot's effortless shift from gear
down to gear? At all the old cafés, look, how
even as he passes by, the aging citizens steam

the windows and miss him, remembering his boy's
way of entering a scene just to break it, his
pink legs working whole crowds into longing.

## ∾ King of Hearts

Somewhere now, someone is missing him,
since here he is for the taking, nicked
at three of his four corners, decked out

in the fade of much play, his two heads
laid prone on the sidewalk before you.

Like you, in this heat and humidity, no
wind, when it comes, moves him. Like you,

he knows a thing, maybe, about wilting—
how, like sleep or some particularly

miserable defeat played over but this time
in slow motion, it has its own fine beauty.

> *

Tonight,
        once you've found him, when you've

brought him home, the man with a face as
close as you'll ever get to the other one,

the one it was easy enough, earlier, not to
pick up, to step on, even, and move slowly

but unbothered away from, you'll only remember

the part about wilting.
                And even that, as

you lift his ass toward you, as your hands
spread it open until it resembles nothing

so much as a raw heart but with a seemingly
endless hole through it—even that will

fade.
        Him, between drink and the good money

you've paid, doing whatever you tell him.
Him throwing back whatever words you hand out.

*You're the king, you're the king,* him saying.


## ∾ Toys

Seeing them like this,
arranged according to size,
sectioned off by color,

I think it's not so much their being
made mostly for men, nor anything in
their being man-made; it's what

they are made *of* disturbs me: rubber
and urethane, plastic aiming for
the plastic of flesh,

and just missing. Growing up, I was
told once that, somewhere in the Vatican,
there's a room still, where—

ordered and numbered, as if
awaiting recall—lie all the phalluses
of stone, granite, tufa, fine marble,

that were removed from pagan statues
for lacking what any leaf, it seems,
can provide: some decorum.

I've never seen them, but their beauty, I
imagine, is twofold: what they're
made of, for one—what, in cracking,

suggests more than just the body that
came first, but the peril,
the vulnerability

that is all the flesh means to say,
singing; then, what even these
imitations before me—lesser somehow

but, to the eye and to touch, finally
more accurate, in being true
to an absurdity that is always there

in the real thing—even these seem
like wanting to tell about beauty,
that it also comes this way, in parts.


## ∾ Luna Moth

No eye that sees could fail to remark you:
like any leaf the rain leaves fixed to and
flat against the barn's gray shingle. But

what leaf, this time of year, is so pale,
the pale of leaves when they've lost just
enough green to become the green that *means*

loss and more loss, approaching? Give up
the flesh enough times, and whatever is lost
gets forgotten: that was the thought that I

woke to, those words in my head. I rose,
I did not dress, I left no particular body
sleeping and, stepping into the hour, I saw

you, strange sign, at once transparent and
impossible to entirely see through, and how
still: the still of being unmoved, and then

the still of no longer being able to be
moved. If I think of a heart, his, as I've
found it. . . . If I think of, increasingly, my

own. . . . If I look at you now, as from above,
and see the diva when she is caught in mid-
triumph, arms half-raised, the body as if

set at last free of the green sheath that has—
how many nights?—held her, it is not
without remembering another I once saw:

like you, except that something, a bird, some
wild and necessary hunger, had gotten to it;
and like the diva, but now broken, splayed

and torn, the green torn piecemeal from her.
I remember the hands, and—how small they
seemed, bringing the small ripped thing to me.


## ∾ Alba: Come

—as he did. Then
go down to the water, to where
he finally closed his slit of mouth,
and died, the world distancing,
more distant, gone. Don't forget
there were two, the one who died,
and the one who made him, whose
feet as they approached, rising
from and drowning among the dry
prone-to-crack leaves, must have
—as yours are now—been also birds
flushed from their cover and brought
abruptly down. His feet like that,

his mouth like any mouth when it opens
to say *You want, I'll suck you off:*
not like threat, but offering; a gift.

The rest—This is the light as it
found him. Take it. Put it on.
This of course is not the exact
same light, but the same moon
appearing to leave, the same sun
appearing. This is the light, this
is the way he was found inside it:
naked, not counting the small
rain all over, not counting the blood
that still, despite rain, glazed
his chest, the blood coming
from what—severed and lifted
from its nest—the hand did not
so much hold anymore as wear,
Egyptian, the scarab worn in death,
the guarantee, safe passage away.


## ∿ Tunnel

> *Come now, if ever.*
> *When it is raining this gentle*
> *and the first thought is of semen,*
> *and the second thought is of lilies*
> *when by their own pale weight*
> *they bend, sing to the ground something,*
> *and the third thought is of*
> *what joy or sadness can be*
> *available to what is finally a lily*
> *and can't sing.*
> :

And you said *It is wind* and *It is heat,*
hearing the doors shift in their frames.

Because you could not say what also
to call it: God as what is relentless,
God as oil, redolent, proffered;
the final, necessary cross-stitch of
death whose meaning is that everything
finds closure; or the meaningless,
already tipped, disembodied scales
in which we are all of us, inescapably,
found wanting, because how can we
not want?

       :

    —In the street below, the latest version of cool need, his
      black car shining in such a way as to make all of it (that
      any children around follow, that each longs to see his own
      face given back, and the one boy, that he is chosen, is
      getting in) seem natural, inevitable.

       :

the body, bright thing and holy   *the body as raft-like*

the ocean beneath it as waves    *the waves as many small fans*

the one you loved, he is dead    *the one I love, he is dead*

each wave beneath him is blue   *—blue, collapsing*

       :

—Sunday morning, the Greek diner. The men in pairs from
    last night. Again the different, more difficult
    tenderness that is two men with only their briefly shared
    flesh in common as they eat and don't eat much, together
    At the window *brush/fail, brush/fail* go the leaves.

       :

After Patroklos, impatient, took the armor of Achilles,
after he put it on his own body
and rode into battle, and then died,
Achilles fell into grief—
not for the loss of the armor that was his,
but for love of the man who had last worn it,
who could never, now,
be brought back.
His goddess-mother Thetis, hearing

as far away as the sea's floor
his uncontrollable cries, hurried to him.
A lot of words, armor, a new shield . . .

      :

> *Here is the sun.*
> *Take some.*
> *Here is the rain, in no apparent way*
> *holy, but serving still.*
> *Wash.*
> *Drink.*
> *Here is the body.*
> *Do not imagine now balm.*
> *The wounds are to be*
> *left open.*

*for Frank*

## ∾ As from a Quiver of Arrows

What do we do with the body, do we
burn it, do we set it in dirt or in
stone, do we wrap it in balm, honey,
oil, and then gauze and tip it onto
and trust it to a raft and to water?

What will happen to the memory of his
body, if one of us doesn't hurry now
and write it down fast? Will it be
salt or late light that it melts like?
Floss, rubber gloves, a chewed cap

to a pen elsewhere—how are we to
regard his effects, do we throw them
or use them away, do we say they are
relics and so treat them like relics?
Does his soiled linen count? If so,

would we be wrong then, to wash it?
There are no instructions whether it
should go to where are those with no
linen, or whether by night we should
memorially wear it ourselves, by day

reflect upon it folded, shelved, empty.
Here, on the floor behind his bed is
a bent photo—why? Were the two of
them lovers? Does it mean, where we
found it, that he forgot it or lost it

or intended a safekeeping? Should we
attempt to make contact? What if this
other man too is dead? Or alive, but
doesn't want to remember, is human?
Is it okay to be human, and fall away

from oblation and memory, if we forget,
and can't sometimes help it and sometimes
it is all that we want? How long, in
dawns or new cocks, does that take?
What if it is rest and nothing else that

we want? Is it a findable thing, small?
In what hole is it hidden? Is it, maybe,
a country? Will a guide be required who
will say to us how? Do we fly? Do we
swim? What will I do now, with my hands?


## ∾ Meditation: Surrender

As when,
into the canyon that means,
whose name—translated—
means *Without Measure, Sorrow*

from the hand that,
for so long, has meant
*give,*
but now—broken—gives in,

is released
the garland   /swag   /bouquet
(that—look,
look again—means

only as much as what it is:
eucalyptus,
kangaroo's paw,
the grass called eel),

that he, impossibly, might catch it.

## ❧ Noli Me Tangere

In the sex club, a quivering
Indian reaches out to touch
our blond god's world class abs.

Jesus shrieks, "Please don't touch! I
*like* feeling like
a hunk

of sacrificial
anonymity: politics
ain't possible

until one melts the self away
into the mind, man's inhumanity
one's point of entry

into the droning
ohm, a zillion arms twisting
in the loud gloom, our trembling

limbs entwined, the sperm
of loners spattered
everywhere."

## ❧ Sangre de Cristo

An aging intellectual collected evergreens
in the green gravel of his art museum's back yard.
Did he want my love? "The force
of my own personality has always

seemed enough for me," he whispered,
screaming when I crowned his big
bronze statue of a stallion
with my tear-soaked Speedos.

I rode alone through twinkling dust,
loving the sunset, crooning anthems
to a brand new herd of bison
minting silhouettes across the cash-green grass . . .

crossing the bridge, I bowed out
over my curled-in ram horn handlebars,
admiring my fat shadow hugging
the freshet's
        surface, its quick-
                silver glass glints . . .

in an abandoned Penitente morada,
its adobe walls like melting flesh,
I prayed, With all this beauty all
around us, does it matter if I harden?

Come again? That last late night,
a black pit bull yapped into our bedroom.
Drunk on Irish whiskey, he hollered,
"Holy hell! A hedgehog! At last!"

His nightmare was absolutely suicidal.

Red peppers dangled
from the eave of the gazebo
in which an orchestra of soldiers
droned golden oldies,

a shirtless fighter pilot waking up, humming

in damp clover.

# ❧ The Knower of the Field

Horny, tired, stumbling
down Phuket ("fuckit"?) Beach,
I suppose one can only think
about that vision of white light
I came to Asia praying
I might have. Evening burns.
The wet beach glimmers, golden.
My torso's shadow buries
this dropped coconut, split
open. I step back:
the silhouette of my bust's filled
with both the halves, as if
the brown shell were my broken
skull, the white meat, freckled
with pink sand, my exposed
brain. A boy toy watches me.
He wears nothing but cut-offs,
his hooking fingers hanged
through his belt loops.
He tiptoes closer, asks, am I
married? I nod, lying.
I glance down at his fly.
"I go back to your room."
"No," I mumble, "I can't pay
for sex." I walk away.
Just past the surf's reach,
in white, dry sand, children
built a castle of wet sand,
its keep surrounded by high
crenellated walls. Between
the beach and street, in evergreens,
the locusts scream. Another sky-
scraping hotel's under construction,
its metal skeleton erect
behind the tee-shirt shacks,

the grind and crunch of dragging
chains hurting my brain, the boy
behind me, suddenly, sobbing,
"I go your room, I have no cash,
I need to eat." "I'm sorry, I can't
give you money to make love."
My red legs throb. I feel
surrounded by the world's heat rising
from this sand like powdered bone.
The body, or the trying
to get into it
and out of it
at the same time
right now seems
the root of all
madness.


## ∾ The Pseudo-Homosexual

Hopkins had to glance away from pretty boys.
He felt safe, loving untouchables.
Moses marched down with the Word
and glared at men in make-up worshiping
the touchy-feely image.
At the Young Men's Christian Association
gym, *anyone* might freak
out,
trying to see butterflies turn into buffy bunnies,
trying to avoid their glassy glances
down
at the dumbbell rolling closer
to one's tongue.
If others make us
into positivists, can't
the shattering of all relationships
be called transcendence?

Why not toss off love,
ejaculate loudly into a squad car?
From the salad bar, I took a hunk of tuna.
In my kitchen, I set it down upon
the stomach-pink floor tiles: the fat lad deep inside me,
my sad past's inner child
whom I hate, intend to get,
scuttled out from under the icebox,
nibbled at that offering
like two men gnawing
at each other's flinching
faces. Under
my back porch,
a black bitch twists,
starving for the milk
you
*have* to put out, fucker,
more than once.


## ∾ Why Not Pleasure the Bigot's Body

The beautiful black boy, thin and strong, his abs world class, swivels
toward me, then
away.

He leaps, he's on his knees, he stretches himself flat across the stage, his tongue
twisting: he needs

anyone at all to stick
into his tighty whities
one damn dollar bill.

Pushed up against
the mirror wall,
he torques his torso, and watches

CHRISTOPHER DAVIS                                                   393

the white irises rise
into his eyes—
afraid to peek out into our faces?

My buddy believes he's defensive: "Why
can't he make eye contact?" Obviously, he can
feel

all around him our disgust: a fat
fuck just announced he don't
do chocolate.

Let me tell you,
I like my black guys
hung, not hanged.

Imagine that little nigger
dragging me into his bedroom,
allowing me to bow into his lap.

He'd fling me away,
his baby girl shrieking,
ignored, in her bedroom.

We split Illusions.
Marching across the parking lot,
I pick up a dead limb, shake it

at two buzzards circling on high,
cruising a pickup, an old troll waiting
to be picked up, maybe

loved. Waiting. Waiting.
Always caught in traffic.
Just let them try.

# ∿ Nod

In this mind
beyond dry cornstalks
I come across
my patriarch's abandoned Cadillac

the door gapes
I crawl in
try turning the wheel
it does turn

I tease the radio's knob
twiddling it between pointer and thumb
clicking it on off
clicking it on off

turning it up "all the way"
hearing nothing
taking in the pain
singing in the pain

Enough. Enough. We interrupt this whining
to broadcast more cowboy yodeling,
the starting of your engines,
gentlemen.

Who'd jump this old thang?
Poisonous pokeweed prods through the bumper.
Why not kiss its dents, fate's public sculpture?
Let it rust out here a few more days.

It might yet get us
where we need to go
if there's no solid place to go
no world called home

CHRISTOPHER DAVIS

# ∾ Against the See-Through Plastic Curtain of the West

1.

In the frigid master bedroom, the black shadow
of a negro phone cable, breeze-bothered beyond
the frost-clouded pane, snakes across the ivory wall,
whipping the sad visage of Abe Lincoln.

I picked up that print at an auction.
I bid against a bitch, her finger lifting
again, again, her bland expression clashing
with her greed: she, too, loved freedom,

or at least craved the zillion
nicks in the cheap frame, the brain-shaped grapes
carved in the comers, not by hand. Actually,
I just dropped acid, and I'm squatting

on the toilet as we speak, watching
closely the plastic curtain: see
the bamboo wiggle? Behind it,
the shower's hot fall steams.

I bow over a penny,
my bust's silhouette burying
the profile of our gentle guy,
brains blown in a theater.

2.

Trembling in a terminal, at the round end
of a glass concourse, my inner child
shrieks at its mother, "You made me
into a freak!" Around

her curls, the curving
window flares: high noon burns
the caul, fading even further
the blood-red rug, piercing

youth's forehead: youth howls
at the flashpoint, a flesh match, its voice
searing its tongue. The sun, hitting
tiny windows in the fighter touching

down, seems
to make the surface quiver
like touched water, nuking
away all the oil stains

from the forehead and the fingertips of a boy
who once pressed his whole torso to this world
to try to feel close to the transport
on which his father disappeared.

3.

Sir, even in this adult bookstore,
the cloud-white partition between you
and I hiding in twin buddy booths

can, I swear
to God, become
see-through: please

press that red
buddy button glowing
near your right temple.

Reflected in the semen-poisoned pane,
half-mirror, half-window, my body
blends with bits of thine, half-

shadowed: from your video screen,
light flickers like razors
over some stud's churning jaw,

your choice the same as mine,
the edges of our visions overlapping
in the plastic glass, jaw gnawing jaw.

My torso quivers within yours.
You tug your cock, threading
your body into thin air.

Rabbits scamper
from a runway,
then leap into a green ditch.

I rub my navel against the border
through this invisible electric fence
around my touching, moving corpse

and you,
you fucker,
cut me off,

the clear page suddenly
opaque, as white
as marble, as your come,

the black span of your arm,
at head level,
a rat in mist,

the stink of your cigar trying
to sting me
blind.

4.

The beautiful white cockatiel is dead.
Its feathers feel so smooth, so cold.
Poking my fingers through the bars,
I brush the pinion feathers of its wing

distended across the shit-caked front page.
Above its heart, a smear of red.
Had a rat wormed into the garage,
sniffed the seed inside the cage,

then bit the soft, defensive angel?
Earlier, flip-flopping around under her perch,
her wings abandoned, she bit Nancy's fingertip,
then flopped backward. Nancy's an ex-hooker.

She has AIDS. For her two girls, she penned
a poem: a drop welled through her fingerprint,
its sworls, and became petals, a blooming rose.
Across their cheeks, she smeared red war paint.

Curled in its black trash sack, the corpse
feels too heavy, too cold through this plastic,
as if death added ice to the stilled meat,
having swiped fire.

CHRISTOPHER DAVIS

## ∾ Blood Test

As the needle goes into my arm
I think of the moment
we first got into bed together:
your body prone along mine,
your shaved head against
my ribs. I kiss the stubble,
think how your anger
is the only thing you have left
as your body fails, blood cell
by blood cell. The nurse
fingers my pulse, asks
if I have nightsweats, any
unhealed marks on my body
and when I say *no,* I
hear your question as you
reach for the extra-strong
condoms on the table. You
hover over me, I
feel your swelling
between my thighs, you could
tear my inner membranes, expose
my blood to your own
and when I say no, you
want me to say it
again and again, your eyes
closing as you fling your
seed across my body until
I hear the nurse say she's
going to take the needle
out of my arm, straight
out of me. She's
quick to place the round

of cotton over the opening
and I think of the coin
placed over the eyes of
the dead. I
see the white drops of your
sperm on my stomach, watch
as your eyes open and
you see that I want it
off my body. You wet
your fingertips with the glutinous
fluid, shake them in my
face, saying *this is it, man,*
*the only life we have now.*


## ❧ Your Feet

When we climbed the black stone,
I was already in love
with your feet. I hadn't
seen them up close, so
when we made it to the top
and you lifted them into my lap,
I was shocked at how small they were.
I rubbed my palm along the arch
and thought of the Chinese girl
whose mother broke her bones
and bound her feet in the rough
sackcloth, I pulled
your socks off and pressed
the rounded bone at the ball
of your sole, you moaned
*that must be where my liver is,*
toe joints I cracked,
that must be where your spine is.
So I held your spine and massaged
your brain—and that night

RICHARD TAYSON                                                     401

we molded our bodies together
for the first time, we kissed
for five years, twenty-three days
until the first purple spot
appeared on your foot.
You cried, I
cradled it, held it
to my mouth and sucked
the death cells out, I kissed
the lesion away, arch bone,
ankle joint, fibula, I learned
to love small things,
your mouth, fist
of earth, first snow, for better
and for worse, we
settled in for the duration.


## ∽ In Sickness and in Health

For a week you lie beneath one sheet,
the fever comes, your face
darkens, the way a boy's face will
flush, the forehead hairs
dampen when his father comes at him
with a fire prod. Then the chill
comes, you sleep
beneath five blankets, your body
shaking, as a boy will freeze
and crack along a fracture line
when his parents lock him out
on the coldest night of the year.
Your head rests heavily on the pillow,
your face pale then bright
with the pink blooms like bruises,
and I know you were a boy whose father
struck him with whatever was handy—
a rifle butt, a baseball bat,

a brick, once—
and I lift the blankets
as if parting the veil that separates
us from the next world. I touch
your underwear, checking for wetness,
smell your urine on my fingers
sweet as the life still in you,
slide the cloth down
your skinny hips and skinny legs,
take the sponge from the bowl
and clean you off. I wipe
the sticky sweet from your penis,
see how shriveled and clammy the skin is,
how the tiny hairs are braided
together, curled
as if frozen beneath ice
and I come even closer, see the pink
flush of the head, the greenish
web of veins on your thighs,
the mole on your left testicle.
I think how many times
you have wanted me to explore
your body, in love, and I
dry you off, pull up
a fresh pair of underwear, climb
into bed beside you. I press
my clothed body against your ribs,
shoulders, your fine intelligent face
with the nose I've come to love
despite its imperfection,
I feel your eyelids move
beneath my fingers
as you wake for the first time
in two days, and I kiss
your forehead and dirty
silver hair, comb out
the knots, your whole life
opening in the room.

RICHARD TAYSON

[gary asleep in his recliner.  this prison work clobbers him.  today let the men stand unguarded]

gary asleep in his recliner.      this prison work clobbers him.      today let the men stand unguarded
he is overwhelmed by his own cells.      a furtive shiv behind his eyes:      searchbearns opaque and anil

he dreams a wall:   desert beyond where nothing is not jagged or barbed.      breathing hard he scales
hands numb nopales:      swollen but withering inward nerveless.      the sensation of pinpricks

one long last watch:      ectomorphic lockdown.      he draws the early pension.      incomplete his sentence

# [tall and thin *and young and lovely* the michael with kaposi's sarcoma *goes walking*]

tall and thin *and young and lovely* the michael with kaposi's sarcoma *goes walking*
*and when he passes each one he passes goes* "whisperwhisperwhisper."   star of beach blanket babylon

the sea washes his ankles with its white hair.        he sambas past the empty lifeguard tower
days like these who wouldn't swim at own risk:   the horizon smiles like a karaoke drag queen
broad shoulders of surf shimmy forth as if to say "aw baby, sell it, sell it."      he's working again

towels lie farther apart.        the final stages:   he can still do a dazzling turn *but each day*
smiles grow a little sharper.        he blames it on the bossanova.        he writes his own new arrangements

[now the mirrored rooms seem comic. shattered light: I once entered the world through dryice fog]

"this was the season disco finally died"
—Kevin Killian, *Bedrooms Have Windows*

now the mirrored rooms seem comic.     shattered light:     I once entered the world through dryice fog
not quite fabulous.     just young and dumb and full.     come let me show you a sweep of constellations:

16, I was anybody's.     favorite song:  *dance into my life* [donna summer] and they did dance

16, first fake i.d.     I liked *walk* away  [donna summer]  I ran with the big boys

18, by now I knew how to move.     on top of the speakers.          *give me a break* [vivien vee]

19, no one could touch me.   donna summer found god.   I didn't care.    *state of independence*

20, the year I went through the windshield.          sylvester sang *I want to be with you in heaven*
I said "you go" and "scared of you."   I listened to pamala stanley *I don't want to talk about it*

[this is my last trick: if he has eyes they are escaping. the neighbors won't be able to describe]

a song of Sal Mineo

this is my last trick:    if he has eyes they are escaping.    the neighbors won't be able to describe
when he flees his mane fans through the alley.    jerusalem palms beating against the doorway

in the blue hollywood hills behind the white hollywood sign where the falcons nest:    I had lain
every letter shivered delighted under the swooping.    my feet drawn up into a careful vee

in the restroom at *the probe* I welcomed a sweet thrust.    pomegranate droplets dotted the commode

he was the disembodied voice of the planetarium.    I want to pretend it did not happen in the dark

[how would ed lower himself to sleep with her. an elaborate rigging of wheels and piano wire]

how would ed lower himself to sleep with her.      an elaborate rigging of wheels and piano wire
butching up for the role:     "tell the katzenjarnrners to amscray."      he'd banish her barnes
or he'd swagger her out to the supper club:     the perfect beard.      cupping her hand on his arm

& bob might never have known.      no latent signs:     ed ogling skirts.      mounding potatoes like breasts
he didn't come home late & stanky.      smelling of imitation passion [by lez taylor] & warm kootchie

yes bob understood infidelity:      elevated it to a high art.      a social circle ripe with peccadillos
but the strings were known and pulled with masterful care:      punch & punch.      punch & no judy

[only the cruisy toilets will suffer this rascal. mmm, darlings . . . your smiles taste like porcelain]

only the cruisy toilets will suffer this rascal.            mmm, darlings . . . your smiles taste like porcelain
have I told you lately blahblahblah oh no?            pity.            but I hear the curfew knell & so must bid adieu

you alone would believe in the fictive heart:            scarified as you are with that shape it's given

no permanent fixture the flesh.            remember a match skating in a urinal.            I escape like a gasp

your names are unsummonable.            extinguished cigs.            I reach toward your ceiling.            dangled man

D. A. POWELL

## [sheet wrapped as a burnoose. about his head]

sheet wrapped as a burnoose.    about his head
tubes fill his mouth with opium:  diversions

keep him occupied:  a palestine whose defenses
are suppressed.    territory lost.    frail arms
impuissant:   his sky is a rattling dry gourd

here is a man from a country without borders
anyone can cross over:    share his bed.    lazaretto


## [your torso: enticing to insects. like me]

your torso:  enticing to insects.    like me
they want to bug you.    bugger you.    cocoons
pupate in those buttocks of adobe:    anthills

untimely your nectar draws me:    bouquet
exchanged for a pinwheel.    the foiled sentinel
over the stone sayonara which brailles itself
as a curious welcome mat: you took it for a hat

webs are your veil:    tumulus beetles the maids
scramble to catch those spikenards.    a demimonde
by whom you are compromised.    in this position
imagination might have wedded us.    to share

# [you're thin again handsome. in our last]

you're thin again handsome.    in our last
hour together I'll be dabbing gravy off
your lip:  stuck out.    an infirmary stoop

how can anything perplex us more than words
the pause in which we chew:  parapraxia
I feed you lines.    you're a poor actor now
flubbing the bit part.    indignant us both

I'll want better for you than institutional
lunch in white paper.    pee stained underwear
a brief brief career as the delicious romantic lead


# [third-world hunger strikes you. midtown bus]

*a song of the virus*

third-world hunger strikes you.    midtown bus
passion settles in the tenderloin.    ravenous

you thrive on the gaunt busboy:  chops
respond pavlovian to the tinkling of poverty

your wallet can afford you.  some protection
an allowance to rut among the cheaper cuts
a scavenger:  you feed off them.    skinny skinny legs

D. A. POWELL

## [you don't have syphilis. the doctor says]

you don't have syphilis.    the doctor says
you don't have hepatitis.    he says
you aren't diabetic.    the doctor says

cholesterol level normal.    blood pressure
good.    he says you've got great reflexes
the doctor says these things.    he's the doctor

he says I *do* have a bit of bad news.    he says
just like that: I *do* have a bit of bad news
not a *real* doctor remember: a physician's *assistant*


## [cherry elixir: the first medication. so mary poppins]

cherry elixir: the first medication.    so mary poppins
a chance to acclimate: an infant dose.    a baby step
supplanting pneumonia half a teaspoon at a time

until the tablet can be tolerated.    with adult strength
my throat constricts around unspeckled eggs:  rosy boa

everybody talks about the cocktail:  sounds delicious
I think in jello flavors.    picturing umbrellas in tall glass
the cocktail up.    the cocktail over.    straws and serviettes

not a steel spansule.    not a fistful of bloated tictacs.    no burn
in the bowels the belly & the mouth.    want my goddamn cocktail

## ∾ A Plague for Kit Marlowe

*In Memory of Derek Jarman:*
*"I place a delphinium, Blue, upon your grave."*

I

I don't trust beauty anymore, when will I stop
believing it, repeating wilted petals? He loves
me not. Delphinium, cornflower, lupine, flowers
I've never seen: forget-me-not, fringed gentian,
lobelia, love-in-a-mist, old names of a world
that never was mine, the last of England's green
and pleasant island, sheer blue above the whited
Dover cliffs. Blue fog spelled out across an August sky
the blinded retina keeps, blue frost of a February
dawn, blue hour where you're dead. Agapanthus, also
called lily-of-the-Nile, closer to my lost continent. Pressed
in this anthology of hours, the serifed letters keep
for years of pages, film on water. Scilla, flax, large periwinkle.
Nothing is wasted but regret. Bluebell, blue flag.

II

The gardens of Adonis wither like burnt pages. Beauty
is an infection, I see now, the paper-thin skin written on water
like hyacinth, lily and anemone floating to decay. The filmy blossoms
fall apart like my hands, like *shallow rivers to whose falls*
*Melodious birds sing madrigals.* Narcissus was pushed, drowned in
a flood of song; Leander's white shoulder is coral echoing
the Dardanelles. *For in his looks were all that men desire.*

I tramp through a closed garden of cures, Foscarnet, Retrovir,
Zovirax, gaudy bouquets which wilt expensively
before ever reaching you. Roferon, Sporanox,
Leukine and Cytovene: those plastic flowers lose color
in the windows of a funeral home, pink wax and wire
accumulating dust like any dead. *And I will make thee*
*beds of roses And a thousand fragrant posies.*

III

*Saw ye him whom my soul loveth?* Will culture cure me, keep me
from harm? It let him die. I wanted some white immortality,
but find *I from myself am banish'd* in these lines, ghost body
of the light I poured away. My hands are stained and helpless
here, black ink spilled uselessly as any blood. The heart
is attached to a branching tree of capillaries, veins and arteries,
oxygen flowering like amaryllis, rose of Sharon, vermilion trumpets
forced in January, Sebastian's month. *Why should you love him*
*whom the world hates so?* The heart wants to keep opening
for seven years of any kind of luck, for any body's blood. Small bells
of paperwhite narcissus fill someone's winter with an idea of scent,
released of color, shape, or sense of touch. Who wouldn't wish
to linger in the sensual world that won't spare me, or let me hold
a living hand to him, *the king in whose bosom let me die.*

IV

I wanted something musical for you, notes floating
on the margins of a stranger's days and works: a lark, an air
of spring somewhere, my voice not clouded under error
just this once. How fine the song I wanted then,
changing from major to minor and, strangely,
back again. The knowing gods must think so little
of my minor wishes, all the sentimental tunes
I've memorized off-key: repeating every error helplessly
to make a song's my one refrain. I suppose I die

a little every day, not noticing it yet. I'm gathering dust
from an occasional shaft of light, I'm dotting all the i's
whole notes repeat, like why or cry. There's no finer tune
than afternoons clouded with luck all spring, the margin of error
I'd call a song. This happens every time I try to say good-bye.


## ∾ Nights and Days of Nineteen-Something

*For Marilyn Hacker*

Midsummer with other men's lovers, fumbles
on a living room couch, significance asleep
upstairs: I come through the door, I come
through the door, I came and was

conquered by tensed thighs, taut buttocks.
Asses, asses, lust from lust, a must
of sweat on matted hair, a spill of semen
down my thigh. (Classicism revised, or

what shall we do with a drunken
torso, machine shop of body parts, some
of them functional. Pink petals
of an asshole opening under tongue,

pink cockhead swollen to bursting
purple balloon. It caught in the trees.)
Who am I to think that
I'm not always on my knees

taking in some stranger strayed too far
from what he wouldn't want
to work for, paying out the line
we've always used. *Hey, do you want*

*a ride?* I'm walking through a field
of safety glass without my shoes; it itches,
like a sneeze. (Say it, no things but in
ideas: desire, denial; define, defiler. Decide,

then choose for me. Mother may I
go down on this man?) The tuck
in my jeans itches afterward, salt
smudge under my knees. This

is for your body made out of words,
the worse for wear if you were there, or
where I wanted me to be. *And where
were you last night young man?* (Here's

a rumor someone passed along: I believed in
his present tense, wrapped in tinfoil and a tissue
paper ribbon, his cock worn to the right
and the several layers that kept me from it,

the shirt and several layers most of all.)
*If you have many desires your life
will be interesting,* a modernism of poverty
and stained sheets, twin bed he went to

with me, came up for air and other things.
It was never sex I wanted, the grand et cetera
with a paper towel to wipe it up. I wanted him
to talk to me about Rimbaud while

I sucked him off in the park, drunk
as any wooden boat and tasting of old cigarettes
and Bailey's Irish Cream, my juvenilia. *Don't talk
with your mouth full.* (In the clearing

at the bottom of the artificial hill, his two hands
covered every part of me until I couldn't be seen,
a darkness past the burnt-out lamp post.
We came up empty-handed. *You're so empty*

*-headed sometimes.)* I never wanted love
from him, his needs adhesive, clinging like
cold sweat, old sperm; I never wanted him
to ask anything of me but *suck my big*

*white cock.* I come home sticky with
his secrecies, wash them all
off. You were my justice, just my means
to sex itself, end justified by the mean

size of the American penis. Just keep going
that way. You'd like to sleep, you'd like to be
left alone for miles of near-misses, missteps, mirrors
in a public bathroom, all mistake

and brief apology. (My lakefront myths of you
all insufficient to the taste of come
lapping my tongue.) The jogging path
curves up into that dark place in the trees

just past the rusted totem pole. Let me
lick salt from white skin in the moon's first light
when it lies brightest: argent, ardent, concrete
and utter falsehood. Comely, my comeuppance,

comfort me: come to mind at any time,
come again for me. Take me to the boy.

REGINALD SHEPHERD

# ∾ The Beautiful

incertitudes are buying shirts
across the street, shopping for another
guise, layer of gauze, mottle
across the mystery of no anyone
in any light. All power lacking

matter, gods (decoys of gods)
that approximate: ghost bodies
somewhat like men. Who wouldn't
own such excellence, own up to damage
done already? Flushed out

of yellowed brick and stone
by attention's blue smoke,
the visible world stumbles
into form: a grammar of wander
and spectacle sidewalks learn

from newsprint and pasted petals
that precede the leaves, flimmer
from branch to ground. To walk behind
beauty as a shadow at noon, perfected
perpendicular, is difference, sundial

gnomon's pain (the manifest
pinned to pure principle, Mediterranean
rêve): proximate loss left in the other
life, where body arrests its tasks
to break for the last instance

but one. (Bracket this, boy murdered
in old paper, asleep across the fold's
spoiled ink: chest open
for inspection, three-color separation
blood soiling the reading

fingertips. Bees build a honeycomb
to seal his halted-open mouth, his carrion
tongue, an eloquence of liquid light
seeps out of bloated lips the clumsy gods
have broken into.) The gods

go home alone, a lake's
translucent body reiterates my face
in dissolve: smudge of stigma blotting
day's remains, a surf of stuttering
stars singing *I'll never fall.*


## ❧ Les Semblables

Stringent syntax of brick dust, cracked
leaves, broken up
pavement and a dead finch, dun
feathers dusted with brick
grit, all the same
color, mine:
                    something
will be built there
I can't afford, blue sky
of your terrifying mouth,
my roof without a ceiling
leaking wind
                    Adore, a door
burnt open, lintel, jamb still
standing, salvaged brick
and timber:
                    "carrying the load
above an opening"
                              Persistent drone
of sky, high tension wire, jet
contrail, drift of Canada

geese incised on sky, clouds
cut off mid-shape, trailing
water particles
                    Wingspan at meridian
turned on an anecdotal wheel
a clutch of ruined wind

Strict noon criteria, qualifying,
qualifying, when isn't a god unlucky
for his lovers

## ∾ Semantics at Four P.M.

He smiles, says *What's happening?*
and I say somewhere
someone's setting electrodes to someone's testicles
who's been immersed two hours in ice water

up to his shoulders, he can't remember
what day it used to be. Somewhere someone
is being disemboweled with a
serrated blade, fish-knife

to slit open two fresh trout
he had for dinner last
week, Wednesday celebration
sizzling in its battered aluminum pan

over an open campfire
in a clearing, gleaming
pan and fish and fire and the water
that put out the fire, and

he looks down at his intestines, small
and large uncoiling, spoiling
by the unpaved road, surprised
the slick should glisten so, even

at noon, this close
to the equator, is it still summer
there, I never can remember
seasons. Several things are

happening, someone is being kicked repeatedly
in the ribs by three cops (he's black, blue
by now too, purple boot
marks, bruise treads), someone else

keeps falling against the wet cement floor
of his holding cell, he can't stop
falling, somebody
stop him, then he does, stopped watch, old

-fashioned, with a broken
spring coil mechanism, and someone
could find it face-down on the sidewalk, hold it
up to the light, say *I can fix this,*

but doesn't. Somewhere four teenaged boys
are playing hackeysack by a stream bed
on the verge of story, one of them
has an erection he wants

to go down, and someone thinks about
dinner, someone says *Sure looks like rain.*

Reginald Shepherd

# ❧ Little Hands

1.


Here actors estrange themselves
from acts. Glare ladles light
across the radius, high canopies
luxuriant with epiphytes, trees
are shaken into green, drench
of wind disturbing leaves
to drunken semaphores: little
hands designing new catamites
for outmoded gods.


2.


At this time every year
divinity died, the Adonis
flowed red with his blood:
clay run-off from the Lebanon.


3.


Chipped singing of arrowheads
and off-white statuary scree
plowed up in a burnt west field
declining a little into afternoon
(some columns broken-off
mid-thought) rings against
well-rusted blades: a waste
of monuments, miles of ravens
and manure, rivers
with the names of trees,
the Cedar flooding summer.

Rome's staple crop
was wheat—called corn—, along

with barley, raised for stock
feed and some places
for beer: peas and beans
also, though forbidden
by Pythagoras. The slow
-maturing olive; figs, pome
-granates, plums; grapevines
trained on a variety of trees.

4.

The man becomes a boy eventually
(blank body a white page
where wishes write themselves): shape
left behind by the sculpture wind,
but stamped with it nonetheless. Certain
human behaviors propagate gods,
nostalgia for the whole he's been
referred to: an exercise of will
around the block, through the park
and down the hill, the possibilities
still unexhausted. Some are games
and some have numbers, some
are hollow, make a ringing sound.

5.

Silence, item, silence.

6.

The god fucks himself with a fig branch
above the open grave, admirer
of hopeless machines—starling
pasted to the street, dysfunctional
flying contraption—, the god
forsakes himself for his own sake

(pledged to slick feathers
frescoed on funerary pavement),
takes himself back to him. *Whore,*
they honor him in caves
and tearoom stalls, alleys
and temple courtyards. Color
is light's continuity, the stem
still new to the trunk, leaf
darkening to fruit, to seeds.

6.

Mere world, where every man's
the artist of himself, body
his medium, interference (an inference
at most). The statues sweating, overflowing
with the fear of form, prefabricated
weather on the other side of glass:
cute guys in various states of disrepair
sighted from across the burning bridge,
and voices in salt water singing
"pale Gomorrah." I walked into my ocean,
meet me under the whale.

## ❧ A Poet's Education

*for Derek Walcott*

In fact, the classroom overlooked a street
That ended in a parking lot. "How quaint,"
I thought, a bit annoyed by my small desk.
I wasn't nervous really, I was mad.
The river they referred to in the ad
Was far enough away—across Bay State
(The asphalt driveway had a name), then down
A grassy knoll that bordered Storrow Drive,
Beyond which, yes, one *"glimpsed"* the briny Charles—
I had a better chance of seeing Cuba

When gazing through that dingy window pane.
Of course, I wanted it to be romantic
I wanted it to be unlike the stiff
Cadavers I had picked apart in labs
At Harvard Med; I wanted it to *be* alive,
The pounding pulse of lambs telling me
The body's truths in terms I understood.
I thought of Bishop, Lowell, Sexton, Plath—
Their workshops where the heart was bared without
The scalpel's blade, by instruments more sharp.
I wasn't nervous; serious for sure,

And proud I'd gotten in on scholarship.
I'd practiced how I'd introduce myself,
Respectfully, but not obsequious,
Perhaps a droll remark that showed I'd read
His work. The street and parking lot below
Provided little inspiration; still,
I thought I could impress him with a line

Or two of his I'd memorized. OK,
It's true, I was afraid of what he'd think
Of me—a careless dilettante, a wanna-be,
A fake, a ruffled-pink-sleeved *mariachi*
Who danced a bit too awkwardly, my feet

As much ungainly as they were too broad.
I worried that my peers had planned applause,
Or worse, cold apples polished to a shine
So bright that even a St. Lucian might
Be tempted. Mangos and cigars, the buzz
Of black mosquitos, the ocean's wish
To eat the island in its roaring jaws
Of waves—the fruits of my experience,
I hoped despite my nagging reticence,
Might still appeal. Each pun, each lively rhyme
Internalized by all my prison time—
Three years had passed when not a single word

Escaped from me to find the freedom of
The page—seemed ready for *his* medicine,
Seemed eager to express a kind of love,
To reinvent my lost Caribbean.
Then suddenly, as if on cue, he entered:
So dignified yet rumpled, stifling a yawn.
The words he spoke I wish I still remembered—
I've lost them in the spotlight that my awe
Directed toward the star that took the stage.
He outlined what his expectations were,
And warned us if we didn't read, his rage
Would be exacted on our timid verse
Which, by the way, we would not read in class—
Too many *finished* poems awaited us.

So much for my ingratiating chatter.
Hart Crane it was, then Auden, Dickinson—
We memorized, and scanned because it mattered—

Then Dante, xeroxed for us in Italian,
He challenged us to sound it out until
The language and the rhymes had filled
Our mouths with music we could taste, if not
Completely figure out. I learned to see
A loveliness that never tried to be,
The beauty in what once had seemed mundane—
What Mr. Bleaney took so properly
In hand, those prepositions ending lines
While Gunn's sad captains turned away.
Then Meredith's raw sonnets came one day:
So utterly redemptive, mordantly gay,

And written more as drama than as verse.
Performance! Even in a failing marriage,
The strange bravado to acknowledge
That poetry is singing in a voice
Undampened by its small, constricted space—
He said that resoluteness was the key.
My sonnets, sheaves of them, came back to me
With qualified encouragement, his face
Betraying humor when he said he hoped
I'd write a hundred more someday. I sulked
At first, convinced he thought my writing sucked.
The last of winter's dirty snow in heaps
Along that semblance of a street, I left
That day pretending I would not return.
Yet something stopped me. Something I had learned.
His dusty classroom beckoned, high aloft.

# ✧ The Battle Hymn of the Republic

Defending you, my country, hurts
My eyes. I see the drums, the glory,
The marching through the gory
Unthinkable mud of soldier's guts

And opened hearts: I want to serve.
I join the military,
Somehow knowing that I'll never marry.
The barracks' silence as I shave

Is secretive and full of cocks.
I think to myself, *What if I'm a queer,*
*What if too many years*
*Go by and then my brain unlocks—*

The days seem uniformed,
Crisp salutes in all the trees;
A sandstorm buries the casualties
Of a war. *What if I were born*

*This way,* I think to myself,
*What if I were dead,*
*An enemy bullet in my head?*
I see the oil burning in the Gulf,

Which hurts my eyes. My sergeant cries.
Now he's a real man—
I sucked his cock behind a van
In the Presidio, beneath a sky

So full of orange clouds
I thought I was in love.
I think to myself, *What have*
*I become?* I lose myself in the crowds

Of the Castro, the months go by
And suddenly they want to lift the ban.
I don't think they can.
I still want to die

My death of honor, I want to die
Defending values I don't understand;
The men I see walking hand in hand
Bring this love song to my mind.

## ❧ Difficult Body

A story: There was a cow in the road, struck by a semi—
half-moon of carcass and jutting legs, eyes
already milky with dust and snow, rolled upward

as if tired of this world tilted on its side.
We drove through the pink light of the police cruiser,
her broken flank blowing steam in the air.

Minutes later, a deer sprang onto the road
and we hit her, crushed her pelvis—the drama reversed,
first consequence, then action—but the doe,

not dead, pulled herself with front legs
into the ditch. My father went to her, stunned her
with a tire iron before cutting her throat, and today I think

of the body of St. Francis in the Arizona desert,
carved from wood and laid in the casket,
lovingly dressed in red and white satin

covered in petitions—medals, locks of hair,
photos of infants, his head lifted and stroked,
the grain of his brow kissed by the penitent.

O wooden saint, dry body. I will not be like you,
carapace. A chalky shell scooped of its life.
I will leave less than this behind me.

# ◯ Unmade Bed

You remember the billboard of the unmade bed on Lafayette and Fourth? It's finally down. It peeled and faded and last week they took it down. The city changes like that, after so much of the same. Things get erased or gone over again.

Three days ago I read about these men who steal cows—curious. They don't take them alive, but bring a truck into the pasture and slaughter the beasts right out in the open, in the middle of the night. They pack the meat, cut in rough shapes, and leave the hides and innards, bones, for dogs to scrap over and haul to duty yards. Farmers wake and find nothing left, their fences cut wide open, a gaped mouth in the morning, the field empty.

Went shopping with C. and spent an hour finding her lipstick. It was so important, just the right shade, you know? We kept smearing them on the backs of our hands, little cosmetic bruises, turning each tongue down its silver throat, dozens, each wrong. I have this tissue with her lip print, perfect *Russian Sable*, not too much brown, though not garish, and I've promised to buy her several if I ever find a match.

And me thinking of the panels of your body pinning me down, your hair. I haven't had it that good since. I saw a doctor. There was a lecture I could have done without, and I'm fine, so don't worry. When they took the blood and I saw the three vials on the counter, little jewels, so red—I could almost see the cells colliding, a galaxy. Forgive me. There will be more mornings, waking alone, when a print of me in the bed is laundered and pinned on a line, is gone.

## ∾ No Place Like Home

On the Kansas highway I see children being useful, driving cars. Twelve or thirteen years old, boys mostly, peering over dashboards in pickups with rusted wheel wells and gravel on the floor. At a stop sign in Hays I catch myself staring at the tanned bare arm hanging out of a truck window. We are landlocked. The sky stretching out above us is huge and useless. I look up at this boy, at his brown face and wheat-blond head, and my heart catches and I panic.

In rest stops all across America, men wait in cars for sex to happen to them, the burning cities of their radios glowing, the voices ringing out like instructions for a new route home. There is that altitude that happens after sex, a heady chime like crystal, and thumbing their vinyl steering wheels I imagine the men hear it too. I have stopped to read the graffiti on the bathroom's beetle-colored walls. A crude phallus points the way to an empty stall, and dates tell of dozens of afternoons spent parked under a low tree's blunt canopy, eyes peeled on the soda machine, waiting for no one.

When did it all begin? I spend the evening staring out the motel window, a man gone thin and unhappy with diligence, my fear at this place generous. At the grocery the woman at the check-out smiles and I see something familiar in the way her grin pulls at her eyes, slipping my carton of milk in a bag and handing it over, a secret between just her and me. I pay and walk outside, gun the engine, drive out on the empty strip.

This is America—beetles clustered with the harvest, dust roads trundling off at perfect angles, and signs proclaiming unbearable roadside attractions.

❧ Slutty

> *Life is inevitably disgusting*
> —Auden

We couldn't get near the bathroom
    with all the models

holding back their hair
over the porcelain bowls.

The chef barely knew how to fling
parsley, so in the end    no one mourned

the hors d'oeuvres' demise.
The champagne was another story.

    A great mystery
to me as well you should be,

your legs seemed longer when
you cartwheeled under the streetlights:

*Straddle me and I'll give you*
*all the gossip, all the sugar.*

    —What would one do
with *all* the sugar anyway?

Caress can still be the right word,
the streets    dark and aflash

with rain    sliding through the city
on its way. A third party wants

in, that warmth.  You love
the noise stars make when they fall.

In the morning        we are knocked around
by the wind        of approaching trains.

You play the drawn-on eyebrow,
        you play the figure-me-out—

        I'd like something too
                to tear at me.


## ∾ Knowing You Could Is Better than Knowing You Will

I must see you; let's meet at the fringes of respectability
at quarter past nine.  We could straddle the oft-licked
curb, it's the repetition we like.  I promise not to say
anything louche when you buss the backs of my fingers.

What is that noise coming from the other side of the river—
maybe pavement being set perfectly straight, or a woozy guitar.
In light like this we become automatic and can reach each other—
what a difficult noise to hold and clearly making love is all that.

Juiced, I'm sure we're taller than before and don't miss
what we've lost track of.  Meanwhile, the streetlights blush
in their globes as if they could tell how the party towed us
along like a chain of rollerblading kids latched onto a bus.

If you want, we can go swimming down by the electrical plant
since, as you know, the water runs out warmest from its pipes.
Bring on the horse tranquilizers
for my listing heart is pecker-fretted, truculent and true.

# ∾ Shine

I got your letter thanks it nearly kicked
me in the heart would have fallen
into the lily-mouth of a collapsing star

as though the whole continent were made
of glycerin your slightest movement
could create a ripple to reach this

warp and shimmer at the core leaving
an imprint of your body still next to me
and could keep you if I ever managed

o wretched word to align our radio waves
as I am yours spread my fingers break
apart the light when you shine you shine


# ∾ Tingling in the Extremities

Here is a misplaced forecast from the spring:

a big *Sorry* in the al fresco restaurant,
your whole posse gathered to see
what you've become.

Nothing worth repeating
        over the tin-can telephone—
the one you love fills your water glass
and is gone.

You cut your finger on the lobster
and glide down the walk.

Swift now.


MARK BIBBINS

A summer of traffic,
        the stereo works
and the sun cooperates.

        We are forever going down
        for the sand, the quivering air
holding the bodies aloft.

The music blurs and everyone
involved is in on it.

        *You'll love our m-m-malts.*
        "I love a promise," you confide.

We have forgotten the need
for transitions,

or haven't learned it yet
        beside the clam shacks

where we act
alluring and young.

# JUSTIN CHIN (1969-)

## ❧ Cocksucker's Blues

Beauty does not come cheap
but there are enough discount stores out there.
Pennies turn to dimes,
dimes into nothing but hard time.
I walk the city with my eyes shut
against the flesh crawl of need,
ducking into alleyways and bookstores
lined with pathetic creatures begging for blow
and a buffed jock named Chad begging
for one more token, one more day
at a time. It's enough to keep
the saddest cocksucker happy.

You said you used to be so beautiful
that people would pay to suck you off
and you didn't even have to cum to collect
but now you would let anyone have you
you have no choice, you said,
and I agreed and tried to make you
feel like a million bucks for $4.99.

Buy your beauty:
At 10, it tastes like spit
      at 20: melted government margarine
      at 30: Elmer's glue paste
      at 40: vaseline
don't bother going any higher,
*pack your bags, and hit the road, Jack,*
it'll never taste like what you paid for
no matter how high you can get.

You crowned yourself Queen of the Poppers.
Sucked so much amyl nitrate
that the vapors were the only thing
holding your tongue together,
the Tic-Tac of your dependency coats your words.
Your silk suit crumpled, your body in a cold sweat
your flaccid penis tasting like stale elbow grease
your icy balls stretched into a tight bruised blue
to match your lips that turned turquoise hours ago.
You said, you needed a few more lines to turn it up.
Damaged goods, but who isn't these days?

In Vegas at the Mirage,
Sigfried and Roy's white Tigers trapped
in a perpetual daylight, 24 hours of fake light
in a plexiglass cage with a glittering waterfall
landscape out of The Snow Queen.
Poor tigers held up to the scrutiny
of the ugly sour-faced masses
decked in sequins, appliques and wash-and-wear,
spongy folk who have lost so much currency
shoved down metal slots.
Only impotence can drive someone
to look at tigers at 3 in the morning.

At 3 in the morning,
I follow reflections and piss-stained corridors
to bedsits and broomsticks.
The first time the first time the first time.
He was a wino a bum a banker a chemist a greengrocer.
He was a lawyer a doctor a systems analyst.
*His name was Rico, he wore a diamond.*
He slapped me around he fucked my face
he came in my mouth when I asked him not to.
He showed me pictures of younger boys
polaroids of bodies without heads, hands holding dicks,
fingers in asses, smooth armpits

and said I want you to be just like that.
I wanted to die when he got too mean and too rough
I wanted to kill him when he apologized
and offered a sandwich, a ride home when it was done
I wanted to swallow more, swallow more.
Maybe that wasn't the first time,
it could have been the 2nd or 3rd
it could have been every subsequent time.
It could also be nothing but a done-up jack-off lie.
*Just one for my baby and one for the road.*

I crawl out at dawn
into the soup of light and scarred gratitude.

A crazed Born-Again bearing a sandwich board
approaches, gives me a tract
that will save me from the evils of the material world.
*Repent*, he says, *repent.*
*There is healing in the blood in the Lamb of Christ.*

580 billion babies have died in my mouth.
580 billion more will follow, their daddies abandoning them,
like AIDS-infected darlings, in spit and in confession.
I repent nothing.

I would do much more.

I would dance barefoot on shards of your broken beauty.
I would call you Daddy in the face of my sadist master.

I would match Rod Stewart's record
12 pints and they won't have to pump it out of me,
I will choke it down and keep it down.

Ask me anything. Tell me anything.
I want all beauty to weep for me.
I wear my wounds on my tongue,

JUSTIN CHIN

my dependency is my king,
and my immortal imperfection, my fractured wings.


## ∾ Buffed Fag

I want to be a buffed fag.

When I walk down the street I want folks to do a double take, gawk in disbelief, mouths agape, and say, "Oh my god! That faggot is so buffed!"

I'll spend six hours in the gym every day, blasting my quads, doing leg lifts, squats and presses and curls so I will be The Buffed Fag Of Your Dreams. I will pose and flex my muscles while having sex because that's what turns the boys on. I will have them worship my muscles and tell me how good I look as they chow down on my glutes. I'll bench press until I look like the Tazmanian Devil of Bugs Bunny cartoons, as I walk down the street in all my big chest skinny waist top heavy neanderthal arm drag swagger, thinking I'm the hottest shit in the universe and I am . . .

Because I am a Buffed Fag (at least I want to be). I will have sex with the towel boy at Muscle Systems, the guy who makes the protein shakes at Gold's, and the trainer at Market Street Gym; and I too will be able to pull off the bad fag attitude thing, previously reserved solely for store clerks at Tower Records and Video.

Oh, I do so want to be a Buffed Fag, hanging out in the locker rooms of gyms to pick up other buffed fags and to score injectable steroids, remembering to wash my needles with bleach and never sharing them, because I don't want to be a diseased fag, just a buffed fag with a dick shrunken to the size of a Vick's inhaler; but I won't care, because I am a buffed fag.

I will scan the L. L. Bean, J. Crew, and International Male catalogs and pick who I will marry; last week it was the one-piece perforated lycra jumpsuit, this week it's the low cut eazy-breathe fundoshi, next week it's the tan-thru bikini underwear, and folks will believe me as I partake of my fantasies because I'm a buffed fag and I have the god-given right to sail through the world being *just like everybody else,* to have the whole puny world owe me a living because everybody loves a Buffed Fag (even though they're assholes), and everybody listens to a buffed fag (even though they have the IQ and personality of a box of cat hair).

You know you too want to be a buffed fag, you can't help it as you watch them waddle down the street sure that folks would move out of their way, downing their protein shakes, spirulina shakes, shaking their way down into the psyche of Ooo-Ooo-Baby-Hot-Baby, boogieing on down to their little techno-trance dance clubs breeding ground display cases for buffed fag bodies. So c'mon, what's stopping you? Decency? Pride? (Forget it.) A sense of self-worth? (Ha.) Intelligence? A semblance of a life? (Forget that). Let's all be Buffed Fags and the whole damn scrawny world will belong to us.

## ❧ Lick My Butt

Lick the dry shit out of my sweaty buttcheeks

I've had my hepatitis shots so it's okay

Lick my butt
cos I'm an angry ethnic fag
& I'm in so much pain
so lick my butt

& the next time
when there's a multicultural extravaganza
& I'm asked for referrals
I can say
   "I know this guy,
   he's really cool,
   he licked my butt."

Lick my butt & tell me about
Michel Foucault's theories of deconstruction
& how it applies to popular culture,
a depressed economy & this overwhelming
tide of alienation.

Lick my butt from the center to the margins
& all the way back again.

JUSTIN CHIN            

Read Noam Chomsky in bed to me & lick my butt.

Lick my butt & give me my Prozac.
Lick my butt & call your mother, she misses you.
Flea-dip the cat & lick my butt.
Recycle & lick my butt.

Lick my butt like you really mean it.
Don't just put your tongue there
because you think it's something you should do
Do it cos you really really want to lick my butt.

My butt didn't always liked to be licked;
on the contrary, it hated anything wet
and sloppy, poking blindly
at its puckered dour grimace.
All it wanted was a nice pat,
an occasional squeeze,
a good warm seat and snug underwear.

It was happy with those,
but then all those other butts started
crashing in on its turf,
on the sidewalks and under my bed,
there were all these butts that said,
          no, demanded,
LICK ME.
My butt got tired of all that shit
& it just had to see what the fuss was all about.

At first it approached
the licking with extreme caution,
making sure all the checks
& balances were clearly present.

Hey—my butt had ever reason to be careful
it knows where it's been;

it's had enough of this bigotry &
poverty & violence
it's been on the wrong end of muggings & bashings
it's been working like a damn dog for years to make ends meet
it's been on the lam, on the block, on the contrary
& on sale for far too long

       so when that first slobber, smack,
slurp found its way into that
crack & up that uptight little asshole
it was like the Gay Pride Parade,
the Ice Capades, the Macy's Thanksgiving Day Parade
and Christmas happening all at once.

Now when I walk down the street
and you see me smiling
it's because I'm imagining
your tongue nestled in my buttcheeks
flicking away like a lizard
in a mad tweak.

Lick my butt & I'll lick yours;
we'll deal with shit of the world later.


## ᔌ Communion, Said the Barfly

    There are so many good-looking men here tonight, did you meet anyone
yet, I always meet bloody tourists who only wanna fuck, then love you long
distance, make you stupid promises of going to Alaska together or Washington
together, suck dick in Redwood HahaLand, did you meet anyone yet, what you
like anyway, look at that one over there, I wanna fuck him, he looks sick
though, sometimes I worry though, I want another drink, you want something,
I met five guys in the last two days, all out-of-towners, no hope to find anyone
who stays here in this provincial hick town, everybody is such pussyshit ugly
trolls, I hate being troll bait, how can you stand it, I wanna leave this place,

there's so many good-looking men around, don't call me by my real name, I don't want anyone to know, what do you drink.

Stick the dick bottle up your fuck nosehole and breathe like your nose up Mel Gibson's ass tasting his crack hairs and drinking it in till your tongue and spit taste like Ribena Pepto cough syrup minty mouthwash Listerine sting, don't spit into my mouth with that flavor breath and make your balls bust cock tip split and flow the cum in my face, anybody seen his poppers, no, he's a popper junkie can't cum can't rim can't fuck think about fucking without the smell of Liquid Paper thinner up his throat, climb into the dumpster to look for the last bottle while I lie in bed on my stomach press my dick hard into the mattress pretend it's him, wait till he comes back and puts rubbing alcohol to pep it up and he wants to fuck now, every part of his body wants to fuck now that it is ready to crack open his artery temples sinuses syndicated psychedelic orgasmic dreamworld nightmare wetcum dream life.

Oi woman get a life and get that peroxide poodle attacking your scalp off first stupid Chink woman thinks she's Haole wannabe fuck white eat white drink white shriek Oh look, look at all those short people, short people repeated like nobody gives a shit, gives me attitude bitch, try dying your crotch blonde and watch your pubic hairs fall out one by one.

I want to fuck the men who look like Jesus, fuzzy beards and chests, bless me Jesus with tattoos and pierced tits, pierced cocks, nipple clamps, nail the skin of my balls to your heavenly bed, make me cum in heaven baby, o angels sing primal piss in my mouth, clip my tits to Jesus's ring, rub my pubes into his, o show me no mercy merciful, o bless me, o fuck me godhead.

Pledging undying love with a gold ring inset with a diamond the size of an eyeball he says, Baby you can never have enough diamonds, Baby everlasting is a long time but is it real, Baby is it too big to be real, what's the point, Baby doesn't it end, is the rhythm wrong, Baby what can you do to make me love you.

Your cock is so ugly, it's so small and wrinkled, you can't fuck with it, it's only good for beating off, why are you so rude to me, is it some sort of racism, you don't know who you just fucked over, I'll have the cops on your tail, I'm not finished with you buddy, hey, fuck you buddy.

Die, Mr. Medallion Man, die. Take your Disco Divas with you, Mr. Medallion Man and die, die and leave us alone. Take your polyester and your Brut. Take your gold and your chains. Take your platform shoes and die, Mr. Medallion Man, die. You are Pisces, I am Virgo. You are Taurus, I am not.

Take your astrology, take your flares and die. We will not be virgins no more for you. Our hymens, asses and sphincters have broken and you can't fix it, Mr. Medallion Man, so die. Take your haircuts and your thinly tapered shirts. Take your discos and your Bee Gees. Take your sideburns and your hairy chests. Take your Listerine Breath Spray, Mr. Medallion Man and die.

Will good-looking men love me when I die, will they press their hunky bodies against my dead ass, slowly lick my dead crack, shoot warm cum up on my cold lips, let the cum slip into the dead mouth, onto the tongue, O let my swollen tongue taste it, will they finger fuck my dead ass will they huh, will they flex and pump their hard bodies so I can jerk-off dead cum, rub it into their shoulders, will they kiss me on the back of my neck and spit in the hollow of my throat, will they huh, will good-looking men love me at all when I'm dead?

He was a sailor but now he's a cab driver from Yugoslavia, why'd you have to blow him, why'd you have to suck him off while he took you home, lick his tits and play with his chest like you wanna fuck his dick, did you really enjoy it, George was a cabbie too, yeah in New York, got twenty bucks cos his passenger wanted to smell his shoes, got fifty bucks to smell his feet, why'd you have to suck him, why.

Sometimes your heart tastes better when you drown it in Buds and blow cigarette smoke through the cracks, patch the holes with cornnuts and popcorn pop trivia piss quiz birthday Carly Simon tunes, sometimes your heart feels much better when you cook it in KY Vaseline pot stogie puff blow paste and hang it up to dry beside Conair toasters yuppie heaven man, treat it good baby, love it like your CDs bonds and bedposts, treat it baby good, treat it next to your plague remover, kiss it baby, cos sometimes your heart sounds like rice cakes soaked in one part vodka, one part gin, one part Coke, one part Tutti Frutti Juicy, one part goo, one part jism, one part heaven, one part hell, one part fucking, one part fisting, one part AA, one part words, one part rimming, one part love.

# ❧ On ~~Ass Tactics~~,
## ~~Aztec Ticks~~,
### Aesthetics

What does cultural aesthetics mean in a world that is changing rapidly, where identities and cultures are in flux, in the blender on frappé, where celebrity Buddhists and white Hindus run rock festivals to save the world, and where culture has become so commodified that you can assume another as easily as going to the mall, guided by last month's full-colored spread in *Elle*, *Family Circle*, or *Needlepoint Digest?* In the spirit of individuality and tolerance, assimilation and acculturation, the Suzie W(r)ong doll is repackaged and paraded as bitchin' Filipino-Irish-Cantonese-Alien B-girl rapper Suzie W.; as Suzie-StarChild, transgendered hippy-vegan militia guru; as Steve, gay Latino Republican for Choice in Deportation; as Suzan Whong, dressed as Pocahontas as Fa MuLan as Miss Eskimo Hawaiian Tropic in fake fur bikini and Keds, pillar-box red Candies (panties are optional, of course).

*Aesthetics* was one of those words that I couldn't spell without the help of my spell-checker or my trusty American Heritage Dictionary of the English Language (three books for three bucks + postage, such a deal). Cultural asstactics exist in the same way that fleas of the dead family dog do, still biting after darling Fido has been crushed under the wheels of the biggest fucking lorry in the world, driven by Mr. Moto, the guy who used to be an accountant for Jacoby, Ramirez, Wong, Wong & Fonzirelli, until he discovered the sacred floating lotus within himself.

Cow-churrail aztec-ticks exist and they don't.

Cowlture means very different things to different people. Identity politics is a maddeningly individual thing, and the joy is finding others who subscribe to your particular lottery numbers and want to play with you at the next drawing.

We are influenced by who and what we are, how we live, and how living is done around us. I am a queer Asian guy, a writer and performance artist, a first-generation immigrant who came into my queerness in the Day-Glo soaked eighties. Obviously, what it means to be Asian in America, Asian-American, queer, part of the Asian diaspora, or any combo platter of those (no substitutions please, 49¢ to supersize soft drink and fries) will be different for me than it would for someone else even in the same straits.

The problems occur when audiences and arts administrators and pro-grammers don't feel that I am playing the carl-cheer right. They demand yet another ethnic dance festival, another trip to the chink-o-rama with the big Ferris wheels, spinning Ethnic McNuggets in convenient packs of six, eight, or sixteen. Something to stick up on the shelf between the Michener books, the *Joy Luck Club* laser disc, and the souvenirs (oooh! big fan, rice-paddy hat, straw mat, sarong, sarong, sarong) from Asia-fest '95.

There will always be work that is deemed not queer enough for the queers, not Asian enough for the Asians, not Asian enough for the queers, too Asian for queers, too queer for the Asians, too much, too little, too bad. A tub of eels of fears and inadequacies to fill the *unagi-maki* roll of cultural consumption (comes with miso soup!), waiting for Goldilocks to learn how to use chopsticks (or at least ask for a fork, dammit, or use her fingers) so she can find the right morsel to take to the right BacoLounger before crawling into the right futon, dreaming of pork chops, bacon, and everything else Just Right.

Ooo. I'm having a thought: (serious voice) Cultural aesthetics is important as long as cultural politics is important, as long as identity politics have been a long hard-worn struggle and fight.

Cull-chew-real asstack-ticks? I'm not too sure what it really is anymore, but I do know that if you buy into it too much as an artist and especially as an audience, it can be severely limiting. It's good to know what you like from art, and what you identify with, but it's much better to be open to the sea of possibilities and the different, challenging, opposing discourses that you might find in there. Cultural aesthetics is a good starting point, and starting points are just that—hopefully they lead somewhere and the roads ahead are not filled with dodos (the extinct bird, not the idiots in our lives) running back-wards. Remember to wait at least thirty minutes after eating. You may start when you're ready.

# Rodney Phillips

# AFTERWORD

In his introduction to this volume, Timothy Liu says he doesn't trust the notion of a gay sensibility. Most of us are of course a little nervous about our separatism, our appropriating tendencies. We are wary of making oh, say, Walt Whitman a modern Act-Up man. Nevertheless we too want our usable past, so we dig up the past to invent the present. We have created a gay culture, a constellation of signs and symbols, rituals, rhythms and attitudes, coming of age tests and ceremonies. It is also complete with various lists of heroes and enemies. It is this constellation most of us live within, sometimes consciously and actively, and sometimes only in reaction and disregard.

One of the most powerful creationary tools of any cultural tradition is canon making, and one of the most useful tools in this endeavor is the anthology. Anthologies serve the double purpose of bringing out the new and unknown and blessing again the known and the famous. *Word of Mouth* is like any anthology, a gathering of flowers, like Tottel's *Songs and Sonnets* (1556). It is a beginning shot at establishing the most important (for lack of other maybe reprehensible adjectives like best and greatest) gay poets in the second half of the century. In this, *Word of Mouth* is also like for instance, Francis Palgrave's *Golden Treasury of English Songs and Lyrics* (1861 and on) or one of the Oxford Books of verse in the hand of Yeats, Gardner, or Larkin. I expect that, like these anthologies, *Word of Mouth* will become influential and that gay anthologists of the future will have to pay attention to it. But of course, this particular anthology is, like any self-respecting anthology, a documentary snapshot of the present, not the future.

Today, Mr. Liu says, these poets, who are pretty much self identified as gay, also identify themselves just as importantly as poets. In fact, each of these "qualities" seems pretty much equal in this anthology, I think perhaps for the first time as far as gay anthologies go. That is, the poets included herein could and have appeared in straight anthologies just as easily. Which is not to say that even one of these poets just happens to be gay. Each and every one of them has struggled in his poetry to define his sexuality and each in his own way writes love poems. The idea isn't that anyone herein, or you or I, is only gay, but gay and . . . and a lot of other things. The gay part isn't everything, but it dramatically informs the sensibilities presented in this volume. The local is not assimilated into the universality of the human feelings which are represented. As a warning, let me say however, that there is no word about aesthetic "excellence" here. This is a documentary, not an award ceremony, not a test.

*Word of Mouth* is also a work of art in itself. The editor's choice of poets and poems provides a ton of interconnections, reflecting the regard of these gay poets for each other, for each other as teacher, mentor, god, hero and lover. See for instance Stephen Jonas' appropriation of Spicer's poet as radio metaphor, or Frank Bidart's poem for Joe Brainard (one of many) or one of Jimmy Schuyler's also many beautiful poems for Tom Carey or Ronald Johnson's poem dedicated to Robert Duncan. You know, of course, this is not the homintern, but the angels of light, if that's not going too far. It's at least the very creation of community. Perhaps this is because Timothy Liu is an accomplished poet himself and is a part of that community (of his own poems, at least "Highway 6,""Men Without," "Crepuscule with Mother," and "March on Washington, 1993" should have been included in this volume).

This volume resists the excesses of some of its contemporaries, its cover lacking for instance the half or wholly nude, very attractive male bodies that grace the covers of Michael Lasell's *Eros in Boystown* and Gavin Dillard's *A Day for a Lay*. It also lacks some of the more obvious work that fills those volumes. *Word of Mouth* is I think the first of the gay anthologies that can be considered seriously "standard" in the sense of defining the tradition in the last half of the century. It culminates the work of its predecessors including, Winston Leyland's *Angels of the Lyre: A Gay Poetry Anthology* (Panjandrum Press, 1965), Ian Young's *The Male Muse: Gay Poetry Anthology* (Crossing Press, 1963), Winston Leyland's *Orgasms of Light* (Gay Sunshine Press, 1966), Ian Young's *The Son of the Male Muse: Gay Poetry Anthology* (Crossing Press, 1983), *The Penguin Book of Homosexual Verse*, edited by Stephen Coote (Penguin, 1986), Joan Larkin and Carl Morse's *Gay and Lesbian Poetry of Our Time* (St. Martin's, 1988) and Rudy Kikel's *Gents, Bad Boys & Barbarians* (Allyson, 1995).

As a documentarian, Liu has dug up poets such as Edgar Bowers or William Bronk who have not been in any previous anthology (because their work wasn't so obviously gay, or because no one who didn't know them personally knew they were gay?). His work should also allow us to pay some more attention to poets like Stephen Jonas, Ronald Johnson or evan Jack Spicer, who have small but intense followings already but not necessarily in the gay community. He is also introducing to the larger community of gays and lesbians, to writers and we hope to the general public, a variety of really good work by established poets such as Carl Phillips, Richard McCann, Daniel Hall, and the late Tim Dlugos. These poets deserve a lot more exposure. Among the very new and youngest poets, the work of D. A. Powell, is I think, one of the treasures of this volume (there is always one real find in every anthology). This shows how far indeed we have come, Virginia. And hints at how many more there are to come.

Berg Collection, New York Public Library
31 December 1999.

# SELECTED BIBLIOGRAPHY

Jack Anderson: *Selected Poems* (Release Press, 1983); *Field Trips on the Rapid Transit* (Hanging Loose, 1989); *Traffic: New and Selected Prose Poems* (New Rivers, 1998).

John Ashbery: *Selected Poems* (Viking, 1985); *April Galleons* (Viking, 1986); *Flow Chart* (Knopf, 1991); *Hotel Lautreamont* (Knopf, 1992); *And the Stars Were Shining* (Farrar Straus Giroux, 1994); *Can You Hear, Bird* (Farrar Straus Giroux, 1995); *Wakefulness* (Farrar Straus Giroux, 1998); *Girls on the Run* (Farrar Straus Giroux, 1999).

W. H. Auden: *Collected Poems* (Random House, 1966).

Dan Bellm: *One Hand on the Wheel* (Roundhouse Press, 1999); *Buried Treasure* (Cleveland State, 1999).

Mark Bibbins: *Swerve* (Graywolf, 1998).

Frank Bidart: *In the Western Night: Collected Poems 1965-90* (Farrar Straus Giroux, 1990); *Desire* (Farrar Straus Giroux, 1996).

Robin Blaser: *The Holy Forest* (Coach House, 1993).

Edgar Bowers: *Collected Poems* (Knopf, 1996).

Joe Brainard: *I Remember* (Angel Hair, 1960); *More I Remember* (Angel Hair, 1962); *More I Remember More* (Angel Hair, 1963); *New Work* (Black Sparrow, 1963).

William Bronk: *Life Supports: New and Collected Poems* (North Point, 1981); *Careless Love and Its Apostrophes* (1985); *Manifest; and Furthermore* (North Point, 1986); *Death Is the Place* (North Point, 1989); *Living Instead* (North Point, 1991); *Some Words* (Moyer, Bell, 1992); *The Mild Day* (Talisman, 1993); *Our Selves* (Talisman, 1994); *The Cage of Age* (Talisman, 1996); *All of What We Loved* (Talisman, 1998); *Metaphor of Trees and Last Poems* (Talisman, 1999).

James Broughton: *Packing Up for Paradise: Selected Poems 1946-1996* (Black Sparrow, 1996).

Rafael Campo: *The Other Man Was Me* (Arte Publico, 1994); *What the Body Told* (Duke, 1996); *Diva* (Duke, 1999).

Tom Carey: *Desire* (Painted Leaf, 1996).

Cyrus Cassells: *The Mud Actor* (Holt, 1982); *Soul Make a Path Through Shouting* (Copper Canyon, 1994); *Beautiful Signor* (Copper Canyon, 1996)

Justin Chin: *Bite Hard* (Manic D, 1996); *Mongrel* (St. Martin's, 1998).

Dennis Cooper: *The Dream Police: Selected Poems 1969-1993* (Grove, 1995).

Alfred Corn: *Present* (Counterpoint, 1996); *Stake: Selected Poems 1962-1992* (Counterpoint, 1999).

Christopher Davis: *The Tyrant of the Past, the Slave of the Future* (Texas Tech, 1989); *The Patriot* (University of Georgia, 1998).

Edwin Denby: *The Complete Poems* (Random House, 1985).

William Dickey: *Of the Festivity* (Yale, 1959); *More Under Saturn* (Wesleyan, 1963); *The Rainbow Grocery* (Massachusetts, 1968); *The Education of Desire* (Wesleyan, 1996).

Tim Dlugos: *Powerless: Selected Poems 1963-1990* (High Risk, 1996).

Mark Doty: *Turtle, Swan* (Godine, 1986); *Bethlehem in Broad Daylight* (Godine, 1991); *My Alexandria* (University of Illinois, 1993); *Atlantis* (HarperCollins, 1995); *Sweet Machine* (Harper Collins, 1998).

Robert Duncan: *The Opening of the Field* (New Directions, 1960); *Roots and Branches* (New Directions, 1964); *Bending the Bow* (New Directions, 1968); *Ground Work: Before the War* (New Directions, 1984); *Ground Work II: In the Dark* (New Directions, 1986); *Selected Poems: Revised and Enlarged* (New Directions, 1996).

Kenward Elmslie: *Routine Disruptions: Selected Poems* (Coffee House Press, 1998).

Edward Field: *Counting Myself Lucky: Selected Poems 1963-1992* (Black Sparrow, 1992); *A Frieze for a Temple of Love* (Black Sparrow, 1998).

Allen Ginsberg: *Collected Poems: 1946-1980* (Harper & Row 1984); *White Shroud: Poems 1980-1985* (Harper & Row, 1986); *Cosmopolitan Greetings: Poems 1986-1992* (HarperCollins, 1994); *Death & Fame: Poems 1993-1996* (HarperCollins, 1999).

John Giorno: *You Got to Burn to Shine: New and Selected Writings* (High Risk, 1994).

Brad Gooch: *The Daily News* (Z Press, 1978).

Thom Gunn: *Collected Poems* (Farrar Straus Giroux, 1994); Boss Cupid (Farrar Straus Giroux, 2000).

Daniel Hall: *Hermit with Landscape* (Yale, 1990); *Strange Relation* (Penguin, 1996).

Forrest Hamer: *Call & Response* (Alice James, 1994).

Leland Hickman: *Tiresias I:9:B: GREAT LAKE SLAVE SUITE* (Momentum, 1980).

Richard Howard: *Untitled Subjects* (Atheneum, 1969); *Findings* (Atheneum, 1961); *Two-Part Inventions* (Atheneum, 1964); *Fellow Feelings* (Atheneum, 1966); *Misgivings* (Atheneum, 1969); *Lining Up* (Atheneum, 1983); *No Traveller* (Knopf, 1989); *Like Most Revelations* (Pantheon, 1994); *Trappings* (Turtle Point, 1999).

Ronald Johnson: *ARK* (Living Batch, 1996); *To Do As Adam Did: Selected Poems* (Talisman, 2000)

Stephen Jonas: *Selected Poems* (Talisman, 1994).

Kevin Killian: *Argento Series* (Meow, 1996), *I Cry Like a Baby* (Hard Press, 2000)

Wayne Koestenbaum: *Ode to Anna Moffo and Other Poems* (Persea, 1990); *Rhapsodies of a Repeat Offender* (Persea, 1994); *The Milk of Inquiry* (Persea, 1999).

Gerrit Lansing: *Heavenly Tree / Soluble Forest* (Talisman, 1995).

Timothy Liu: *Vox Angelica* (Alice James, 1992); *Burnt Offerings* (Copper Canyon, 1995); *Say Goodnight* (Copper Canyon, 1998).

Jaime Manrique: *My Night with Frederico Garcia Lorca* (Painted Leaf, 1996).

Richard McCann: *Ghost Letters* (Alice James, 1993).

J. D. McClatchy: *The Rest of the Way* (Knopf, 1990); *Ten Commandments* (Knopf, 1998).

Taylor Mead: *Excerpts from the Anonymous Diary of a New York Youth* (1961); *Second Excerpts from the Anonymous Diary of a New York Youth* (1962); *On Amphetamine and in Europe: Excerpts from the Anonymous Diary of a New York Youth Vol. 3* (Boss, 1968); *Son of Andy Warhol* (Hanuman, 1986).

James Merrill: *The Changing Light at Sandover* (Atheneum, 1982); *The Inner Room* (Knopf, 1988); *Selected Poems: 1946-1985* (Knopf, 1992); *A Scattering of Salts* (Knopf, 1995).

Thomas Meyer: *The Umbrella of Aesculapius* (Jargon Society, 1965); *Staves Calends Legends* (Jargon Society, 1969); *Sappho's Raft* (Jargon Society, 1982); *At Dusk Iridescent* (Jargon Society, 1999)

WORD OF MOUTH

Frank O'Hara: *Meditations in an Emergency* (Grove, 1956); *Lunch Poems* (City Lights, 1964); *The Collected Poems of Frank O'Hara* (Knopf, 1961); *Early Writing: 1946-1950* (Grey Fox, 1966); *Poems Retrieved: 1950-1966* (Grey Fox, 1966).

Carl Phillips: *In the Blood* (Northeastern, 1992); *Cortege* (Graywolf, 1998); *From the Devotions* (Graywolf, 1998); *Pastoral* (Graywolf, 2000).

D. A. Powell: *tea* (Wesleyan, 1996); *lunch* (Wesleyan, 2000).

Boyer Rickel: *arreboles* (Wesleyan, 1991).

James Schuyler: *Collected Poems* (Farrar Straus Giroux, 1993).

Reginald Shepherd: *Some Are Drowning* (University of Pittsburgh, 1994); *Angel, Interrupted* (University of Pittsburgh, 1996); *Wrong* (University of Pittsburgh, 1999).

Aaron Shurin: *A's Dream* (O Books, 1989); *Into Distances* (Sun & Moon, 1993); *Unbound: A Book of AIDS* (Sun & Moon, 1996); *The Paradise of Forms: Selected Poems* (Talisman, 1999); *A Door* (Talisman, 2000).

Jack Spicer: *The Collected Books of Jack Spicer* (Black Sparrow, 1965); *One Night Stand and Other Poems* (Grey Fox, 1980).

Richard Tayson: *The Apprentice of Fever* (Kent State, 1998).

David Trinidad: *Hand Over Heart: Poems 1981-1988* (Amethyst, 1991); *Answer Song* (High Risk, 1994); *Plasticville* (Turtle Point, 2000).

James White: *The Salt Ecstasies* (Graywolf, 1982).

John Wieners: *Selected Poems: 1958-1984* (Black Sparrow, 1986); *Cultural Affairs in Boston: Poetry and Prose, 1956-1985* (Black Sparrow, 1988); *The Journal of John Wieners Is to Be Called 606 Scott Street for Billie Holiday, 1959* (Sun & Moon, 1996).

Jonathan Williams: *An Ear in Bartram's Tree: Selected Poems, 1956-1966* (University of North Carolina, 1969).

Mark Wunderlich: *The Anchorage* (University of Massachusetts, 1999).

# RECOMMENDED READING

Agha Shahid Ali: *A Nostalgist's Map of America* (Norton, 1991).

John Ash: *The Burnt Pages* (Random House, 1991).

Thomas Avena: *A Dream of Order* (Mercury House, 1996).

Ben Belitt: *This Scribe, My Hand* (Louisiana State, 1999).

Steve Benson: *Blue Book* (The Figures, 1989); *Reverse Order* (Potes & Poets, 1989).

David Bergman: *Heroic Measures* (Ohio State, 1998).

Walta Borawski: *Sexually Dangerous Poet* (Good Gay Poets, 1984).

John Cage: *Silence* (Wesleyan, 1961); *I-VI* (Wesleyan, 1996).

Turner Cassity: *The Destructive Element: New and Selected Poems* (Ohio, 1998).

Henri Cole: *The Look of Things* (Knopf, 1995); *The Visible Man* (Knopf, 1998).

Douglas Crase: *The Revisionist* (Little Brown, 1981).

Melvin Dixon: *Love's Instruments* (Tia Chucha, 1995)

Jim Elledge, *Into the Arms of the Universe* (Stonewall, 1995).

Paul Goodman: *Collected Poems* (Random House, 1963).

Essex Hemphill: *Ceremonies* (Plume, 1992).

Daryl Hine: *In and Out: A Confessional Poem* (Knopf, 1989).

Benjamin Ivry: *Paradise for the Portugese Queen* (Orchises, 1998)

Thomas James: *Letters to a Stranger* (Houghton Mifflin, 1973).

John Keene: *Annotations* (New Directions).

Maurice Kenney: *Between Two Rivers: Selected Poems 1956-1984* (White Pine, 1992).

Michael Klein: *1990* (Provincetown Arts, 1993).

Dean Kostos: *The Sentence that Ends with a Comma* (Painted Leaf, 1999).

Michael Lassell: *A Flame for the Touch that Matters* (Painted Leaf, 1998).

Russell Leong: *The Country of Dreams and Dust* (New Mexico, 1994).

John Logan: *Only the Dreamer Can Change the Dream: Selected Poems* (Ecco, 1981).

Paul Mariah: *This Light Will Spread: Selected Poems 1960-1965* (Manroot, 1968).

David Melnick: *Men in Aida: Book One* (Tuumba, 1983).

William Meredith: *An Effort at Speech: New and Selected Poems* (TriQuarterly, 1996).

Paul Monette: *Love Alone: 18 Elegies for Rog* (St. Martin's, 1988).

Herbert Morris: *Dream Palace* (Harper & Row, 1985).

Howard Moss: *New and Selected Poems* (Atheneum, 1985).

Harold Norse: *Hotel Nirvana* (City Lights, 1964).

Dwight Okita: *Crossing with the Light* (Tia Chucha, 1992).

Peter Orlovsky: *Clean Asshole Poems and Smiling Vegetable Songs* (City Lights, 1968).

Jim Powell: *It Was Fever that Made the World* (Chicago, 1989).

Assotto Saint: *Stations* (Galiens, 1989).

George Stanley: *Beyond Love* (Open Space, 1968).

Philip Whalen: *Overtime: Selected Poems* (Penguin, 1999).

Marvin K. White: *Last Rites* (Alyson, 1999).

Designed by
Samuel Retsov

Text: 11 pt Minion

acid-free paper

Printed by
McNaughton & Gunn